On Location

Cinema and Film in the Anglophone Caribbean

Keith Q. Warner

CARIBBEAN

Dedication
For Berna, and for Jade, Billy, Daria and Reece, for whom Caribbean films will be especially important.

First published 2000 by
MACMILLAN EDUCATION LTD
London and Oxford
Companies and representatives throughout the world

www.macmillan-caribbean.com

ISBN 0-333-79211-4

10   9   8   7   6   5   4   3   2   1
09   08   07   06   05   04   03   02   01   00

This book is printed on paper suitable for recycling and made from fully managed and sustained forest sources.

Printed in China

A catalogue record for this book is available from the British Library.

Cover illustration taken from the poster of the film
The Harder They Come, courtesy of Perry Henzell, International Films Ltd

Series preface

In this latest addition to the series Professor Warner, a specialist in French and French West Indian literature and Trinidadian popular culture, has crafted a book full of rare information, analyses, prescriptions and suggestive insights out of what, at first sight, might seem an unpromising subject. With only a dozen or so films produced in the anglophone Caribbean over three decades how can we speak of cinema and film when Hollywood produces as many films in a single month? In this stark contrast lies the central problem addressed in this book which, for its importance and implications, deserves to be read not only by Caribbeanists but by those working in media and cultural studies, and those concerned with the effects of cultural dependency.

How can a Caribbean film industry develop without a mass audience, adequate funding, committed government support, willing investors, commercial expertise and access to advertising and distribution facilities? How can Caribbean films hope to make any impact on world cinema let alone compete with foreign imports in the domestic market? The odd prestigious award at international film festivals is no guarantee of wide distribution. Talent is not lacking and film-going has been an integral part of West Indian popular culture, but although there have been rare successes there has been no take-off comparable to the international impact of the music industry or even that of West Indian writers (many of whose works are crying out for screen adaptation).

The book concentrates on the plots and treatment of the few full-length feature films (rather than documentaries or short features) produced in the English-speaking Caribbean as well as in the diaspora in Canada and England. The reasons for the popularity of foreign films, especially the Western, gangster, war and action movies are analysed, as well as the sociology of West Indian cinema-going, the role of critics, and the make-believe world of the West Indian poor. The problem of a fragmented market is well illustrated by differences in audience reactions. What is popular in Jamaica may not be so in Trinidad where distribution and cinema ownership is concentrated in the hands of Indians and where Bombay rivals Hollywood. African films and films with African content are either not distributed or tend not to be popular. Also discussed are the role and influence of foreign film companies which choose the Caribbean as a location and in doing so project an outsider's image of people and places.

Overall, Hollywood dominates. The book thus poses the key question of cultural identities. How can these be nurtured in an age of accelerating technologies when viewers are bombarded by a bewildering array of images and ideas of foreign provenance which perpetuate stereotypes with their inaccuracies and misrepresentations and which tend to be conditioned by the commercial demands of the box-office? A pernicious aspect of these pressures is the influence which can be exerted on Caribbean film-makers financed by backers who are aware of the damaging effects which the depiction of controversial issues, such as drugs or violence, can have on a tourist industry on which small island economies increasingly depend.

The most important, although the shortest, chapter contains Professor Warner's prescriptions for a Caribbean cinema. To these might be added two others. In free societies where the market rules the box office is too often the arbiter of taste. There is no easy solution to the impasse. The Cuban way – state support, unwittingly aided by an arbitrary US embargo – forced the Cubans to go it alone, thus sparing them from the fate of the early Mexican film industry of being co-opted by Hollywood. Remarkably the Cubans were able to create a unique film industry which achieved world recognition, becoming a model for Third World film directors, to be institutionalized in 1985 by the establishment, under the inspiration of Gabriel Garciá Marquéz, of the Foundation for New Latin American Cinema. Collaboration with the Cubans in co-productions under the auspices of the Association of Caribbean States, of which Cuba is a member, could be one way of developing a genuine Caribbean film industry. Another might be collaboration in co-productions with states of the European Union anxious to escape from US cultural hegemony. The putative revival of the British film industry as well as success of television productions on Caribbean themes might encourage the earmarking of funds for future co-productions.

Professor Warner's book appears at an opportune moment and is a valuable addition to those books in the series on aspects of popular culture which have already appeared – on Jamaica, Cooper's *Noises in the Blood*; on Trinidad Carnival, van Konigsbruggen's book of that name and Warner's own essay on calypso in Yelvington (ed) *Trinidad Ethnicity*; and the forthcoming volume by Best on Barbados. Also forthcoming, in *The Cultures of the Hispanic Caribbean* edited by

James and Perivolaris are two pungent analyses of the effects of Hollywood and commercial cinema on the Caribbean generally.

This is an important and, hopefully, should be an influential book which it is a pleasure to have in the series.

Alistair Hennessy

Warwick University Caribbean Studies

Series Editors: Alistair Hennessy and Gad Heuman

Contents

List of plates

Acknowledgements

It is almost impossible to complete a study of this nature without help from many sources. I hope that those whose names I do not mention will forgive the omission, and consider themselves included in my blanket expression of gratitude to all who took time to offer advice, to point me in a particular direction, or simply to listen.

In Trinidad, Sita Bridgemohan, Randy Hezekiah and Roseanne Mee Chong all seemed to drop whatever they were doing to help me find what I was looking for. Deoraj Sirjoo, Anthony Maharaj and Anthony King, distributors at the Film Centre, were generous with their time and information. Horace Ové, Liz and Cliff Seedansingh, Tony Hall, Barbara Jenson, Aiyegoro Ome and Christopher Laird of Banyan also provided useful insights. I thank Brenda Hughes for sharing ideas and perspectives that proved very helpful as I gathered material.

For my visit to Jamaica, Hilary Brown put me in touch with key people, while Beverley Phillips, Carolyn Cooper, Heather Shields and Michael Dash made my stay both pleasant and fruitful. I thank Franklyn St Juste and Carl Bradshaw for graciously granting interviews at short notice, and Melanie Graham for sharing information about her company, Palace Amusements.

In England, Frances-Anne Solomon, June Givanni, Julien Henriques and Menelik Shabazz willingly talked about their work, and suggested relevant contacts. They all contributed more than they could imagine to the completion of this study. The fact that I have published only Menelik Shabazz's interview means only that I had limited space at my disposal. Suzanne Roberston's recollection of her husband's involvement with film-making in Trinidad helped a great deal.

Finally, back in the United States, I was heartened by the interest all my department colleagues showed in my work, and by the immediate assistance I received from film people like Mickey Nivelli, Bruce Paddington, Kamalo Deen and Andrew Millington when I called upon them. Thanks are also due to Cynthia Mahabir, Ray Funk,

John Cowley, and Françoise Pfaff for sharing material, and to Kevin Yelvington for putting me in touch with a group of dedicated publishers at Macmillan. Their unflagging interest in my work was a great motivator.

The quotations from V. S. Naipaul's *Miguel Street*, copyright 1959, are reprinted with the permission of Gillon Aitken Associates Ltd and reproduced by permission of Peuguin Books Ltd. The bibliography and notes give complete citations and details of pages quoted.

Keith Q. Warner

Introduction

There are enough faces of the Caribbean to cater to a multiplicity of tastes, styles, and cultures. The former colonial powers – the British, Dutch, French and Spanish – have left their indelible marks on a chain of islands that have become associated with exoticism, with beautiful beaches, with rhythmical music and with fun in the sun. These stereo-typical images have appeared in a variety of feature films which often show a side of the Caribbean that is more in the mind of the film-maker than in the eyes of the viewer. This book examines one set of faces, namely those from the parts of the Caribbean formerly or still under British colonial rule.

The study looks at images of the anglophone Caribbean and its people both in non-Caribbean feature films shot on location in the region, and in films the anglophone Caribbean has produced on its own. In doing so, it acknowledges that what was brought to the former Dutch, French and Spanish colonies, as well as what was eventually produced by these territories, was in some way different from what would be found in the anglophone countries. In other words, the multi-faceted, multi-cultural, and multi-lingual nature of the Caribbean is reflected in the world of the arts, and thus in cinema and film as well. Film professional Bruce Paddington sums up the situation quite adequately:

> Reaching a mass audience in the Caribbean is not a simple matter. The region is still fragmented, and contacts between the English, Dutch, French and Spanish countries are still difficult. There is no effective regional distribution system. Because there is no common language, distribution requires effective dubbing or sub-titling facilities. And above all it requires an assault on popular tastes which are now deeply attached to the ceaseless flow of entertainment from American television, film and video.[1]

This continued dominance of American fare will make it increasingly difficult for the anglophone Caribbean to develop its own cinema industry.

Paradoxically, the extent to which American films dominate in the anglophone Caribbean is highlighted by the situation in Cuba, where no such domination is permitted. The political and economic isolation of this country has forced it to develop its own institutions. In so doing, it has become a role model, and its achievement in cinema has been hailed worldwide.

Although in many aspects of their life they have problems similar to those of their counterparts in other areas of the Caribbean, the Cubans have found their identity in cinema and film. They have done so with the full knowledge that they have virtually no one in the West to whom they can turn. Cuba's internationally acclaimed director, the late Tomás Gutiérrez Alea (*Memorias del subdesarrollo / Memories of Underdevelopment, Fresa y Chocolate / Strawberry and Chocolate, Guantanamera*) maintained that:

> The cinema has a great influence on the people, and we have a great need to recognise ourselves on the screen, to reflect our own problems and to build our own identity. I think it is very important that people have a sense of ownership of the media and of their own identity.[2]

To this end, Cuba set up a film institute in 1959, the Instituto Cubano de Arte e Industria Cinematográfica (ICAIC), and gradually carved a place for itself as a respected force in Third World and Latin American film production. In 1979 it inaugurated the International Festival of New Latin American Cinema in Havana, where, in 1985, the Foundation of the New Latin American Cinema was established, under the chairmanship of Nobel laureate Gabriel García Marquez. According to film scholar Zuzanna Pick, this foundation's most ambitious undertaking was the establishment of the Film and Television School of the Three Worlds, with the aim of training young film-makers from Asia, Africa, and Latin America.[3]

The Cuban example shows that it is possible to be productive even in the face of the voluminous output generated by mainstream cinema in the United States. However, given the political ramifications of association with Cuba, and the barrier of language, the anglophone Caribbean has not aligned itself too closely with this nation, and has not emulated its achievement in film. Nor has it aligned itself with the French-speaking Caribbean – technically part of France. The former British colonies keep their eyes steadfastly focused on the United Kingdom and on North America, and on the films they produce; the former French colonies similarly direct their gazes to France. It was only when Martiniquan Euzhan Palcy's faithful and elegant movie adaptation of *La Rue Cases-Nègres*, the novel by her compatriot

Joseph Zobel, became an international success in the mid-1980s that many in the anglophone Caribbean realized that there were other film-makers in islands not too far from them. In this regard, Bruce Paddington's assertion that the names of leading Caribbean film-makers and their work remain unknown to most Caribbean people is certainly true.[4]

The present study, which is *not* a history of cinema in the Caribbean, deals with most of the film-makers of the anglophone terri-tories. Inevitably, there will be film-makers who will not find their work mentioned, because I felt I had sufficient information in the films at my disposal. My approach is not unlike the one taken by scholars of literature, who choose from a vast array of writers and works to make their point.

I also do not deal with non-anglophone Caribbean film-makers, but readers should, at the very least, be aware of the main ones among them. In addition to Tomás Gutiérrez Alea, there are in Cuba Humberto Solás, Santiago Alvarez, Sergio Giral and Daniel Diaz Torrez; from the Dominican Republic comes Agliberto Melendez, who made the award-winning feature *Un Pasaje de Ida;* and from Puerto Rico, Spanish-speaking but with US commonwealth status, we have Jacobo Marales and Marcos Zorinaga. In Dutch-speaking Curaçao, there are Felix de Rooy and Norman de Palm, who have worked together on *Almacita di Desolato* and *Ava and Gabriel*, the latter achieving the highest film award in Holland. In the francophone islands, we can add Christian Lara from Guadeloupe to Euzhan Palcy from Martinique; and from Haiti, officially francophone but *de facto* Creole-speaking, there are Rassoul Labuchin and Raoul Peck, whose *L'Homme sur les Quais* is set in Haiti during the Duvalier dictatorship.[5]

My focus on fictional feature-length films naturally excludes many outstanding documentaries and short features, which probably do well in festivals, but are hardly ever seen by the average viewer – also the subject of my study. Unfortunately, in too many instances, this viewer had never had the opportunity to see the features examined in this study because the runs had been cut short, or distribution had been limited. But such is the nature of the film and cinema business: losses are great, many feature films never make it to the cinema, and some suffer aborted runs.

The study begins with a look at cinema and Caribbean conscious-ness, the aim being to show how readily the masses took to the cinema, and how they identified with the films shown. The second chapter deals with the way non-Caribbean films, mainly out of the United States, portrayed the Caribbean when they were shot on location. Chapter 3 discusses Caribbean-made feature films, looking at what the region does when it controls images of itself, while Chapter 4 is devoted to the film-makers of Caribbean descent operating outside of the region, and to their treatment of the immigrant experience. Finally, Chapter 5 looks at what is involved in the development of a Caribbean film industry and offers some suggestions for its future.

Despite my best efforts, I was unable to view afresh some of the films I had seen when they were first released. I have in such instances relied on contemporary reviews to jog my memory. I interviewed several people during the course of research for this book, with the intention of culling information from what I heard in the exchange. When I began to transcribe the tapes, however, I felt it a shame not to share with readers some of what I learned. As a result, I have appended four of the interviews with key people in the film-making world: an actor, a director of photography, a director and a distributor.

Notes

1   Bruce Paddington (1992), 19.
2   Reported in Paddington (1992). See note 1 above.
3   Zuzanna M. Pick (1993), 32–3.
4   Paddington (1992), 18.
5   I am indebted to Bruce Paddington's article (1992) for the information given in this paragraph. For a more detailed overview, see Mbye Cham's 'Shape and Shaping of Caribbean Cinema,' in his compilation *Ex-Iles: Essays on Caribbean Cinema* (1992), 1–43.

1 | Cinema and Caribbean consciousness: believing make-believe

All Port of Spain is a twelve-thirty show.
Derek Walcott, 'The Spoiler's Return'

Television did not come to the anglophone Caribbean until the early 1960s, a period coinciding with the attainment of independence by both Jamaica and Trinidad and Tobago, the earliest of the former British colonies to do so. Prior to the introduction of this medium, all of the moving images of the world beyond the shores washed by the Caribbean Sea came via the cinema. The region's colonized subjects, who would rarely have had the opportunity or the means to travel beyond the islands, dutifully stood for 'God Save the King' (or 'Queen' later on) at the start of the show, then settled back to enjoy the wonder of moving pictures. They reacted with enthusiasm and fascination to what they saw of a world that had hitherto only been imagined through written or oral descriptions, and seen in drawings and still photographs. In addition to the newsreels of contemporary world events, the make-believe universe of fictional feature films took hold of the imagination of large sections of the population, who often ended up believing the make-believe.

This fascination with the world of make-believe is amply documented by various artists in Caribbean society, from calypso singers and carnival masqueraders to steelband players and writers of fiction. They show beyond any doubt that films and cinema have penetrated the consciousness of the society as a whole, and of certain sectors of it in particular. Our initial look will be at the writers, for, as Nobel laureate Toni Morrison has written, 'writers are among the most sensitive, the most intellectually anarchic, most representative, most probing of artists.'[1]

Writers on the cinema

From one end of the archipelago to the other, from Jamaica to Trinidad, the lure of the cinema – popularly referred to as 'pictures' or 'theatre' – was inescapable. It provided a relatively inexpensive activity for the masses, affording them a look at another world beyond the confines of the islands, and allowing them to submerge themselves in other adventures, albeit from a distance. Even in those islands without established cinema houses, movies were shown to the public from mobile units. Going to the cinema also provided a wonderful communal opportunity for sections of the population to indulge in open grandstanding, to show off their home-grown expertise in directing, and to hone their skills in visual literary analysis and fundamental film theory. Writing in *The Middle Passage*, V. S. Naipaul notes that:

> Newspapers and radio were ... only the ancillaries of the cinema, whose influence was incalculable. The Trinidad audience actively participates in the action on the screen. 'Where do you come from?' Lauren Bacall is asked in *To Have and Have Not*. 'Port of Spain, Trinidad,' she replies, and the audience shouts delightedly, 'You lie! You lie!' So the audience continually shouts advice and comments; it grunts at every blow in a fight; it roars with delight when the once-spurned hero returns wealthy and impeccably dressed (this is important) to revenge himself on his past tormentor; it grows derisive when the hero finally rejects and perhaps slaps the Hollywood 'bad' woman (of the *Leave Her to Heaven* type). It responds, in short, to every stock situation of the American cinema.[2]

A similar reaction is observed in Jamaica:

> As anyone who has attended the cinema in predominantly oral societies will attest, film is an art-form in which an open-ended dialogue with the narrative/visual text is transacted. Loud comments on the action, not simply non-verbal laughter or tears, articulate the viewer's response to this intimate medium. Characters are addressed directly and are often warned of impending danger; the viewer, after all, is more knowing than they and can 'read' the meaning of events the character merely experiences.[3]

In their own primal way, these audiences constituted our first generation of film critics. They knew exactly what they wanted, what seemed plausible, what worked, and what did not. They knew when they were being cheated by a projectionist who, anxious to go home, had 'cut' the picture. They knew that the sound of violins and the sight of waves crashing against rocks were a poor substitute for clever camera work when two lovers went to bed. They noticed where rules of etiquette and hygiene had been bent or overlooked, and had no qualms about reminding a coy heroine, still in bed and about to be kissed by the gallant hero early in the morning, that she had not brushed her teeth. 'There was no such thing as watching in silence,' writes the narrator in *The Harder They Come*, the Jamaican novel spawned by the film of the same name. 'The identification was high and a contagious excitement spilled down from the screen and rolled in waves through the theatre'.[4] Films were seen repeatedly; favourites were brought back, and certain double features became standard: *Latin Lovers* with *Sombrero*, *Ride Diablo* with *Duel at Silver Creek*, *High Noon* with *Gunfight at the OK Corral*; or as boys in the Port of Spain of V. S. Naipaul's *A House for Mr. Biswas* knew, *Jesse James* with *The Return of Frank James*, and *When the Daltons Rode* with *The Daltons Ride Again*.[5] Many in the audience thus knew by heart the key dialogues and plot twists. Outside the cinema, it was not unusual to hear dialogue from a popular movie being quoted. 'The boys reenacted the good scenes. With amazing memory and mimicry they drawled the best lines through their noses, walked the walks with hands hanging like claws above imaginary holsters, and made the moves' (*THTC*, p. 194). Not being able to reproduce a particular line when challenged by a film-lover – and in a feigned American accent at that – was a sure sign that one was slipping, and meant a definite loss of face among one's peers.

The majority of films shown in the pre-independence period – and after it, as it turns out – were American. V. S. Naipaul provides a telling glimpse of what and who were popular in Trinidad: '*Casablanca* with Humphrey Bogart; *Till the Clouds Roll By*; the Errol Flynn, John Wayne, James Cagney, Edward G. Robinson and Richard Widmark films; vintage Westerns like *Dodge City* and *Jesse James*; and every film Bogart made' (*MP*, 63). Interestingly, we see some of the same actors mentioned as popular in Jamaica: 'Of course there were certain names: Humphrey Bogart, Edward G. Robinson, Richard Widmark, Sidney Greenstreet, or George Raft, which evoked a certain style, a cynical tight-lipped toughness' (*THTC*, 195). It mattered not that all these actors were white, and that their admirers were of predominantly African (or Indian) descent; the latter were so engrossed in the make-believe that style and bravado transcended race. The pioneering performances of Harry Belafonte, or Sidney

Poitier, or of many of the black actors who desegregated Hollywood's stranglehold on the film industry, came long after the bonding had developed between the cinema-going public and its favourite actors. There was, literally, no hero-worship of black actors *qua* black actors.

Naipaul provides us with an astute observation with regard to the way blacks in Trinidad viewed Stepin Fetchit, admittedly not the ideal black actor to pit against the likes of Humphrey Bogart and Richard Widmark:

> Stepin Fetchit was adored in my childhood by the blacks of Trinidad. He was adored not only because he was funny and did wonderful things with his seemingly disjointed body and had a wonderful walk and a wonderful voice, and was given extravagant words to speak; he was adored by Trinidad people because he appeared in films, at a time when Hollywood stood for an almost impossible glamour; and he was also adored – most importantly – because, at a time when various races of Trinidad were socially separate and the world seemed fixed forever that way, with segregation to the north in the United States, with Africa ruled by Europe, with South Africa the way it was (and not at all a subject of local black concern), and Australia and New Zealand the way they were – at that time in Trinidad, Stepin Fetchit was seen on the screen in the company of white people. And to Trinidad blacks – who looked down at that time on Africans, and laughed and shouted and hooted in the cinema whenever Africans were shown dancing or with spears – the sight of Stepin Fetchit with white people was like a dream of a happier world.[6]

The time of which Naipaul spoke in this observation, that of his childhood, would correspond to the early 1940s, when, as he noted with accuracy, awareness of the problems of racism worldwide was not as acute as it became a couple of decades later. What seemed so paradoxical to Naipaul fell naturally into place within the framework of colonization, where nearly everything in the society conspired to keep blacks in their position of subservience.

Black audiences were mesmerized by what Naipaul called the 'almost impossible glamour' of Hollywood. They saw no incongruity in identifying with white actors and what they were portraying, thus virtually imagining themselves in the very films they were mimicking. The reason for this situation in Trinidad is explained by Naipaul as follows:

In its stars the Trinidad audience looks for a special quality of style … For the Trinidadian an actor has style when he is seen to fulfill certain aspirations of the audience: the virility of Bogart, the man-on-the-run romanticism of Garfield, the pimpishness and menace of Duryea, the ice-cold sadism of Widmark (*MP*, 64).

As far as the young Jamaican moviegoers were concerned:

their identification was with the actors, not with the characters they played who were obviously ephemeral and transitory. It was the ability of the actors that made the characters *bad* and which endured, so that arguments took place over whether Bogart was *badder* than Widmark (*THTC*, 199; emphasis in the original).

Many viewers, enthralled by the American films, had no hesitation in taking as nicknames the names of their favourite actors. In one of his first pieces of sustained writing, later published as *Miguel Street*, Naipaul named one of his characters Bogart, and gave the following possible explanation for the origin of the nickname:

It was something of a mystery why he was called Bogart; but I suspect that it was Hat who gave him the name. I don't know if you remember the year the film *Casablanca* was made. That was the year when Bogart's fame spread like fire through Port of Spain and hundreds of young men began adopting the hard-boiled Bogartian attitude.[7]

A Bogart also turns up in the Kingston of *The Harder They Come* alongside Bendix, Cagney, and Widmark. 'They answered to the tough-sounding two-syllable surnames that were the stock in trade of Hollywood press agents – names of consequence and with the right resonances that could be spat out with sharp, dangerous inflections' (199). In like manner, the places where these young men spent a great portion of their time were also baptized with names that came straight off the screen: Salt Lake City Ranch, Dodge City, Hell's Kitchen, Boot Hill, El Paso, Durango, and even Nikosia (201). Indeed, any corner of their turf could instantly be transformed into a Hollywood set, as is evidenced by this Kingston street scene from the novel:

Suddenly Bogart bent over wheezing for breath. A fit of hollow, consumptive and explosive coughs rattled in his chest. He made an effort to control the coughing, failed, and was thrown to one knee by the vehemence of the fit. He didn't seem to have long for this world. Then he stood, gasping uneven gusts of air into his tortured chest, with an open ratchet knife dangling ever so casually from his hand. The expression on his face was one of pure malevolence.

'Oowee' Ivan shouted, laughing with delight and unfeigned admiration. 'Doc Holliday to raas!'

He recognized the scene: Kirk Douglas as the consumptive and deadly Doctor. In that single performance Douglas nearly ruined the lungs and throats of a whole generation of West Kingston youth (*THTC*, 197).

Over and over, we see instances where Caribbean young men made an almost instant connection and association with the world of the cinema – in speech, in dress, in their every action. Westerns were particularly admired; the fact that many of these young men had never even touched a real horse was of no significance. They could, like Derek Walcott's Jackson in *Pantomime*, resort to 'creole acting', turning any object into an imaginary revolver: 'JACKSON: Yes. Creole acting. I wonder what kind o' acting dat is. (*Spins the hammer in the air and does or does not catch it*) Yul Brynner. *Magnificent Seven*. Picture, papa!'[8] Their vivid imaginations would make up for any lacunae in their life style. It was simple, really, and as such we read of Ivan in *The Harder They Come*:

Then night transformed him, into a desperado of the imagination. He prowled the streets with Bogart and the boys, went to blues dances where highly amplified black-American music dominated, faced down other gangs, fled the clutches of Babylon, and rode with John Wayne, Gary Cooper, and Wild Bill Elliott out of places with names like Fort Apache and Rio Lobo (203).

Westerns

This world of make-believe was dominated by men, a situation which, upon reflection, was not unusual, given the aura of mimicry that pervaded the entire atmosphere in which these young Caribbean men lived. Westerns were dominated by men trying to carve out their turf, to establish their manhood through their quick draw and their overall toughness. They showed values that appealed to the spirit of adventure and fair play in the hearts of many of those cheering on the cowboy, the star boy who could not die – or in any event, not till the last reel:

Those values are in the image of a single man who wears a gun on his thigh. The gun tells us that he lives in a world of violence, and even that he 'believes in violence'. But the drama is one of self-restraint: the moment of violence must come in its own time and according to its special laws, or else it is valueless. There is little cruelty in Western movies, and little sentimentality; our eyes are not focused on the sufferings of the defeated but on the deportment of the hero. Really, it is not violence at all which is the 'point' of the Western movie, but a certain image of man, a style, which expresses itself most clearly in violence. Watch a child with his toy guns and you will see: what most interests him is not (as we so much fear) the fantasy of hurting others, but to work out how a man might look when he shoots or is shot. A hero is one who looks like a hero.[9]

There was an air of 'triumph of the underdog' combined with 'might is right' that permeated many westerns, a tailor-made situation for a colonized citizen anxious to prove his mettle, if only subconsciously, against a colonial master. The western, *par excellence*, typified the struggle of the good guy versus the bad guy, and the colonial filmgoer could identify with both elements as it suited his fancy. This duality of association explains the ability of the Caribbean viewer to identify with John Wayne leading his assault against native American Indians, who were defending lands they had held for centuries before the arrival of the white settlers, and who were made in many instances to be the villains.

Women in the westerns played subservient roles for the most part, and if these Caribbean men were to carry their fantasy to the logical conclusion, then their women would also have to play subservient roles. The roaming and exploring of territory we see done by the men is not duplicated by the women – just as in the films, and there is hardly any mention in the writing of women who patterned themselves on anything or anyone they saw on the screen. Of course, one might argue, the role models were few and far between, and if women did pattern themselves after screen heroines, they would most likely have ended up staying at home and being good wives anyway, for such was the example they would have seen being portrayed in the films.

Women – at least the sisters and mates of the young men about whom we have been speaking – attended the cinema, but the circumstances of their attendance were slightly different from the men's. They avoided, or were clearly uncomfortable in, the enclaves of males who staked out little territories in the section of the cinema closest to the screen, an area that gained a formidable reputation in Trinidad as 'pit':

Nearly all the movie theatres in Port of Spain are divided into three sections. Tickets to the *balcony* section are the most expensive, and this is where all white and middle-class patrons sit. Occasionally there is a poor, ghetto couple here, their choice of seats reflecting the occasion of a special date. There is almost never any noise in this part of the theatre, and the patrons who select these seats disdain those in the more rowdy sections of the cinema. The *house* usually includes the back half of the orchestra section; tickets are less expensive than for the balcony, and the audience here is mixed, though most of the poorer, black patrons sitting here are single women, couples or the elderly. The *pit* is the front half of the orchestra, and contains seats considerably shabbier than those elsewhere in the theatre but also considerably cheaper. While there is a common entrance for those who purchase balcony and house tickets located at the front of the theatre – near the rest rooms and next to the nicer refreshment stands – there is a separate entrance to the pit at the rear. This entrance is usually a single, narrow door, making entry into the cinema very uncomfortable for pit patrons. Inside the theatre there is a physical barrier between the house and pit sections which is intended to prevent patrons sitting in the pit from climbing over into the house and bothering the patrons there. The composition of the pit is nearly exclusively black, male, poor and young. Women rarely sit in this section, and a man who would normally choose to sit here when alone will buy house seats if he is accompanying a woman.[10]

Pit was clearly not an environment for women aspiring to the upper rungs of the social ladder, and, as the quoted passage reminded us, if they were on a date, then that was not the section for them although V. S. Naipaul does equate entering pit with entering 'a dungeon of romance'.[11] The situation described above related to the cinema scene as observed toward the end of the 1970s, but was apparently not very different from what obtained already in Trinidad of the 1930s, the time frame of the novel *Crown Jewel* by Trinidadian novelist Ralph de Boissière.

Popito Luna is attracted to Cassie, a maid who is experiencing financial difficulties, and a pivotal character in the novel. He has found a job, and, with a relatively large sum of money in his pocket, is emboldened to invite her to the pictures:

They went to the Empire Theatre. He wore his good suit, she a flowered frock her sister had made for her. Even more attractive did she seem to him than on that day he had met her going to San Juan. She had thought they would sit in the pit with the workers but to her joy and pride they went through the front entrance among the well-dressed white and coloured folks and sat in the soft seats of the stalls. He put several bars of chocolate in her lap. She was amused.[12]

Popito's desire to appear respectable is seen in his wearing his 'good suit', and in his purchasing the nicer refreshment Michael Lieber referred to (as opposed to salted peanuts, channa, or mints). But he also understands what it means for his lady friend not to have to sit among the cruder patrons in pit. Being taken to theatre was almost *de rigueur* as a first date for the lower classes, who did not have the range of entertainment opportunities that an improved standard of living would bring a couple of decades after independence. It was therefore important that the right impression be made if the relationship was to be successful, and taking a prospective girlfriend to pit was out of the question to all but the poorest. Even the calypsonian, the traditional voice of the masses in Trinidad, but also the traditional underdog, understood this, and took his 'Nice Señorita' to theatre. The Mighty Sparrow sang in the 1950s:

> I have a nice señorita
> Last night I took her to theatre
> Then I told her I love her
> And I want her forever
> She say 'Sparrow, me no compran
> Talk in Spanish for me to understand.'

This young lady is from a Spanish-speaking country, no doubt nearby Venezuela, and is probably of fairer complexion. The calypsonian therefore wants to do everything possible to impress her, including trying to speak Spanish, and, like Popito in *Crown Jewel*, buying an assortment of nicer refreshment, though he does add peanuts. Since this date is special, the best seats are chosen, though the couple is still not guaranteed privacy for what the calypsonian obviously has in mind. He wants to 'prove his manhood', and has 'no time to look on the screen', bent as he is on the conquest of this 'Spanish queen.' Things do not go well. She is 'real disagreeable', despite the fact that, apart from the ticket collector, they are the only patrons in balcony:

> The ticket collector in balcony
> Sit down on a chair playing sleepy
> But I myself whey so tricky
> Better than he couldn't catch me

> He play he sleeping, but I know he peeping
> So to make certain, I pull the curtain
> And I gone back to the Spanish
> I ain't even know the picture finish.

Sparrow did switch to a simplified Spanish to make his conquest, for we hear in his chorus:

I say 'well, dame, dame la cosa	[… give me the thing]
Mi amor, yo te quiero	[My love, I love you]
Mucho, ay mamaita	[A lot, ay mamaita]
Dame la cosa, caramba'.	[Give me the thing, caramba]

Still, the calypso, like the picture, comes to an end, and we are left to laugh at the luckless calypsonian, who is also laughing at himself, though the public knows that it won't be long before he gets his revenge in another calypso of successful conquest. There were no more similar attempts chronicled in Sparrow's repertoire.

It emerges, then, that over the years Caribbean moviegoers, in large part comprised of young men, have come to appreciate not only the films they saw in the cinema, but also the 'territorial protocol that obtained there' (*THTC*, 195). The young men were able to frequent the cinema even if they were unemployed, for the admission price could easily be begged for, a situation we see in Jamaica:

> A group of younger boys passed along, imploring likely prospects. 'Maastah', one said, holding out a palmful of change in evidence, 'Ah need a smalls fe mek up de fare; let me go, maastah!' (*THTC*, 144).

and in Trinidad, when we hear in Sparrow's 'Royal Jail' how the apparently unemployed young ruffians of the day begged their way into the cinema:

> When you pass by Strand
> They stretching they hand,

and were not afraid to use violence if their requests were turned down:

> Ay, pardner, gimme something dey
> You ain't have, so you walk away
> Next morning you wake up in a ravine
> You' head bust, you' pocket clean.

If such gangster-like scenarios were not the rule of the day, sheer trickster tact was used, either to advance to the head of the queue, or to gain admission free of charge:

'Ah a bring out a new breddah, y'know. Is me new walkin' partner dis'. He pulled a thoroughly flattered Ivan forward: 'Him name Rhygin'. Jose introduced the group: '"Bogart", "School Bwai", "Easy Boat", "Peter Lorre"'. Low, cool murmurs of acknowledgement. Ivan attributed the easy and affable acceptance to Jose's patronage. They stood talking, Jose completely ignoring the people behind him as if breaking the line were the furthest thing from his mind. But after some short time had passed and he made no effort to move away a challenging voice shouted.

'Wha' happen, maastah, is bruk unu out to bruk de line?'

Jose turned, slow, deliberate, a study in understated danger, all the more menacing because it was so cool and controlled, so stylish. 'What you say, sweets?' he asked with a mocking sneer calculated to sharpen the insult.

'Ah say it look like you out to bruk de line', a tall youth with a scarred, hardbitten face said flatly, and glowered at him.

'No, y'know, breddah'. Jose laughed affably, after they had exchanged a long stare. 'Why you t'ink I'd do somet'ing like dat?' With a disarming shrug he strolled off, drawing all eyes and leaving Ivan unnoticed in the middle of his friends.

Ivan bought the tickets (*THTC*, 144–5).

The scene plays well, with no condemnation of the trickster who uses his wits and street smarts to survive, even if it means being openly selfish. Style, Naipaul has told us, is admired.

Youthful Caribbean guile is also manifest in Sparrow's 'Renegades', which tells how a band of prospective patrons manages to enter the cinema for the 12.30 show, clearly the preferred performance time for this group, and renowned among lovers of pit. 'Going twelve-thirty' had its own mystique, but also its own social stigma:

> Everyday they going theatre twelve-thirty
> And, believe me, they going in free
> One will call the gate man here
> Talk in he ears, ten gone through there
> The gate man rush to put a stop
> They push him down and the whole theatre full up.

The fact that these young men could go to the cinema every day at 12.30 probably meant that they were unemployed, and thus had a lot of time on their hands not only to get into mischief, but also to absorb aspects of the various *personas* being constantly beamed at them. In this regard, they reflected the thinking in colonial society, quick to believe that whatever came from the outside was necessarily better than what was produced on the inside. Derek Walcott, a keen observer of *mores* in Trinidad, compared its capital precisely to the goings-on at one of these shows when he writes in 'The Spoiler's Return' that:

> All Port of Spain is a twelve-thirty show
> Some play Kojak, some Fidel Castro.[13]

It was these 'wu'tless youngmen', as Tantie calls them in Merle Hodge's *Crick Crack, Monkey*, who patronized every cinema ('t'eater') they could find. Tantie chides Mickey: '... "yu t'ink blasted saga-clothes an' t'eater does grow on tree? An' before you look to help-out yu mother and she forty-nine chirren no yu prefer siddong on yu arse wid them long wu'tless youngmen down at that bridge'".[14]

On this bridge, we discover, 'the fellows mainly discussed last weekend's Tarzan picture or Western,' or gave the floor to the character Manhatt'n, who liked to claim that, while up Stateside, he had outdrawn the sheriff in Dodge City during an encounter:

> But when one day someone maliciously murmured 'Crick-crack!' at the end of one of these accounts in perfect Western drawl, Manhatt'n in his rage forgot to screw his mouth to one side before starting to speak.
> 'Crick-crack yu mother! Is true whe ah tell yu – yu only blasted jealous it ain' you! Crick-crack? Ah go crick-crack yu stones gi' yu!' (*CCM*, 15).

The 'crick-crack' broke the spell. The narrator knew immediately his listeners saw him as nothing more than a poor version of Brer Anancy, teller of folk tales. The Dodge City story was pure playing to the gallery, and taken straight from the screen, since so much of daily intercourse revolved around the profound influence the cinema had on these youths:

> There was one memorable time when Mickey took us along to the bridge. When we arrived a discussion was in full swing. Lamp-post was enthusing.
> 'Western in yu arse, boy, Western in yu arse!' and Joe was recreating the climax with a lovely pantomime: '"ey boy, forty-million o' them against the star-boy and the rest o' them ridin comin and then he bullets run-out ... ."'

'And then the other guys reach, an' then, ol'-man, then yu jus' see Red-Indian fallin-dong all over the place – ba-da-da-da-da – pretty, boy, pretty!' mused Krishna (*CCM*, 16).

Soon after this incident, Mickey and 'a young man going by the appellation Audie-Murphy (there was also a Rock-Hudson and a Gary-Cooper in the company)' get into a fight. The outcome is not serious, and Mickey slouches home, the hem of his jersey half torn loose and 'draping his hips drunkenly like a gunbelt' (*CCM*, 18). Commenting on the way the writer handled this flirtation with make-believe, Wilfred Cartey noted that she had captured:

> the effervescence and vitality of the street boys through images of figures borrowed from and mimicking Hollywood movies, which gives an immediacy to the social reality she delineates. So much of this interplay becomes theatre, street theatre at its best.[15]

From very early in her novel, then, Merle Hodge shows that her young men are typically Caribbean in at least one respect – their love for the cinema and the films that were shown.

Post-independence cinema fare featured a wider range of films, with so-called action and *kung-fu* (kick-up) films bringing the majority of patrons, but it had to compete with in-home television in a way the early westerns did not. However, even with Hollywood's evolution away from the genre, the western remained the essential film-lover's movie, which explains why accounts of reaction to it, or of intoxication with it, turn up so readily. Two novelists in particular, Earl Lovelace in *The Dragon Can't Dance*, and Michael Thelwell in *The Harder They Come,* have underscored the total identification of a couple of characters with the world of the cinema. Both writers have used the figure of the cowboy as the *alter ego* of urban youth at odds with a system he does not fully understand, and as a result cannot master.

It is no doubt ironic that the section of the Caribbean population most enthralled by the cinema was the one that seemingly had the most to lose in this fixation with make-believe. One could easily fault the characters who indulged in what Carolyn Cooper called the 'lonely fantasies of vicarious power',[16] that is if one lost sight of the fact that they were usually at the bottom rung of the social ladder desperately reaching out for anything that would even remotely begin the process of moving them up. Fisheye in *The Dragon Can't Dance* is in such a situation.

Shortly after the Second World War, Fisheye comes to town from Moruga, one of Trinidad's most remote villages, where he would surely not have had any exposure to films. He arrives in Port of Spain full of enthusiasm, and parades his natural strength as proof of what Moruga (hence simple and unpretentious) people can do. Soon, however, a sense of uselessness takes hold of him, and his attempt to combat it leads him to films:

> He began to go to the cinema. Every night almost, he went to Royal or Empire, whichever was showing a western double; and after the show, walking home up the Hill, the picture fresh in his mind, walking kinda slow, he would feel for a few moments his strength, his youth, his promise fill him, and he would walk, the fastest gun alive, his long hands stiff at his sides, his fingers ready to go for the guns he imagined holstered low on his hips. But no one wanted to draw against him; and he would pick his way between the garbage and the dog shit with his secret power and invisible guns, his eyes searching the shadows for a hidden gunman – in which movie was it that someone had said: 'Every shadow is a gunman?' – but all he saw was maybe a few fellars gambling under the street light, or a man and his woman quarreling. Back in his room, he felt crushed by his own strength, spun by the quickness in him. Now and again he would punch the boards of the partition, and he would overhear his neighbour's resigned comment: 'The devil in there with that boy'. The devil remained with him.[17]

The initial transformation is mostly cerebral, as the picture he has just seen causes inner strength to radiate throughout his body, restoring him, he imagines, to his former self. However, with no apparent external manifestation of his metamorphosis, he is disappointed that 'the fastest gun alive' is denied the opportunity to show his mettle. As a result, a further development is in order:

> He began to develop a crawl, a way of walking that was kinda dragging and slow, in which his knees barely bent, his feet were kept close and his legs spread apart to give the appearance of being bow-legged from riding a horse. He walked, crawled to and from work, to and from the cinema, tall, slow, a bow-legged cowboy, with his hair combed up on his head in a big muff, his shirt pushed into his pants resting low on his waist, his hands hanging loose and empty at his sides; that and the cut of his head, his bulging eyes, and the

soft sullenness of his lips issuing a challenge, just waiting for a man to snicker or say a rough word to him so he could cuff him down; but, his readiness was its own warning, and he went, almost a spectacle, unmolested through the streets, nobody wanting to tackle him (*TDCD*, 65).

Gradually, Fisheye confuses make-believe with reality, with the result that when he provokes a confrontation in a parlour by refusing to pay for a meal he has already consumed, he 'stood his ground and watched the old man coming towards him, feeling very tall and very much a bandit like in a western movie – and the people in the place watching like in a western too' (*TDCD*, 65).

In the ensuing melee, when the police have arrived, Lovelace's narrative adopts the modern cinematic technique of the slow-motion presentation of key action scenes:

> Then he knew he had this baton in his hand and he saw one policeman fall and he heard the people screaming and he heard a police whistle blasting, and he had this baton in his hand, and before he could decide what to do with it, for the two policemen were on the ground, he saw a whole crowd of grey-shirted policemen coming towards him, a whole army of them, like in *Guns Across the River*, and he was standing there with the baton in his hand swinging, and he tasted blood in his mouth, and then he was floating down very slow, falling down very slow, like he had all the time in the world to fall, and it would be the last thing he would do, forever and forever fall (*TDCD*, 66).

The budding bad John is frozen in time as the cowboy, the desperado to be admired by patrons in pit. The 'might is right' attitude of the western sweeps Fisheye along the path to violence and rebellion, and he ends up pitting himself against the entire system. He highjacks a couple of policemen in their jeep, doing so in the name of the People's Liberation Army, an organization that had no structure, no real existence, until he and his buddies created it on an impulse. The entire scenario is worthy of a movie script:

> That was when Fisheye said the words that he would recall to his death: 'Nobody ain't moving on', and when the policeman turned to the voice, they would see him standing beside the jeep and a little behind them, his hat brim pushed up from his eyes, his legs spread apart, slightly bow-legged, leaning back a little, with a pistol in his hand, a cowboy in a Western movie, braced against one of those storms of dust

that always seem to sweep across the street, rolling hoops of
brambles, just at the moment of the showdown between two
nerveless rival gunmen. 'And take your hand off your
holster' (*TDCD*, 186–7).

The cowboy-turned-rebel-turned-revolutionary is arrested, tried, and
sentenced to seven years in prison. This marks the second failure for
Fisheye, for he had earlier been unsuccessful in preventing the concept
of sponsorship from taking hold among the steelbands, his own
included. He had again taken up the fighting he had stopped, an act of
sabotage of sorts, because 'sponsors did not like violence in bands.
Indeed, one of the conditions of sponsorship was no misbehaving in
the band' (83). There is no stereotypical denouement for Fisheye,
however. We see him totally subdued during his incarceration, and he
turns to philosophizing as opposed to fantasizing:

> Me, I'm smarter. I know now that you have to have real
> power, and if you don't have it, man, you have to survive
> with them that have it. It's a joke, man, this business of being
> bad, a bad John. That is a old long time thing ... . Now a
> man have to learn how to live (*TDCD*, 204).

The reader almost wishes for some action from Fisheye – a
breakout, or a shoot-out in true Hollywood style, but Fisheye has
wizened up, and the make-believe world of the cinema is abandoned
for harsh reality. 'What should be', he concludes, 'and what is is two
different things' (*TDCD*, 204).

Almost two decades after *The Dragon Can't Dance* was first
published, Lovelace again used cinema images to pinpoint aspects of
his characters' lives in the novel *Salt*. The villager Moon, competing
with a more prosperous Gopisingh for the hardware business, takes to
advertising the articles he has for sale by means of a loudspeaker. But
his competition soon retaliates:

> Seeing how successful he Moon was getting, Gopisingh
> bought a loud hailer as well and to get the edge, began to
> play music from the soundtrack of Indian films. Moon hit
> back with chutney singing from Trinidad Indians:
>
> > I see the young girl passing
> > I tell she how de do
> > She have a little garden
> > And her pretty cow does moo,
>
> and when Gopisingh turned up the volume of his own hi-fi,
> Moon added calypso music to his arsenal of musical

bombshells. Every Friday the street was a bedlam of chutney, calypso and songs from Indian films.[18]

We shall return to the significance of Indian movies in the concluding chapter, but suffice it to say that Lovelace is well aware of how readily the villagers would take to the selections from the films as served up by storekeeper Gopisingh. Ironically, Moon's grandson, Sonan, campaigning for election some years after his grandfather's death, would have his electioneering remembered by the people in terms relative to the movies:

> 'If I am called upon to bat for the Democratic Party the best way I can do that is to bat for batting. Because', said he, quoting the poet John Donne: 'No man is an island entire unto itself. Every man is a piece of the continent, a part of the main. Any man's death diminishes me. Because I am involved in mankind and therefore never let me send for whom the bell tolls, it tolls for thee.'
>
> To some it was his most impressive performance and when people met him afterwards they sighed and said, 'For whom the bell tolls,' which they remembered as a picture starring Ingrid Bergman and Gary Cooper (*Salt*, 234).

Sonan also included references to films as he sought to impress the crowds:

> He quoted from the movie *Panhandle*, starring Rod Cameron:
>
> > 'Seems like you got wet, Mr. Sands.'
> > 'Not as much as the men outside.'
>
> … He quoted from the scene in *Billy the Kid* when Doc Holliday asks, 'Why didn't you draw?' And the Kid answers, 'I changed my mind' (*Salt*, 235).

He was aware that such references would have the desired effect because his listeners would quickly follow him into the world of fantasy as created on the cinema screen.

In his novel, *The Harder They Come*, Michael Thelwell completes the make-believe in a way that Lovelace does not – and the star boy even dies in the last reel. More than a mere 'novelisation,' that quick embroidering of some prose around what is essentially a film script, *The Harder They Come* is a sensitively written novel that can stand on its own. The author writes in his preface:

> What I had hoped to achieve was a broader new work into which the action, characters, and scenes of the film could be

organically integrated and which would work as a novel at least nearly as well as the film did as cinema. Stated differently, I tried to write if not the novelistic equivalent of the movie then at least the novel from which the film might have derived were the process reversed, as is more usually the case.[19]

The sub-text of film narrative that runs throughout the movie is admirably captured by Thelwell as he fills in areas that would have made the film too long had they been included. But the visual medium of film can do things with images and with soundtrack that cannot be done in the same manner in the written medium of the novel. Both mediums should be complementary; and if they both succeed, then the 'apples with oranges' comparison is of little consequence. Thelwell can thus dwell on aspects of the lives of the Jamaican youth that populate the novel in a way that the film can only allude to briefly, and the penetration of film and cinema into the consciousness of this section of the population is one such aspect.

Thelwell devotes the first quarter of the novel to preparing the reader for what was the first scene in the film – Ivan coming from country to town by bus, for he, like Lovelace's Fisheye, comes out of the belly of the rural folk. Ivan's exposure to the cinema, again like Fisheye's, must have been quite limited, even non-existent, though the newcomer to Kingston claims to have read about Rialto, one of the cinemas:

> One of the great attractions of the city, and a source of speculation and wonder back home, was the moving picture shows advertised so tantalizingly in the newspapers. What was the name of a theatre? The first one that came to mind was Rialto. Keeping his voice as casual as possible, he asked, 'You know wha' showing at Rialto?'
>
> 'Oh.' Jose looked up surprised. 'What you know 'bout Rialto an' you jus' come from country?'
>
> 'Read 'bout it, man. Read 'bout it,' Ivan said and shrugged disparagingly (*THTC*, 141).

Thelwell's language emphasizes the degree to which Ivan and the rest of the audience were absorbed into the world of moving images. Speaking of the reaction to what was taking place on the screen, the narrator informs us that 'the identification, however *willing* a suspension of disbelief, was also spontaneous and damn near total' (*THTC*, 148). Likewise, we read that Ivan enjoyed the action in his first movie, but 'great as the action was, it was something else that intoxicated him. The world of the movie was harsh and brutal, yes. But it was also one where justice, once aroused, was more elemental and deadly than all the hordes of evil' (*THTC,* 149). The Ivan we are shown not only identifies with the screen heroes, but is also intoxicated by what he sees: 'Ivan ached with the stoical, taciturn Django through vicious physical beatings, grieved with him over the murder of his woman, shared his humiliation and growing anger under the accumulation of outrage and injustice' (*THTC,* 148). Ivan's fellow patrons are similarly sucked into the action on the screen, and they react in a 'visceral' manner:

> A low, approving, anticipatory, visceral growl rose from the audience, becoming a joyous, hysterical, full-throated howl of release, of vindication and righteous satisfaction as Django, grim-faced and alone, the very embodiment of retribution and just vengeance, raked the masked killers, hot, bloody, destruction spitting from the Gatling gun on his hip (*THTC,* 149).

Finally, the excited viewers leave the cinema, Ivan in a virtual daze among them:

> Gradually the howling subsided, and the crowd, muttering excitedly, some running and acting out the ending, filed out in a rush of nervous energy that crackled around them, each nine feet tall, feet barely touching the ground, feeling no pain.
>   His ears still throbbing with the metallic staccato of the gun, images of violence dancing before his eyes, a dazed and blinking Ivan followed Jose into the night (*THTC,* 149).

This marks the start of what some observers have termed Ivan's pathological identification with film heroes, a far cry from 'the discriminating responses of habitual moviegoers in the Caribbean ... who are ultimately able to maintain a sane critical distance from the text.'[20] But, one could argue, those who would maintain this distance are precisely the ones on whom any influence would manifest itself the least. Such gut reaction to mere images on a screen could only be seen as the reflection of an uncultured and unlettered mind, or of someone who, according to the psychological profile a university psychiatrist published based on lyrics to Ivan's songs, 'was "obsessed with a 'wild west' image of himself, had delusions of destined greatness, a typically psycopathic obsession with heroic violence, and a paranoic and unjustified sense of being oppressed"' (*THTC,* 358).

Ultimately, then, the consciousness of which we speak has necessarily to be that of the people, of the masses. Ivan, like Fisheye, is of the 'vulgar' folk, one of that group that had no pretensions to middle-class respectability when it came to enjoying its entertainment, the very group that persevered and eventually won acceptance, and respectability, for reggae in Jamaica, for example, and for steelband and calypso in Trinidad and Tobago.

One of the novel's "improvements" over the film is the author's ability to relate a variety of incidents to their resemblance to film scenarios. Carolyn Cooper's on-target commentary on this aspect of the novel is worth citing:

> For these impressionable young men adrift in the city, local events acquire the resonance of spectacle and are interpreted in terms of film metaphors. When Prince Emmanuel David and his 'strange army' (209) of Rastafarians attempt to capture the city of Kingston and exorcise the spirit of colonialism, Widmark (an appropriated name) moved by the ritual grandeur of the occasion, whispers 'it only want Charlton Heston fe come down wid de commandments now' (207) thus bringing together in a single image both the Rastafarians' identification with the avenging power of the Old Testament Jehovah/Jah, and the young men's vicarious political/moral victories in the idealized world of the cinema. But the waiting crowd of onlookers, like so many film extras, fully enjoying the pure drama of the moment, become annoyed that the Rastafarian takeover seems purely symbolic; they want action ... The Rastafarians soon attempt to capture two 'Babylon' as sacrificial victims, and the crowd is placated: '"Whaiiee, watch de Babylon dem a run. Haw, haw. Me say run Babylon!" The sight of the police in headlong flight pleased them mightily and their good spirits were immediately restored at the prospect of seeing something really unusual like a sacrifice' (211–212). It is Cowboys and Indians, with the cowboys as the villains: the ethos of the film, *The Harder They Come*. In this passage three voices and perspectives converge – Jamaican, biblical English and the language of the tourist/voyeur: the native and the foreign, mediated by the ritual language of film.
>
> When the police assemble their counter-army it is Widmark, again, who remarks 'Spartacus to blood claat' (212). The omniscient narrator/*griot* concurs: 'And indeed, with the Biblical robes of the Rastas and the lines of shields and spiked helmets, the scene resembled nothing so much as the Roman legions against the slaves' (212). After the defeat of the Rastafarians, it is Bogart, 'the cool, the unchallenged

leader, the man of respect ... by day Ezekiel Smith, a mechanic's apprentice' (201) who sums up the profundity of their failure: 'even Victor Mature couldn't help them' (213). And even Bogart's real name, Ezekiel Smith, the visionary worker in metals, returns us via the Old Testament prophet to the film fantasy of *The Ten Commandments* and the apparent failure of Jah to protect the righteous.[21]

Increasingly, Ivan is shown as more obsessed than his counterparts. Films not only filled his consciousness, they transformed him, giving him more fulfilment than the religion others were trying to inculcate in him: 'None of that spiritual stimulation elevated his spirit or captured his imagination in any way comparable to what he felt before the altar of the silver screen. Time for Ivan was measured by the changing of the bill' (*THTC*, 195).

It is not surprising, therefore, that the act that starts him on his life of crime, his fight with Longah, is immediately seen as a clip from a movie. Ivan becomes a spectator to his own real life film:

> Then a strange thing happened. His head cleared and he was there but not there. In one way he seemed detached and floating above it all, seeing himself lying on the ground with a burly figure crouched above him. He saw himself rolling quickly out of Longah's reach, jumping to his feet and whipping out his *okapi*. He saw Longah stop, look alarmed and break off a bottle. It was just like watching a scene in *From Here to Eternity* where Lancaster and Borgnine are in the bar. He heard himself say, 'If it's killing you want Fatso, it's a killing you get.' From a distance he saw himself balancing on the balls of his feet, knees bent, switching the *okapi* from hand to hand as Peter Lorre used to do (*THTC*, 256–7).

The language with which Ivan addresses his adversary is also straight from an imagined film, and the other accouterments of cowboyhood will follow as the novel moves to its showdown-cum-climax. He dresses the part, and acquires guns from the appropriately nicknamed Midnight Cowboy, officially completing the transformation to outlaw gunslinger:

> Ivan hefted the guns again, feeling the balance and marveling again at the natural, steady way they nestled into his grip. He held them together and turned his wrists over to see the play of light on the barrels. He twirled them backward western style by the trigger, pleased at the easy graceful way they settled back against the heel of his hand.

'Rahtid,' Cowboy breathed. 'Gunslingah to raas. Is a star-bwai dis!' (*THTC,* 310).

Such pleasure in owning the firearms could only lead to a burning desire to use them, to complete the fantasy. The opportunity soon presents itself when Ivan, 'in one smooth, unhurried, Randolph Scott motion,' shoots the cop who is pursuing him at the start of a drug bust. The deed done, Ivan is now officially on the run, but overcomes the initial wave of nausea that filled him, and ends up pleased with himself, indeed with the image of himself as 'a calm, cold-eyed and very cunning desperado outsmarting posses and search parties' (*THTC,* 342). The denouement has begun, and there is no turning back, no help from his common-law wife Elsa, who, typically, does not fully understand what drove him to such a despicable deed, for such is the stereotypical role of the cowboy's woman: 'If there is a woman he loves, she is unable to understand his motives; she is against killing and being killed, and he finds it impossible to explain to her that there is no point in being "against" these things: they belong to his world'.[22] The fugitive Ivan sidelines the virtuous Elsa in the heat of pursuit. He relieves his tension with another woman of easy virtue, but even as he tries to forget his predicament in passionate sex, he cannot help the flashback to the cop shooting, and the instant connection to the film-like quality of the entire episode: 'It was pure, abstract motion and power, like something on the screen' (*THTC,* 346).

Glimpses of other movie types – war, for instance – meld with the final western imagery as Ivan is cornered and gunned down, a make-believe cowboy who encounters a real death, one that was foreshadowed in a dream Ivan had while hiding out from the law:

> Then there were scenes from movies he had seen – familiar westerns, but a mysterious, black cowboy astride a Honda kept riding into the scenes, changing the ending. Every time he appeared, guns spitting and engine roaring, the crowd in the theatre would erupt into cheering. A new scene came on, D'Jango was about to make his move. The crowd was watching for the black cowboy but a cold arrogant voice cut into their excitement: "*Show cut. Unu believe me now say show cut?*" The black cowboy did not appear (*THTC,* 374).

Ivan is impatient to play out the last scene. The stage has been set and the wait must not be too long, lest viewers begin to react to the slowdown in the pace of the action:

> 'So what dem a wait for – is *Sands of Iwo Jima* dis to raas? Is mus' Iwo Jima dem t'ink dem deh.'

He had to fight the laughter that rose up in him. Were they real – or another scene from a movie? They certainly seemed in no hurry to move. If he just lay in the thick grass they would never find him. Not cowering on their bellies like that. He realized with a great astonishment that Babylon, with all their long guns, were afraid of him. Eight, or more like twelve, with long-range guns crawling like so many turtles in the sand.

'Me one, an' dem fraid me … Show doan over a raas! Star-bwai can' dead after all… .' He rose to his feet shouting and staggering in the loose sand. 'Cho – done de army business!' he challenged, laughing. 'Who is de bad-man unu have? Sen' 'im out, nuh – one man who can draw. Sen' 'im out!'

He stood rocking in the shifting sand, bawling out his challenge and squinting against the gun's glare.

"Sen' out you fastes' gun – de bes' man unu have. Sen' 'im out!'

The police raised their heads – but were frozen either by fear or disbelief at this apparition.

'What de raas unu waiting for!' Maas' Ray screamed. 'Is him! Shoot!'

A sudden brief silence followed the echoes of his scream. Then, the fierce thunder of automatic rifles. Rhygin crumpled forward and rolled down the dune. The fierce clatter continued long after he was still, except for the impact the bullets made. They continued to pump lead into the dune with the frenzied intensity of a gang of apes battering with clubs the dead body of a leopard.

'STOP!' Maas' Ray bawled. 'Cease fire, nuh' (*THTC*, 390–1).

Christ-like, Ivan/Rhygin dies, only to live again. The final scene of all in the novel shows a small boy at play, in ambush behind a tree:

'Bram, Bram, Bram!' He leapt from cover, guns blazing.

The posse returned fire. 'You dead!' the sheriff shouted. 'Cho man, you dead!'

'Me Ah Rhygin!' the boy shouted back. 'Me can' dead!' (*THTC*, 391–2).

A new generation is about to begin the process all over again. The imitation of the home-grown outlaw by the little boys at play is significant. Ivan had that quality Naipaul saw as necessary to endear him to audiences – he had style.

War films and melodrama

Although we cannot overstate the importance and popularity of westerns as far as large numbers of Caribbean moviegoers were concerned, it must in all fairness be noted that there were other types of feature films that captured their imagination. Trinidadian Anthony Luengo, writing about cinema attendance in the mid-1960s, provides an update to Naipaul's account of what was popular:

> After the ten minutes or so of ads, there followed about another ten minutes of trailers, or 'intros', as they were called locally. The audience would become especially attentive at their appearance. They promised a seemingly endless parade of films ... Westerns with bluff 'star boys' like John Wayne and Robert Mitchum, biblical and medieval epics starring 'classy' actors like Charlton Heston, Stewart Granger, and Robert Taylor; titillating melodramas hinting at off-screen sex with blonde temptresses such as Dorothy Malone, Lana Turner, and Brigitte Bardot (being French, Bardot, of course, showed more skin than any of the others, which elicited an official, blanket condemnation of her films from the local *Catholic News*, thus forbidding Catholics like myself from attending them under threat of eternal hell-fire).[23]

Luengo goes on to state that war films were also lapped up, with many patrons going two and three times to see Audie Murphy's autobiographical *To Hell and Back*. Incidentally, it is this same film that Sparrow refers to in 'Gunslingers', his calypso glorifying the spate of hooliganism that was sweeping Trinidad and Tobago in the dying days of colonialism and the first days of independence:

> Sparrow selling guns nowadays
> That's what really pays
> Nearly every young man is a gunslinger
> With he razor and he steel knuckle on he finger
> Don't mind they dress in suit and bow tie
> All of them looking for guns to buy... .
> When you catch gun fever
> You' two hand does start to shiver
> This time you ready to attack
> Like Audie Murphy in *To Hell and Back*

> If you see a man ain't fraid to get kill
> Is to give him a one-way ticket to Boot Hill
> Just get a couple of you' friends
> Swear him 'way, you did it in self-defense.

In all fairness to Sparrow, one must point out that as he matured, a decade into independence, he too turned on the would-be bandits who were aping what they saw on the screen. He lambasted their obsession with so-called spaghetti westerns in his calypso 'Rope':

> Idle all day, don't work no way
> And have more cash than who get pay
> Spend it all on Italian western to learn more gunplay
> Thirsty, thirsty to practice it on Carnival day
> Ah warning all them Sancho and Django
> This year won't be so.

Sparrow let the potential evil-doers know, in no uncertain terms, that their unsocial behaviour would not be tolerated.

Steelbands and calypsonians and moviegoers

The mixture of war-time heroics and western lore that the calypsonian sang about in 'Gunslingers' was a stark, if amusing, comment on the fascination with feature films by a growing band of society misfits. But there were other artists, other misfits if one believes the bourgeois elements of the society, who, in their way, also reflected this fascination.

Steelbands

Although there are varying accounts about exactly where the steelband originated in Trinidad, there is absolutely no doubt that it came from the belly of the underclass. It is probably this humble origin that made the middle-class elements in society so hostile to its existence in the early years. The instruments were crude: discarded oil drums; the players were either illiterate or, at best, had a few years of elementary schooling. The music was quickly dubbed mere noise, and the derogatory term 'pan' used to dismiss what was clearly an annoyance to the peaceful existence of the quieter neighbourhoods.

In his study of the steelband movement, Stephen Stuempfle writes:

> The creators of the steelband were generally young and of
> African descent. In addition, they belonged to that sector of
> society that Trinidadians refer to as *grass-roots*: the working
> class, the marginally employed, and the unemployed. Their

bands were based in different neighborhoods and villages and intense rivalries ensued as they developed their new instruments. The grass-roots basis of the music and the violent clashes in which bands sometimes engaged evoked much hostility from the middle and upper classes and even from many members of the grass-roots class itself. Essentially the new music was perceived as a threat to the social order and legal restrictions were soon placed on its performance.[24]

From its very inception the steelband attracted the type of adherents who, as we have seen, would be most likely to be ardent cinema fans: young, poor, and black for the most part. Thus, it was not surprising that one of the very first bands called itself 'Alexander's Ragtime Band', directly copying the name from the title of the 1938 film starring Tyrone Power and featuring music by Irving Berlin.[25] This group was probably influenced by the fact that the film showed the triumph of popular music – ragtime – in the face of stiff competition from 'serious' music, a development that the quick minds of the local moviegoers would not have missed.

It was in the cinema, viewing over and over westerns, gangster dramas, war films, and musicals – from which they took many of the songs they played – that the budding steelband members and their followers found the spiritual support that their own society was denying them.

> Through these movies the panmen experienced a foreign world of grandeur, battles, and romance that had a major influence on the cultural style that they were developing... . Similarly, during the war and the immediate postwar years, panmen often named their bands after movies: Casablanca ... Destination Tokyo ... Cross of Lorraine ... Night Invaders ... Desperadoes ... Sun Valley ... Bataan ... Hill 60 ... Pearl Harbour ... . Once the war was over and Carnival was again permitted, the movies had a tremendous impact on military masquerades played by the steelbands. Uniforms, equipment, and maneuvers observed in the cinema were replicated on the streets.[26]

This carnival connection was the key to the survival of the steelband, since this annual festival gave them a focus and the opportunity to show themselves at their best. The rivalry involved in this search for identity and selfhood was intense, and unfortunately manifested itself in many now-famous clashes, which reinforced the feeling among the middle and upper classes that only hooligans would 'beat pan'.

Carnival celebrations had been held long before the steelband started participating in them. It was only grudgingly that the French creole element that controlled carnival acceded to the obvious enthusiasm of revellers as they enjoyed what the *Trinidad Guardian* disparagingly called in 1941 'the biscuit-drum and dustbin orchestras'. To their credit, though, the steelbands persevered, and even defied attempts to muzzle them though they were banned from the streets for the duration of the war. This defiance could be seen in the name changes that many of them underwent, in most instances the new appellation reflecting some popular Hollywood movie: 'Merry Boys' to 'Casablanca'; 'Oval Boys' to 'Invaders'; 'Laventille Boys' to 'Desperadoes'; 'John John Band' to 'Destination Tokyo'.[27] These were names that 'even today invoke loyalties and set passions aflame among the pan community'.[28] In the case of Casablanca, its former leader and later steelband historian, Oscar Pile, 'proudly displaying his tattoo of the Cross of Lorraine' to a *Sunday Guardian* staff writer, explained in the resulting article that members of his band identified with the movie *Casablanca* because of the 'guts the French showed against the Germans'.[29] The fact that the cross was also emblazoned in the centre of the band's flag as a rallying emblem also shows how powerful the movie influence was, allowing one group that had absolutely no connection with the other to use the latter's symbol as a unifying force.

The steelband players and their followers, once allowed into the regular carnival celebrations, quickly solidified their support and popularity, and even began to attract more and more followers from the middle and upper classes. Soon, their favourite costumes for the carnival celebrations, now that they were participating in their own right, were replicas of sailor uniforms. This development was possibly occasioned by the fact that the war had brought American sailors to Trinidad, and their presence had had a profound effect on the population – chronicled at length in many calypsos. 'Sailor mas', as it came to be known, was also popular because it was relatively inexpensive and the same costume, with minor adjustments, could be used year after year. But the many war movies being shown also accounted for this popularity, for the sailor costume was easily part of the military re-enactments that the carnival bands loved to stage. 'In 1948, for example, Red Army played its namesake with "officers and high-ranking generals in their red coats and dark trousers."'[30] As carnival developed and the portrayals became more complex, band leaders, whether directly involved with steelbands or not, tried to outdo one another in order to cop the various prizes that confirmed superiority in mas'. Errol Hill provides an account of the keen nature of the competition:

While sailor bands have grown fanciful, the masquerades of army, marine, and air corps personnel have tended to become more realistic. Frequently, a section of these bands appears in battle dress, camouflaged with bits of shrubbery, carrying rifles, machine guns, and other weapons of modern warfare. Others drive real jeeps and life-sized tanks discharging rockets and smoke. Arriving on the carnival competition stage, the marines reenact a commando raid. They crawl on hands and knees, shoot from prostrate position, get wounded, and are helped off by fighting companions, all in the best tradition of American war movies. For the ten minutes that it takes the band to cross the stage, a desperate battle is in progress from which every one of hundreds of maskers emerges a war hero.[31]

Carnival, then, like the cinema, allowed participants to live vicariously, if only for two days a year. As the spectacle of lavish costumes took on added importance with the emphasis on competition among band leaders, Hollywood-type productions began to be imitated. In this regard, Harold Saldenha is cited as the leader who did the most to pattern his portrayals on what was being shown on the screen, and among carnival aficionados he came to be known as the local Cecil B. De Mille. Errol Hill's study further informs us that:

> By the time Harold Saldenha came on the scene, in 1952, historical bands were growing larger, more professional, and more authentic. Mr. Saldenha began by basing his first bands on film extravaganzas like *Quo Vadis* and *Samson and Delilah*. For costume designs he used still pictures put out as advertising material by the motion picture companies, and he even wrote to Hollywood for additional information.[32]

Anthony Luengo also tells of audience reaction to film epics like *The Ten Commandments, The Prodigal, The Robe, Quo Vadis,* and *Samson and Delilah*:

> Among the celluloid persecuted and their persecutors appeared instantly recognizable actors – Kirk Douglas, Jack Palance, Yul Brynner, Anthony Quinn, Tony Curtis – whose on-screen behaviour prompted continual chronic commentary from the ground-level crowd: 'Dem pagans bad, eh?' 'Oh, God, he go dead,' 'Kill he now!' 'Dat is a good mas' (the last comment reflecting the audience's keen attention to cinema costume, an important source of inspiration for upcoming Carnival bands).[33]

Carnival provided an excellent opportunity for one section of the Caribbean population to believe make-believe, and the cinema's contribution to this phenomenon was undeniable.

Calypsonians

Carnival had other performers whose work is closely associated with the annual festivity. Traditionally referred to as the voice of the people, calypsonians provide a virtual running commentary on what is going on in Trinidad society in particular, and in the rest of the world in general. Each year brings new calypsoes, resulting in a wealth of songs on every subject imaginable. Paradoxically, though, given this wealth, calypsos dealing with films and the cinema are relatively scarce, a situation apparently also reflected in Jamaican reggae songs. The calypsos that did deal with cinema and film nonetheless provide a window to the mindset of the average Trinidadian.

In 1936, the Growling Tiger[34] recorded a calypso called 'Movie Stars' listing all his, and presumably the country's, favourites. On western stars he sang:

> With my western stars I won't go too far
> I bound to mention Gary Cooper
> Ton Keene, a favorite in Trinidad,
> Tom Mix, Richard Arlen, and Ken Maynard.

The calypso named the movies *Common Clay, The Big Broadcast, Imitation of Life*, and *Song of Soho*, in addition to 42 other actors and artists. The Roaring Lion that same year recorded 'Four Mills Brothers' in which he stated his preference for the singing siblings over Bing Crosby in *We're Not Dressing*, and how much he enjoyed them as they accompanied Cab Calloway in *The Big Broadcast*. Lion devoted an entire calypso to 'Bing Crosby' in 1939, mentioning songs from *We're Not Dressing* and *Pennies From Heaven*; and in 1956 Lord Invader recorded 'Grace Kelly Wedding' in celebration of that royal event.[35]

We have already seen how calypsos treated the rising crime rate in Trinidad and the whole activity of cinema attendance in a particular context. There were some that merely played on the popularity of film titles, like when Lord Melody had the mother of his children remind them that the 'Creature from the Black Lagoon' was their father; or of film characters, like when Sparrow sang 'Cowboy Melo', relating how 'a cow in the country make a baby just like Melody'. There were others, like Sparrow's 'Jack Palance', that used the film connection as a metaphor for what was occurring in the society. In this case, the calypsonian was complaining about older women, prostitutes to all appearances, who were still 'hustling for a bob' in night clubs and competing with young girls:

> Caroline and Josephine making more than fifty
> And I'm sure without any doubt they could be my granny
> Still they walking 'bout at night with they face like Jack Palance
> Go to France! Step aside and give the Sparrow a chance
> Ah looking for youth not experience.

The gritty hard-boiled face of the well-known actor thus becomes the symbol of the ugliness of the entire situation in which older women are forced to continue plying their flesh trade. Palance's face was good for only Palance. The cinema-savvy public would have understood the analogy instantly.

This same public would also have understood the point the Mighty Spoiler was making, though with tongue slightly in cheek, when he sang his calypso 'Tarzan'. The Afro-Caribbean viewers would have come to accept the original Tarzan, whose alleged superior intelligence had seen him through many adventures with African natives or dim-witted European explorers. If such was the fare presented, then it was best to leave it as such, either because the Caribbean viewers were brainwashed into believing that Tarzan's Africa was the real thing, or because they knew better and tolerated the biased images as an example of Euro-centric arrogance. We cannot take it for granted that Tarzan was seen as an aberration – and Naipaul's quote early in the chapter substantiates this view – given the power of the British-based colonial education system. For many years Caribbean people of African descent were taught that Africa was the Dark Continent, and that it was populated with savages, with whom no self-respecting Caribbean person would want to associate.

As we listen to this calypso, we must keep in mind that the calypsonian is forever the trickster. As such, his uncritical preference for the original Tarzan over the modern version must be seen as part of that most Trinidadian of characteristics: the ability to see humour in almost any situation:

> Ah rather see Mickey Mouse drive a train
> Than to go and see a Tarzan picture again
> Now he riding bike, Tarzan going to dance
> Tarzan eating hot dog, he wearing pants.
> Now he talking fluent more than you or me
> Like he eat up a Webster's dictionary.

We have already become accustomed to the old Tarzan, the singer is saying, and for that, we have to go back to his early films. A cleaned-up, sanitized Tarzan is no Tarzan:

> If they want to get meh money out of meh hand
> Bring back pictures like *Tarzan the Apeman*
> Two pictures again which were very great
> *Tarzan Finds a Son*, *Tarzan and His Mate*.

It is interesting to note that Earl Lovelace's fictional calypsonian in *The Dragon Can't Dance* also invites a fresh look at the Tarzan cycle of films. Philo won the Calypso King crown with 'Women Running Me Down' and 'I Am the Ape Man, Not Tarzan':

> I am the ape man, not Tarzan
> This is something you have to understand
> Tarzan couldn't be no ape
> Anywhere in Africa he land we woulda cook him for dinner
> He couldn't escape (*TDCD*, 244).

Like Spoiler, Philo goes for stereotype, only in this case it is the other one perpetuated by Hollywood – that of the African as cannibal:

> The point he, Philo, was striving to make in the Tarzan calypso was that the African would have eaten Tarzan if he was real. He liked the idea of Africans as cannibals. What a nice wicked sight! Tarzan in a big steaming pot and Africans jumping around waiting for him to cook. Any time he listened to that calypso he laughed (*TDCD*, 245).

The laughter surely would come from the lingering image of such a scene in the cinema, an image reminiscent of the one conjured up by Sparrow in his 'Congo Man':

> Two white women traveling through Africa
> Find themselves in the hands of a cannibal headhunter
> He cook up one and he eat one raw
> They taste so good he wanted more
> More, more … me want more.

Sparrow uses the cannibal imagery as a cover for black sexual conquest of the white female:

> I envy the Congo man
> I wish I coulda go and shake he hand
> He eat until he stomach upset
> And I, ah never eat a white meat yet.

It is this aspect of the calypso that appealed to the basic instinct of the masses. Among listeners of African descent, there was no outrage over Sparrow's negative portrayal of their forefathers; nor was anyone shocked that the fictional Philo could laugh at the thought of Tarzan being cooked by Africans. This absence of reaction shows the extent to which make-believe could at times lull viewers, and listeners, into complacency. This is no small paradox, given the vociferous, down-to-earth, and penetrating critiquing we have seen from those fed on this diet of make-believe.

Make-believe today

Television has naturally expanded what the public sees on a daily basis. The growing affordability of television sets and video-cassette recorders, as well as the increased ability of the region's masses to visit the countries that were only part of their fantasy until a few short years ago, has led to a toning down of the utter fascination with images and characters on the cinema screen. In a way, the romance of the unattainable has cooled considerably. Going to the cinema is still a popular activity, and films still exert a great influence on the population, some of it amusing and healthy, some far less so. Karate, for instance, was noticeably very popular during the period that coincided with the spate of *kung-fu* films. It is noticeable that one hardly hears of young men taking names of film heroes or film stars as nicknames any more, although the Jamaican music scene did produce DJs Dillinger, Charlie Chaplin, Captain Sinbad, and Dennis Alcapone, as well as singer Clint Eastwood. This could very well be because contemporary matinee idols are not viewed with the same awe and fascination that attended Humphrey Bogart, Richard Widmark or Gary Cooper. It could also signal a loss of innocence or *naïvete*, or, as is most likely, the fact that tastes have simply shifted. Cinemas, already fewer in number than two decades ago, will see new patrons join the die-hard regulars – pit has largely disappeared, for example – and the perspective these viewers bring will necessarily be different. Films will continue to amaze and amuse patrons, though computer-generated special effects will probably become the new source of wonder. Be that as it may, the cinema seems destined to remain firmly embedded in the consciousness of the cinema-going population, which will continue to enjoy believing make-believe.

But, one might ask, how did this same population feel when the aura of make-believe was broken by on-screen images of locations familiar to the viewer? Would it believe, as did some early sceptics with regard to fiction by Caribbean authors, that locally conceived stories about life in the region could not be on par with those conceived elsewhere? Would Caribbean-made films ever be seen as worthy of the same adulation and respect as foreign ones? What patrons saw once recognizable locations were shown on screen, and how they reacted to what they saw, is the focus of the following chapters.

Notes

1. Toni Morrison, *Playing in the Dark* (1992), 15.
2. V. S. Naipaul, *The Middle Passage* (1969), 62–3. [*MP*]
3. Carolyn Cooper, *Noises in the Blood* (1993), 96.
4. Michael Thelwell, *The Harder They Come* (1980), 194. [*THTC*]
5. V. S. Naipaul, *A House for Mr Biswas* (1992), 464.
6. V. S. Naipaul, *A Turn in the South* (1990), 109.
7. V. S. Naipaul, *Miguel Street* (1971), 9.
8. Derek Walcott, *Remembrance and Pantomime* (1980), 131.
9. Robert Warshow, 'Movie Chronicle: the Westerner,' (1992), 466.
10. Michael Lieber, *Street Life* (1981), 94–5.
11. V. S. Naipaul, *A House for Mr. Biswas,* 466.
12. Ralph de Boissière, *Crown Jewel* (1981), 123.
13. Derek Walcott, *Collected Poems* (1986), 435. See also Christopher Laird's poem '12:30 Is Life', where he writes:

    > When I come out of a 12:30 brother
    > the whole world is a main street in China,
    > and I is Wang Yu.
    >
    > …
    >
    > 12:30 ain't cinema ner,
    > is life!

    (Quoted with permission of the author.)
14. Merle Hodge, *Crick Crack, Monkey* (1970), 12. [*CCM*]
15. Wilfred Cartey, *Whispers from the Caribbean* (1991), 188.
16 Cooper, *Noises in the Blood*, 98.
17. Earl Lovelace, *The Dragon Can't Dance* (1986), 64–5. [*TDCD*]
18. Earl Lovelace, *Salt* (1996), 220–1.
19. Michael Thelwell *The Harder They Come,* 8. For the author's account of how he came to write this novel, see his article, '*The Harder They Come*: From Film to Novel', (1992), 176–210.
20. Cooper, *Noises in the Blood,* 98.
21. Ibid., 106–7.
22. Warshow, 'Movie Chronicle' (1992), 454.
23. Anthony Luengo, 'Patrons of Empire', (1998), n.p.
24. Stephen Stuempfle, *The Steelband Movement* (1995), 2.
25. Michael Anthony, in *Parade of the Carnivals of Trinidad, 1838–1989* (1989), 153, places this band's first appearance in carnival in 1940: 'People jumped to tamboo-bamboo and bottle-and-spoon in the gray of the morning, and perhaps one of the

most joyous bands was the one from New Town, the old Cavalry tamboo-bamboo band. This was now Alexander's Ragtime Band, but it was calling itself Count Basie this Jour Ouvert'.

26. Stuempfle, *The Steelband Movment*, 49–50.
27. The change to 'Destination Tokyo' is also given as being from 'River Lady'. (See Rory Rostant, 'Star Struck', in *Sunday Guardian Lagniappe Magazine*, 31 December 1995.) Leo Alfred (Stuempfle, 50) and Michael Anthony (169) give the 'John John' version.
28. Rostant, 'Star Struck', 21.
29. Rostant, 'Star Struck', 21.
30. Stuempfle, *The Steelband Movement,* 56.
31. Errol Hill, *The Trinidad Carnival* (1972), 94–5.
32. Ibid., 97.
33. Luengo, 'Patrons of Empire', n.p.
34. Calypsonians usually sing under a sobriquet, and there was one who sang as Lord Brynner, complete with shaven head like his Hollywood namesake. His calypsos did not deal with cinema or film.
35. I am indebted and grateful to John Cowley for providing these calypso references.

2

On location: images, reality and stereotype

Echoing the passage in which V. S. Naipaul reported audience reaction to Lauren Bacall's claiming to be from Port of Spain, Anthony Luengo writes:

> When, at the beginning of the wartime movie *Heaven Knows, Mr. Allison*, it was announced in large text that we were 'Somewhere in the South Pacific,' there was a brief hush, then loud laughter. Above this outburst, someone at the front of the cinema yelled 'You lie!' More loud laughter. The deserted tropical shore on the screen certainly *could* have been in the South Pacific, but the man shouting, like everyone else in the packed audience, knew better.
>
> The cinema was the Empire on upper Frederick Street in Port of Spain, and it was around 1958, just after the movie had been filmed, to much local interest, in nearby Tobago.[1]

What the audience knew was that this film had been shot on location, an occurrence that is not unusual in film-making, but one that takes on significance when the viewer recognizes the location. The excitement of recognition can even interfere with the viewer's enjoyment of the film, clouding the objectivity needed for an unbiased assessment. It is this interference that is at play in the comment by the Port of Spain moviegoer quoted above. It did not matter as much when the location shots were of places to which Caribbean audiences could not relate. But with familiarity would come emotional attachment, as well as added scrutiny to see whether the images of the Caribbean presented were authentic, whether they were close to reality, or whether they were the result of extra-regional stereotyping.

In the theatre, a simple set, a stylized reconstruction of a milieu, can suffice to create the illusion of reality. In the cinema, one expects a closer representation of reality; anything less might lead to viewer dissatisfaction, as has been the case with the glaring artificiality of early sets that purported to show Africa. The eventual solution to the use of

Hollywood back-lots was to take crews on location, an exercise that proved increasingly feasible and manageable as technology condensed the bulk of most of the equipment needed to shoot a film. Naturally, the Caribbean benefited from this development, and 'shot on location in the Caribbean' became a badge of authenticity for a variety of films. But whereas mainland film-makers hoped their films showed a true-to-life Caribbean, island viewers and others with a sympathetic eye often saw these works as dripping with stereotype and negative images. This situation led Kennedy Wilson to the following observation:

> Since Hollywood's early days, filmmakers have depicted the region as an illusory paradise peopled by dubious natives, ravishing temptresses and swashbuckling heroes. Themes of black magic and voodoo, gangsters and spies, and pirates and villains have recurred in nightmarish proportions over the years. As long as the formula seems to work, portrayals of the islands as lawless playgrounds will certainly prevail.[2]

This chapter takes a look at some of the films shot partially or totally on location in the English-speaking Caribbean, and the resulting themes that were part of this search for authenticity. As one film critic has reminded us, a film 'isn't just plot, shots, editing, and music. That's text. It's some other, difficult-to-define *something,* unstated but insistent: a vocabulary of suggested ideas, visual thematics and associational connection. That's subtext.'[3] Our search here is for both text and subtext. The period under consideration extends approximately half a century through to the present, and as such does not cover the very early location films, about which Kennedy Wilson has given us some indication of their frequent treatment of the theme of piracy:

> The Caribbean has long been used by filmmakers as a place of intrigue. *Captain Blood* (1935) was the film that made Errol Flynn a star. He played the eponymous arch pirate who gets the girl, Olivia de Havilland, and becomes Governor of Jamaica. Although this was one of the less swashbuckling of Flynn's movies, it was perhaps the best pirate film ever made.
>
> There followed a spate of made-in-Hollywood pirate films that had Caribbean settings capitalizing on glamour and mystery of the Spanish Main. Seven years after *Captain Blood*, Tyrone Power became Governor of Jamaica and attempted to rid the Caribbean of piracy in *The Black Swan* (1942). In 1948, the famed musical director Vincente Minnelli made *The Pirate*, a musical with his then-wife Judy Garland

mooning over Gene Kelly. The score, by Cole Porter, included references to Martinique, Trinidad, and, inevitably, voodoo.[4]

Ironically, movie historian Pauline Kael, in her short review of *Captain Blood*, says that 'the exteriors were actually Corona, Laguna Beach, and Palm Canyon near Palm Springs',[5] all locations in the United States. Of note, too, is the fact that the all-black cast of *Dirty Gertie from Harlem, USA* (1946), a movie supposedly set entirely in Trinidad, clearly never went anywhere near this or any other island.

We must keep in mind that the films made by Hollywood – the majority of those that came to the Caribbean – were meant primarily for American audiences, who hardly knew, or even cared, where the Caribbean was. They were aware, as was the case with Africa, that there was a certain charm and intrigue that surrounded dealing with foreign peoples and cultures. As such, the films set in the Caribbean had more to do with how the outsider coped with everything from surviving 'hot, humid nights pulsating with tropic rhythms' – a typical description of life after dark in the islands – to finding a local doctor with up-to-date training; from learning the latest dance steps, for there was always music and carnival, to dealing with crooked politicians; and from acquiring the natural lilt of the language to understanding the language of the supernatural. In other words, the films were largely gazes from the outside, giving viewers on occasion the impression of seeing a travelogue meant to promote tourism in the islands.

Affair in Trinidad

In 1952, when Columbia Pictures made *Affair in Trinidad,* even before the title sequence was projected a voice off-camera accompanied a shot that started with the wider western hemisphere and slowly zeroed in on Trinidad.

> Between North and South America [the voice tells viewers] lie the islands of the Caribbean, colorful and exotic. Once remote and little known, history is forcing them out of obscurity into the current of world events. Important among these is the British colony, Trinidad.

It is only well into the film that we learn why Trinidad would be considered important. Its location, it turns out, is quite strategic, and enemy forces would love to gain a foothold there, and have the ability to launch strikes against the United States. As for the plot, the studio-supplied synopsis informs us that:

> Rita Hayworth stars as Chris Emery, a sexy, hip-grinding dancer who works in a Trinidad dive owned by her husband. When he's murdered by an international spy (Alexander Scourby), Chris' life is turned upside down, especially when the police draw her into the investigation. When Glenn Ford, who plays her brother-in-law Steve, arrives in town, the two are drawn deeper into the mystery and ultimately into each other's arms.

It is never fully explained how this American woman has ended up a dancer in a Caribbean nightclub, but she does seem to exude enough sensuality to mesmerize her admirers with what the studio termed her 'wild, uninhibited tropical dance to calypso music'.

The film reunites, according to the studio blurb, 'the screen-scorching team of Rita Hayworth and Glenn Ford' in a 'romantic spy drama of international intrigue and sizzling sensuality.' Its opening shot shows a sign identifying Port of Spain, BWI, but we see mainly white (possibly expatriate) police and customs officials in charge of black (possibly local) officers. Such a situation is not altogether unusual, in view of the colonial status of Trinidad at the time, but when the blacks do speak – and they do so very infrequently – it is clear that they are not Trinidadian, not even Caribbean. The Trinidad/Caribbean ear detects this immediately, but the American ear would not know the difference.

This pseudo-Caribbean accent is heard in the unseen chorus that accompanies the song that Rita Hayworth sings in the nightclub where she works. The song, 'Trinidad Lady', is by Lester Lee and Bob Russell, and is sung by Jo Ann Greer. There are echoes of the Andrews Sisters version of 'Rum and Coca Cola' in the arrangement, an influence that is plausible since the film came not too long after the outstanding success of this calypso on the American hit parade. The club – the Caribee – where Rita Hayworth performs has a predominantly white clientele. Many of them are in uniform, suggesting a military presence on the island, as was the case in post-Second World War Trinidad, the context of the original 'Rum and Coca Cola' calypso by Lord Invader.[6] The musicians in the band that accompanies her seem local, but their music does not have a local ring to it, though there could be perfectly acceptable reasons for this. Once again, the Caribbean ear immediately hears what the American arranger imagines calypso-oriented music to be, and the dance that Rita Hayworth does to this music, while sensuously exotic to the American eye (by the studio's own admission in its blurb), is greeted from the Caribbean viewer's perspective with bemused politeness.

The Trinidad shown in *Affair in Trinidad* is firmly in the grip of colonialism. We never see the colonized citizens in any other role but one of service and subservience. The ones who are probably played by Trinidadian extras – various pedestrians, and a dance group at a party – have no speaking parts. Apart from the local fishermen, played by Americans, the only 'Trinidadian' or 'West Indian' given a speaking role is Dominique, played by American Juanita Moore, the brazen housemaid employed by the heroine. While it is comforting and encouraging to see this woman assert herself, it is also highly unlikely that a black house-maid would have taken such liberties with her white expatriate employer.

Most of the action takes place in settings that do not particularly indicate that we are in the Caribbean, and the architecture has a definite non-Caribbean flavour to it. In this regard, we are far from what would become stereotypical: swaying palm trees and sandy beaches, for instance.

The cars used are nearly all American, complete with left-hand drive interiors in a British colony where cars drive on the left side of the road, though, to be fair to the producers, Trinidad did allow such cars on the roads. The final shot of Trinidad is of a mountain range seen from aboard the ship taking the heroes back to America. We cannot escape the feeling, though, that nothing has been done to help Trinidad emerge from the obscurity mentioned in the film's opening seconds. Columbia Pictures claims that *Affair In Trinidad* out-grossed *Gilda*, its 1946 blockbuster also starring Rita Hayworth and Glenn Ford, by a million dollars at the box office. It is hard to tell what was the principal attraction, beyond the pairing of two favourite actors, but it is reasonable to assume it was not the fact that the movie showed the Caribbean.

Fire Down Below

The studio used Rita Hayworth again in 1957, this time casting her opposite two leading men, Robert Mitchum and Jack Lemmon, in *Fire Down Below*. Columbia described this film as a 'high seas adventure tale of smoldering passion and deception, shot on location in Trinidad. Hayworth is the torrid siren-turned-sailor who comes between two best friends and sends temperatures rising.' Already we can see the pattern emerging: put a character in a tropic setting, add some pulsating rhythms, and sensuality ripples forth. The publicity blurb confirms this impression:

Playing the mysterious Irena was a more challenging assignment than Hayworth's previous roles. But for all the depth she brings to her character, Hayworth's sex appeal is always close to the surface. When Irena joins a carnival crowd, a wild limbo suddenly turns into a sensuous dance solo climaxed by the removal of her high-heeled slippers that has all the power and erotic force of a stripper's final fling.

It is as if Chris Emery of *Affair in Trinidad* has returned, only she is now seen in vivid colour. In fact, the spectacular colours of the region have led at least one observer to conclude that very often 'the Caribbean and its islands are the real stars ... lending hackneyed plots a touch of sunny glamour or a beach-party atmosphere.'[7]

The Caribbean as locus of international intrigue is once more evident. Irena (Rita Hayworth) has arrived in the unidentified island from Havana. She comes with a shady past, is without proper documents, and needs to be taken to another island. Felix (Robert Mitchum) and Tony (Jack Lemmon), best friends until they both fall for this *femme fatale*, make a living operating a boat between the islands. They are hired for the job, and are assisted by Jimmy Jean, played by Trinidadian actor Edric Connor. After the inevitable falling out, Tony decides to make one last trip before marrying Irena, but he and Jimmy Jean are ambushed by the coastguard, though they escape by jumping overboard. Tony feels he was betrayed by Felix, and takes another boat back to home base, but is injured in a collision (in thick fog no less). He is trapped under tons of rubble and needs help to be extricated from a ship that is on the verge of blowing up. Enter Felix once more, risking his life to save his former friend, who still vows to kill him for stealing the woman he loved. He changes his mind when he sees that Irena and Felix are now a couple in love. 'Some days you win, some days you lose,' he concludes.

Edric Connor as Jimmy Jean is the lone Caribbean native with a speaking role. He thus represents a people who have no voice in this movie, and almost no face, apart from the one seen on those providing services – such as the firemen – or on those gawking at events surrounding the fire aboard the boat. There is a shot of uniformed school children singing as they walk along the street under the watchful eye of a nun, but they are seen only from behind. We hear their song, but never see their faces, so that an interesting opportunity to show the look of youth is missed completely. Even the voice that sings the title song, 'Fire Down Below',[8] is that of an unseen Teri Southern. One would have preferred to hear that of Edric Connor, the film's acknowledged singer of folk songs, at least from the Caribbean audience's point of view. As the harpooner Daggoo in *Moby Dick* (1956), he had been allowed by John Huston to have some say in the choice of song to inspire the hunters:

> Though his role was peripheral in *Moby Dick*, Edric made a very important, but easily overlooked, contribution to the film. Daggoo is required to sing a sea shanty to inspire the men in their boats during the whalehunt. From his own repertoire, Connor chose 'Hill an' Gully Rider,' a 150-year-old Jamaican folk song by an anonymous composer. Pearl [his wife] remembers how Edric was fully aware that it would be recognized by Caribbean people in the audience.[9]

Fire Down Below did strive for authenticity in one area. The opening sequence of limbo dancing features the 'Stretch' Cox troupe, one of the more popular performers on the tourist and nightclub circuit of the period. V. S. Naipaul's observation on the significance of limbo at this point in Trinidad and Tobago's history is worth recalling. He wrote in *The Middle Passage* that 'nothing pleases Trinidadians so much as to see their culture being applauded by white American tourists in nightclubs.' He then quoted a piece from the *Trinidad Guardian*, headlined: 'Limbo for W. I. Film Likely', in which the author reported that an Italian film director had flown into Trinidad; that he was looking for talent and possible locations; and that he was considering 'incorporating the limbo in the film' (*MP* 76–7).

The carnival sequence in *Fire Down Below* did give a reasonable sense of what is involved in this festival, but the mixture of revellers, bystanders, and musicians somehow does not tally, especially with the music supplied on the soundtrack. We see the steelband instruments but do not hear them, and the stately dancing couples amidst the revelry are definitely out of place. Finally, one cannot resist a feeling of amusement as one looks at the outsider – Irena – falling under the hypnotic spell of the local rhythms as if on cue, because such is what is expected in this tropical setting. Felix does not succumb to the charm of the milieu the way Irena does, but Tony allows himself to attempt a timid version of the limbo.

As far as Caribbean audiences are concerned, what stands out most of all in this movie is the same distancing apparent in *Affair in Trinidad*. Dominique has now become Jimmy – to show that the islanders can think and speak. Apart from this one character, all the others could just as well have been on a studio lot, rather than on location. The interaction that might have made Caribbean viewers proud to see themselves as characters on screen is limited to their roles as caterers to the tastes and desires of outsiders.

Island in the Sun

The year 1957 also saw the making of *Island in the Sun*, which would go a little further in showing that Caribbean people could be more than domestic servants and boat crew. The film shows that colonialism, portrayed in its rich ceremonial splendour, was nevertheless on its way out, for there is mention of a new constitution, one most probably conferring political independence. 'Do you think the West Indian is ready to govern himself?' a visiting journalist asks the island's governor. The film provides an indirect reply.

Viewers in the Commonwealth Caribbean could easily think that this movie is about them and their situation in the dying days of Britain's hold on the political reins. Shot primarily in Barbados and Grenada in the newly developed Cinemascope, it opens, like *Affair in Trinidad*, with a pinpointing of the geographical setting, only this time it is of the fictional island of Santa Marta.

We are told by voice-over that the island's population is 100 000; that 90 per cent of these inhabitants are of mixed ancestry; that they are ex-slaves who came to the island four and a half centuries ago; that the main crop is sugar; that the island was originally French but is now a British Crown colony. The shot that precedes this narration opens with an aerial view of the complete island, followed by limbo dancing with steelband music. But most importantly, the film's opening soundtrack sequence is of Harry Belafonte singing 'Island in the Sun', with appropriate scenes illustrating the stanzas: workers cutting cane and loading bananas, vendors at the market, fishermen tending their sails, and so on.

Harry Belafonte, who had spent part of his childhood in Jamaica, had brought international recognition to calypso, and to the Caribbean via his recordings of Irving Burgie compositions like 'Jamaica Farewell' and 'The Banana Boat Song'. Trinidadians in particular thought of Belafonte as a lightweight when he sang calypsos, to which they felt only they could do justice. But as singer of pleasant folk songs of life in the region he was more readily accepted. His 'Island in the Sun' was part of Burgie's string of hit songs that immediately identified things Caribbean, and it is unfortunate that the film's credits do not acknowledge Burgie, born in America of a Barbadian mother, as the song's composer. What *Fire Down Below* failed to do, namely use Edric Connor the known singer to cover the title song, would be done in this film, thereby creating a more lasting rapport with Caribbean audiences.

The film tells the story of Maxwell Fleury (James Mason), owner of Belle Fontaine, a decaying colonial family estate. He mistakenly suspects his wife is having a romantic relationship with a gentlemanly ex-colonel (Michael Rennie), whom he ends up murdering. A wily police inspector persuades him to confess. In the meantime, Maxwell's sister Jocelyn (Joan Collins) is trying to decide whether she should accept the advances of the governor's son Euan (Stephen Boyd); and islanders David Boyeur (Harry Belafonte) and Margot Seaton (Dorothy Dandridge) become involved in inter-racial relationships: he with Maxwell's sister-in-law Mavis Norman (Joan Fontaine), and she with the governor's aide-de-camp Dennis Archer (John Justin).

The Caribbean voice in this film is shared between Belafonte, playing a militant labour leader and aspiring politician, and Dorothy Dandridge, playing an ambitious store clerk-turned-stenographer. David Boyeur cannot bring himself to fall in love with Englishwoman Mavis, for this would surely mean having to leave the island just as things are changing for the better for his people. His ambition is to take his militancy through the rest of the islands – to St Kitts, Grenada and Trinidad. He also fears she will never, indeed can never, understand what he experiences as a black man, and might even end up calling him a nigger. The mulatto Margot, on the other hand, has no difficulty being wooed by Dennis Archer, nor any qualms over going off to England with him. Why she does not have a relationship with the handsome David, whom she accompanies to the governor's party early in the film, is never explained, and must have puzzled Caribbean viewers.

The racial problem raised by the movie was seen in an entirely different light in the Caribbean, and led the press to be particularly critical of its treatment.[10] It is almost laughable to see how much the colonial power structure is obsessed with the matter of mixed blood, a subject that would have been controversial in America, but which Caribbean viewers would have taken in their stride. We were even reminded at the opening of the film that some 90 per cent of the population is of mixed heritage, with the result that all the revelations about a Jamaican grandmother and the like seem anti-climatic.

Hollywood's hitherto unwritten prohibition of on-screen inter-racial kissing and love-making, which led the American press to trumpet the many firsts chalked up by this movie, seems similarly ludicrous to the Caribbean viewer. The blight of racism had almost torpedoed *Island in the Sun* in America. Film historian Donald Bogle writes:

> Before its release, some theater owners (mostly Southern) threatened to boycott it. The South Carolina legislature even considered passing a bill to fine any movie house that showed the film $5000. That bill was never passed, but the threats had their effect.[11]

No one would conceive of such a situation in the Caribbean, although many of the islands' black population would acknowledge privately the existence of an unofficial hierarchy of colour. Boyeur's assessment, given to the visiting journalist, that the most important issue on the island is one of colour does not ring true. British colonialism in the islands did not allow race relations to degenerate into absurdity the way they did in the United States at that time.

The film does make it clear, however, that the pomp and circumstance of colonialism, which it shows very well at times, are about to give way to a new disposition, to which the governor seems already resigned. Maxwell Fleury's half-hearted attempt to run for office is effectively countered by David Boyeur, who, as far as Caribbean spectators were concerned, says all the right things in his short campaign. The inside view audiences would have had of the colonial apparatus would have confirmed that it was just as shaky as any other, and that the British were no different from the rest of other mortals. Boyeur's decision to sacrifice love for politics, while praiseworthy, seems hollow at the end of this film, especially when Caribbean audiences were fully aware that many of their black leaders had brought home white wives. In addition, the typical pit audience would have had difficulty understanding how David could prefer Mavis over the stunningly beautiful Margot.

There is the overall look of authenticity in the scenes shot with locals, whether at the beach or on crowded buses. In one of the small speaking parts, a worker explains to the police chief how and where he found the murdered man's wallet, but his language is almost a parody of what the American ear thinks a Caribbean accent sounds like. He comes across as overly subservient to the white police official, almost non-Caribbean in his demeanour.

Carnival as the remover of inhibition is again in evidence, only this time it is the local belle who allows herself to be transported by the bewitching music as she moves among her countrymen. Unlike Irena in *Fire Down Below,* the outsider who falls under the spell of the dance, the English ladies in *Island in the Sun* remain aloof from involvement in island festivities, as do the men. Consequently, what might possibly have served as a useful catalyst for the coming together of the expatriates and the islanders remains just another event that is observed with curious detachment.

The approaching political maturity alluded to in *Island in the Sun*'s Santa Marta was already in the air in the Caribbean when this film was released at the end of the 1950s, making it easy for audiences to relate to Boyeur's circumstances. They could even go beyond his vision, since in 1958 the Commonwealth colonies had united in a

federation, a dream of many early politicians, and an idea never mentioned by Boyeur for all his desire to develop political awareness in
some of the other island territories. Unfortunately for pan-Caribbean
unity, the federation did not last, and by August 1962 it ended when
Jamaica and Trinidad and Tobago each opted for independence. There
were no films advocating a federated Caribbean – either from outside
the region, or from within it. Island cultures and societies would
remain individually portrayed, some films depicting actual islands,
others depicting fictitious ones.

James Bond

One of the first films portraying the anglophone Caribbean to be
shown in the region in the post-independence era was *Dr. No*. It tells
the story of special agent James Bond (Sean Connery), who had been
sent from London to Jamaica to investigate the mysterious disappear-
ance of another agent. Once on the island, Bond soon discovers that
someone wants him dead. All trails lead to the sinister Dr No (Joseph
Wiseman), a nuclear scientist with revenge and destruction on his
mind.

Released a short while after the departure of the British, the film
was made at Pinewood studios in England, and in Jamaica at location
sites such as Kingston, Ocho Rios, Dunn's River Falls, Falmouth, St
Anne's Bay, and the Reynold's Bauxite Pier. It is fairly common
knowledge that Ian Fleming, James Bond's creator, loved Jamaica, and
wrote his novels about the special agent from his hideaway,
Goldeneye, on the island's north coast. Jamaica, then, was the most
natural setting for the first of what would turn out to be an internationally popular sequence of films. It was used again in 1973 for *Live and
Let Die*, with location shots in Montego Bay, Runaway Bay and the
Rose Hall Great House.

Dr. No opens with a shot of three blind men walking in single file.
Even as the credits are still being shown, a male voice on the soundtrack sings what is supposedly a calypso, 'Three Blind Mice' – it men-
tions the men walking along 'to a calypso beat'. We have to believe, in
the absence of any acknowledgment to the contrary in the on-screen
credits, that this 'calypso' is also a composition by Monty Norman,
who co-wrote the music for this and several other Bond films. It is a
simple effort, with the typical beat that most non-Caribbean ears have
come to recognize as calypso, but that Caribbean ears immediately recognize as a watered down version of the real thing. This is one of the
two occasions that 'local' music is heard, apart from when Honey

Ryder (Ursula Andress) and Bond sing snatches of the recurring folk song 'Underneath the Mango Tree'. The other is when Bond visits a club and we see popular Jamaican bandleader Byron Lee, non-credited, and other musicians playing for a group of patrons. The dancing is of the sort seen when foreign visitors unaccustomed to Caribbean music and culture try to 'jump up' (as the song being played invites everyone to do). The over-exuberant movements by one black dancer, who seems out of step for someone attuned to this style of music, make this individual somewhat comic.

James Bond in Jamaica is the typical expatriate. He uses the locals only when he needs information or service, and is whisked into the un-Jamaican world of espionage as soon as he arrives at the airport. His special training makes him adapt very quickly to the island; he seems rattled only by the black tarantula that crawls on his arm as he lies in bed. Naturally, Bond just happens to solve the problem of the Crab Key Island 'dragon' that for some time had mystified terrified islanders, even local boat-owner Quarrel (John Kitzmiller).[12] This knowledgeable go-between plies his boat from the Cayman Islands to Jamaica, and we are led to believe he may be one of the bad guys; it turns out he is a good guy, helping the CIA agent (Jack Lord) in his efforts to ensnare the infamous Dr No. As such, when it is he who is torched by the man-made 'dragon', the film leaves the impression that islanders are so naïve that they would believe just about anything, eventually paying dearly for their gullibility. This is but a rehash of the many scenarios in which mainstream cinema has shown black people petrified with fear, and unable to extricate themselves from a situation because of it.

It is not clear whether the 'three blind mice' of the opening scene of the film are Jamaican, or even Caribbean, and the accent of the driver of their getaway car does not help in this identification. The young lady photographer (Marguerite LeWars), who claims she works for the *Gleaner* when confronted by Bond, sounds local. The apparently poor woman who shows Bond where to find Quarrel, and the boatman who takes Professor Dent (Anthony Dawson) to Crab Key Island, also sound like native islanders. The point in all of this is not to trumpet the fact that ordinary Jamaicans are in a major film, but to examine how they are portrayed when they do appear in one. The newly independent nation would slowly venture onto the international stage, and it was imperative to do so without the pre-judgment of sub-conscious messages sent by films such as *Dr. No*, however innocuous they may appear at first viewing.

A James Bond film crew paid a second visit to Jamaica for location shots of the fictional San Monique in *Live and Let Die*. In the film,

Bond's arrival in the Caribbean is signalled by a cut to Geoffrey Holder doing a dance as Baron Samedi, the traditional voodoo symbol of death, in a scene that is a bit overplayed, no doubt to sustain the mystery of the simple plot. Holder's now-classic 'golden laugh' is much in evidence, though one does get the impression that he is playing to foreigners on screen and off, giving them exactly what they expect of such a character. Secret agent Bond, this time played by Roger Moore, once again immediately familiarizes himself with the territory, and needs very little help adjusting to the tropics. He even finds time to romance black CIA agent Rosie Carver (Gloria Hendry), but it is never clear if she is Caribbean or simply Caribbean-based; her reaction on finding a snake Bond has just singed to death seems unnatural for a Caribbean agent, and, of course, her accent does nothing to lead Caribbean viewers to identify her as an islander.

Unfortunately for *Live and Let Die*, it came after Sean Connery had set the tone for the way Bond handled himself, his adventures, and his villains. San Monique's Dr Kanaga (Yaphet Kotto) seems hopelessly ineffective and singularly non-menacing against a more clever Bond; and alongside Roger Moore's tepid Bond, compared to Sean Connery's, the island villain comes across as incapable of generating the true nail-biting intrigue audiences expect from these films. The situation is such that critics, seeking to find something constructive to say about the film, took to praising the setting. 'Where *Live and Let Die* scores highly is in the great locations ... . The Caribbean islands look quite alluring with their combination of sun and swaying palms.'[13]

Of the English-speaking islands of the Caribbean, Jamaica, for reasons we shall examine in a later chapter, has had the lion's share of location filming done by the major metropolitan studios. Naturally, it matters little when the location is of a generic nature, unless there is something specific about a beach or a landmark. For example, when James Bond does his underwater sequences off Nassau in the Bahamas – in *Thunderball* (1965), *The Spy Who Loved Me* (1977) and *For Your Eyes Only* (1981) – the Caribbean viewer enjoys the beauty of the setting, and has essentially no further comment on its portrayal. This is more or less the situation in a film like *Papillon* (1973), the story of a convict who manages to escape from the infamous French prison on Devil's Island. It was shot on location in Falmouth, Jamaica, which stood in for French Guyana and Honduras. Similarly, St Lucia, with its well-known pitons clearly visible, provided the location of the fantasy floating island at the end of *Dr. Dolittle* (1967), a film that showcased Trinidad's Geoffrey Holder playing island chief William Shakespeare. The atmosphere of fantasy and playfulness made it easy to suspend what would otherwise have been a critical look at how the islanders were portrayed. They are shown as naïve inhabitants whose problems with their animals are solved by the all-knowing European doctor (Rex Harrison). This is Hollywood's classic treatment of Africa and her people, with costumes and tribal rituals reminiscent of several films that purported to depict life on the Dark Continent.

Nineteenth-century locations

In the reverse situation, a non-Caribbean location setting is used for the Caribbean. In *The Story of Adèle H* (1975), the heroine (Isabelle Adjani), Victor Hugo's second daughter, is madly in love with Lieutenant Pinson (Bruce Robinson), a member of Her Majesty's 16th Hussars. She follows him from Guernsey to Halifax, but he rejects her, despite her willingness to let him have other women if he cared to. When he is transferred to Barbados, her obsession with him draws her to the island, where she arrives in a state of virtual insanity. But the Barbados we see seems curiously non-Caribbean, even for 1864. The extras are all dressed in what could be termed African attire and the street urchins are addressed in French, an unlikely scenario for Barbados. The incongruity is cleared up when one reads in the end credits that Dakar, Senegal, is acknowledged.

Another view of the nineteenth-century Caribbean is seen in *Wide Sargasso Sea* (1993), John Duigan's adaptation of the Jean Rhys novel that serves as a 'prequel' to Charlotte Bronte's *Jane Eyre*. When Rochester (Nathaniel Parker) arrives from England to marry the mulatto Antoinette Cosway (Karina Lombard) and lay claim to her vast holdings, he is both charmed by his new bride and baffled by plantation life. He never quite comes to terms with the possible threat of voodoo from their nurse Christophene (Claudia Robinson), nor the fact that the freed slaves won't remain quiet for long. Gradually, his passion for his wife dims, he yearns to return to England; meanwhile, she lapses into a state of insanity.

The Caribbean shown in this film, shot on location in Jamaica, is lush with tropic greenery. It is naturally unspoiled and undeveloped, even somewhat mysterious, as Rochester soon finds out. Of its portrayal, film critic Roger Ebert wrote:

> I have rarely seen a film that more effectively conveyed the climate it takes place in; the island is sunny and humid, the nights warm and damp, and sweat is allowed to glisten on the skins of the actors, instead of being mopped up

and dusted down by the make-up artists. The hothouse atmosphere permeates every scene, creating an unhealthy climate in which young love is perverted, promises become lies, and jealousy is the strongest emotion.[14]

In a scene reminiscent of Rita Hayworth's in both her Caribbean films, Antoinette joins the former slaves in a wild dance that brings out of the bedroom the sensuality viewers see when she and Rochester are together. There is so much sensuality and sexuality that the film-maker was accused of making a soft-porn movie. Sexual passion comes easily under tropical skies, he seems to be saying, and his emphasis is stylized in the posters that advertised the movie. They quoted snatches of the *New York Times* review that Vincent Canby wrote on 16 April 1993: 'Infinitely romantic ... a seriously exotic Gothic romance. [Karina Lombard's] lush beauty and sexual abandon are as intoxicating as the landscape; the film's eroticism is real. A most poetic film.' This reaction to the film, seen as stemming from the reviewer's concept of what a Caribbean landscape is supposed to stimulate, prompted one scholar to remark:

> The semiotic articulation that renders such cultural markers as 'typical' signs of the Caribbean not only generalizes the response into a tourist one, but also ... predetermines such reviews of the film itself. Thus these lines read like a tourist brochure, even if the brochures would tone down the language of anticipated, even natural, sexuality.[15]

It is interesting to speculate on what type of film a Caribbean director would have made. Trinidadian-born Peggy Mohan, a freelance film director living in India, claimed that she attempted to secure the rights to the adaptation. In a *Sunday Express* interview, she said:

> If I can think of a book which I really admired and wished to be the one to make into a film it's *Wide Sargasso Sea*. It was badly made into a silly film by a stupid Australian director – I was the other one bidding for it at that time, and naturally I didn't have the discipline and the contacts he had to be a good boy and get around the producer.[16]

Given her comments, one would hope that Mohan, who grew up and took her first degree in the Caribbean, would not have been as intoxicated with the landscape and the sexuality we see in the Duigan adaptation.

Although in this film we are still a century away from the Caribbean-as-paradise advertising of modern tourist brochures, one can plainly see how such thinking could have developed, independent of the newly emancipated servants. The former slaves are still forced to serve their masters, with the result that little seems to have changed. Christophene is rather forthright with her mistress, even to the point of playing the role of confidante. Her emboldened attitude and power may have come from her knowledge of obeah, which she acknowledges is 'too strong for a white man'.

Rest and relaxation

The Caribbean location in a movie such as *The Story of Adèle H* comes at the very end of the film, and emphasizes the view of the region as one of escape or retirement. It is a formula that would be used over and over. This rest-and-relaxation formula is evident, for instance, in Blake Edwards's *The Tamarind Seed* (1974), based on the novel by Evelyn Anthony, which is set in Barbados. Englishwoman Judith Farrow (Julie Andrews), who works at the British Foreign Office, admits that she is escaping the trauma of her husband's accidental death by taking time to relax at a Barbados hotel. There she meets Russian military attaché Feodor Sverdlov (Omar Sharif), who is also in Barbados 'to get away from people'. The scene shifts back to London for the development of most of the film's intrigue, but the couple eventually returns to Barbados to enjoy more of the balm of tropic sea and sand. In this setting, the Barbados we see is typically tourist-oriented: hotels with uniformed waiters, cane fields, and natural landmarks. It is also a country without voice or significant identity. Voice, even that of a fictitious Caribbean island, and identity would come with a series of films made in the 1980s.

Water

The British-made *Water* (1985), shot in St Lucia, is a light comedy about a neglected British colony in the Caribbean. The fictitious island of Cascara of the early 1980s, a period when many other Caribbean Commonwealth territories had already achieved political independence, has a long list of characters who are nothing short of caricatures of their real selves. This deliberate parody softens the impact of a film that does more to decry the colonial situation than first meets the eye. It is a comedy whose main ingredient is the worst that colonialism and multi-national exploitation have to offer. As such, when all the laughter dies down, what is left is a bitter taste of modern-day

Caribbean reality, even for many of the nations proudly boasting of their independence.

The story revolves around what takes place after the island's peaceful colonial existence is shattered by a series of comical occurrences. An American company, exploring for oil under the guise of shooting a promotional film, discovers unlimited quantities of mineral water instead, setting off an international squabble for the rights to mine it. Meanwhile, a couple of local revolutionaries bungle their way through various subversive activities. One of them, Delgado (Brian Connolly), sings his lines because he has sworn not to talk until he can say 'Cascara is free'. Their attempt to commandeer the island's lone radio station is botched, but the governor suspends their jail term, refusing to make them into martyrs. To complicate matters further, Delgado, the illegitimate son of the white expatriate Presbyterian minister (Fulton Mackay) and a black mother, seeks help in the struggle from two Cuban revolutionaries.

By the end of the movie, there is also a female environmental activist (Valerie Perrine) bent on saving a bat from extinction; the governor's wife Dolores (Brenda Vaccaro) has latched on to Her Majesty's visiting envoy, Sir Malcolm Leveridge (Leonard Rossiter), in her attempt to escape boredom on the island; Delgado takes the country's case for independence to the United Nations, where he sings his presentation accompanied by guest musicians Ringo Starr, Eric Clapton, and George Harrison; the governor himself joins the revolution, which Britain is secretly backing in order to secure bottling rights, and battles invaders trying to seize the mineral water production facilities. In the crowning oddity, the disputed well again begins to produce oil, though this does lead to Cascara's receiving its independence in the film's final seconds.

As can be seen quite readily, the plot does not lend itself to serious interpretation, and director Dick Clement makes no attempt at in-depth analysis. However, whereas international viewers might find certain scenes purely comical, even insignificant, Caribbean viewers nonetheless find that much of the comedy hits very close to home.

The colony's governor (Michael Caine), whose main interest seems to be growing a new strain of marijuana, is technically in charge of a colony that Britain has virtually forgotten. The neglect is such that when Sir Malcolm is about to visit to announce Britain's plan to abandon the colony, the official car must be rescued from dust and a stray cat with her litter. The restoration job is first-class, as are the furniture and fixtures at the governor's house, giving the obvious impression that money can be found when necessary to make the right impression. Yet the island's population is so poor that the radio programmes are beamed to it on loudspeakers. There are a couple of boom boxes in sight, but one is still led to conclude that economic hardship has precluded purchases such as personal radios. Despite its apparent hardships, this population is shown as relatively happy, and not involved in the attempt at revolution. What is uppermost in its mind is the creation of job opportunities once the mine is in operation, for we are told that the island's lack of suitable beaches makes tourism impractical.

In a curious bit of casting, Jimmie Walker plays the DJ at the radio station. His broad American-style humour, which passes muster with audiences in the United States, and his un-Caribbean-like demeanour fall flat in this movie. His fake dreadlocks add to the uneasiness of seeing this outsider trying too hard to look and sound like an insider. In the end, he has to take shelter in stereotype, and the result is demeaning to the image of the Caribbean. One regrets that such a part is not played by a Caribbean actor, the way Geoffrey Holder turns up in *Dr. Dolittle*.

The unfortunate point of a movie like *Water*, at least from a Caribbean perspective, is that the small territories of the Caribbean can ill afford to go it alone. The international scramble seen at the end of the film is only partially a caricature, for this situation actually exists even in those nations that profess to manage their natural resources themselves. In this respect, the closing celebration takes on added import for the Caribbean viewer, who is no doubt aware of the significance of the calypso that is being played on the soundtrack.

Although the music of another Caribbean artist, Eddy Grant, is featured at the start of, and during the film, the final 'jump up' celebrating what promises to be the start of oil-based prosperity for Cascara is to the calypso 'Jack' sung by the Barbadian calypsonian, the Mighty Gabby. This calypso was originally sung as a stinging criticism of the Barbados official who wanted to make it legal to have private beaches on the island, rendering certain spots inaccessible to some citizens. The move, ostensibly intended to protect the tourist industry, was seen as an insult to the local population, and an attempt to capitulate to foreign white interests in a predominantly black country. Gabby's popular attack made it impossible for the measure to be approved. Caribbean audiences would surely have heard this calypso at the time of its popularity, and its use as one of the closing items on *Water*'s soundtrack is filled with great symbolism: protest rising from the belly of the people can sometimes be powerful and effective.

Water is by no means a major film, and it would be futile to make of it more than it is – a light-hearted comedy that takes a tongue-in-cheek look at colonialism in the Caribbean. For most international viewers, this description remains valid. However, because film images are so powerful, there is the risk that what started with comic intent might achieve exactly the opposite effect. The grains of truth in the portrayal thus bear more fruit than originally intended.

Club Paradise

Another Caribbean romp with a potentially serious side is shown in *Club Paradise* (1986), a film that is structurally similar to *Water*. It is set on a fictitious Caribbean island – Saint Nicholas in this case, barely disguising the Jamaica in which it is filmed; there is the ineffective governor-general; there is the talk of dying colonialism and the approaching independence; there is the multi-national battle to develop a product – tourism this time around; there are the islanders scampering to observe what is taking place; and there is the guerrilla warfare by revolutionaries trying to secure a better life for the country's citizens. Of course, there are also the outsiders who come with their eccentricities, and on whom the film focuses, since it is, after all, made by outsiders.

Robin Williams plays the American firefighter Jack Monicker, who uses the insurance money he receives after an on-the-job injury to migrate to the Caribbean, where he goes into the resort business with Ernest Reed (Jimmy Cliff). Once in business on St Nicholas, he alternates between scheming with the has-been governor-general Hayes (Peter O'Toole), convincing a new girlfriend (Twiggy) to stay and enjoy life with him on the island, outsmarting the corrupt prime minister (Adolph Caesar), and avoiding a hostile takeover bid for his hotel, which happens to be situated on prime beachfront. He and his partner, who spends a great deal of movie time performing with his band, have their hands full with a group of visitors who are depicted as stereotypes seen in most Caribbean islands where the main revenue comes from the tourist industry.

Of far more interest to Caribbean moviegoers, however, are the interactions with the St Nicholas population, and the fact that, according to movie critic Leonard Maltin, the 'writers even try to shoehorn a 'serious' subplot about exploitation of the natives into the proceedings'.[17] Seen from the region's point of view, the tourist-oriented Caribbean shown in this film is quite authentic, typically fun-loving and blessed with good weather. The beach and hotel shenanigans are those seen wherever resorts cater to the pleasure and satisfaction of the money-bearing tourist. This means that most of the workers are accustomed to dealing with foreigners, putting their best foot forward, but also suppressing any discontent with their own situation. The only problem we see among the workers is when hotel matron Portia (Louise Bennett) refuses to allow a dreadlocked cook to work in her kitchen. The solution is an oversized chef's hat. Would that all problems on St Nicholas could find that easy a solution.

Britain cannot be very proud of the governor-general in this film.[18] He is half-hearted in his loyalty to the Queen, and equally cagey about improving the standard of living of his citizens, though he has evidently already conceded to himself that Britain's role in the island's affairs is over. His ready relationship with the visiting *New York Times* travel writer (Joanna Cassidy) is seen as the only time in a long while that he has been enthusiastic about anything or anyone.

The island's prime minister, who also holds the portfolios of finance and tourism, is one of whom the Caribbean cannot be very proud. He is willing to sell the country to the highest bidder, and, in personally dunning Ernest Reed for back taxes as a means of forcing him to accept the takeover bid, even stifles local private enterprise for his own gain. Adolph Caesar, playing the Caribbean politician with relative ease, manages to produce a convincing lilt that makes this African American actor sound as though he is really 'from the islands'. In this regard, he is not unlike many of the region's politicians who were schooled outside the Caribbean, and who, upon their return, speak in a mixture of accents.

The social milieu in Club Paradise is noticeably mixed. One is not certain, on the positive side, if this is because the locals are now in a position to mix and mingle with the foreign, and predominantly white, visitors; or, on the negative side, if it is because the hotel has seen better days, and must attract a local clientele to survive. If the latter were to be the case, it would be a sad commentary on the effects of depending too heavily on the tourist dollar. Unfortunately, visitors to Caribbean tourist resorts cannot escape the reality of this state of affairs.

St Nicholas, as a carbon copy of Jamaica, has everything which has made this Caribbean nation both renowned and infamous. There is marijuana to be had; there are Rastafarians and their unique language and rituals; and there is abundant reggae, the hallmark of nearly every movie shot on location in Jamaica. There is also on-screen steelband and limbo, and several calypsos by the Mighty Sparrow on the soundtrack, all of which work to lend the film a distinct Caribbean flavour.

Jimmy Cliff as co-owner of Club Paradise becomes a symbol of black business in an industry that usually does not have a high percentage of local ownership. We are not told how he acquires the business, but his constant vigilance with regard to the welfare of his compatriots, and his subsequent leading of the revolutionary forces, would lead us to believe that he never let an opportunity go a-begging. He becomes a positive role model for the Caribbean viewer, who is not accustomed to see many fellow islanders in such a position. It is similarly refreshing to see established Jamaican actors like Charles Hyatt, Leonie Forbes, Carl Bradshaw and Louise Bennett, and to hear some of them with small speaking parts.

Cocktail and How Stella Got Her Groove Back

Club Paradise is one of the on location films that attempt to show that the island where they are being shot does have something else beside sandy beaches, hotels and workers catering to tourists. Although the development of other aspects of island life is sparse, often comical and satirical, we can at least give the writers credit for being aware of the struggle for political independence, and the desire among the workers to improve their standard of living. Caribbean viewers, having recognized familiar landmarks and the indigenous music, could reasonably be expected to identify with other aspects of what they saw on screen. But in many instances, there is little else to endear the movie to these viewers, especially when the location is not fictitious, and is identified as an actual territory. Such a film is *Cocktail* (1988), in which Tom Cruise plays bartender Brian Flanagan, who goes to Jamaica to work and ponder his next move in life.

After his stint in the army, Brian is determined to become a millionaire, but cannot find the right job to achieve this ambition. He ends up becoming a bartender alongside Doug Coughlin (Bryan Brown), with whom he entertains customers in a disco with a series of bottle-juggling, drink-pouring antics, but he is constantly on the lookout for a 'rich chick' as his ticket to eventually owning his own bar. The two friends quarrel over a girl, and, in a foreshadowing of *How Stella Got Her Groove Back*, Brian goes off to Jamaica. He meets Jordan Mooney (Elisabeth Shue), and appears to fall in love with the vacationing waitress after their honeymoon-like lovemaking. Unfortunately, he also beds a rich Manhattan executive on a dare, and when Jordan sees them together she promptly flies back home. After the executive (Lisa Barnes) takes Brian back to New York, he realizes that he has made a mistake. He is reunited with Jordan, who is both pregnant with his child, and, as it turns out, rich.

The Jamaica that is seen in this film is definitely tourist-oriented. Nearly every black face belongs to a waiter, a hotel maid, a driver, or some such worker, except in the dance scenes when other black couples, presumably Jamaican or Caribbean, though not so identified, are seen on the floor. This is the Jamaica to which the television advertisements beckon visitors with the words 'Come Back to Jamaica'. Portions of the footage could easily be used in such ads, for the camera lingers on all the elements that go to make up the idyllic tropical paradise vacation. The reggae music, which in these later films has replaced carnival and limbo as the remover of inhibition, again works its magic. Brian and Jordan feel so freed from the cares of the world that they also free themselves of their swimsuits while bathing together in this picture-perfect setting, a gesture one hardly ever sees on the part of the islanders. Sexual liberation in these movies is never between the islanders. It is either between the outsiders, who use the tropic locale as their incentive to liberate both mind and body; or between the outsider and an islander, with each party using the opportunity to relive a long-cherished fantasy.

There is absolutely no mention of the non-tourist Jamaica, nor any indication of the aspect of the islands usually shown when films are shot on location: no impending revolution or political upheaval; no oppression of workers; no multi-national bickering for exploitation rights. There is no Jamaica outside of its existence for the pleasure of the outsider, who, inexplicably, has a job. Did Brian need a work permit, for example? These apparently mundane matters are not the concern of the movie – and no one really blames the film-makers for not dealing with them – but when Caribbean eyes see it, they see glaring omissions or incongruities.

As we have already indicated, *Cocktail* foreshadows *How Stella Got Her Groove Back* (1998), the film version of Terry McMillan's popular novel. Stella (Angela Bassett), a 40-year-old divorced single parent, is a successful San Francisco stockbroker, whose success does not spill over to her romantic relationships. Responding to an ad on television inviting her to Jamaica, she and her friend Delilah (Whoopi Goldberg) jet off to Montego Bay, where she meets Winston (Taye Diggs), half her age, still toying with the idea of studying medicine, and available for instant romance. Stella quickly overcomes the older woman/younger guy malaise, and starts to 'get her groove back'. She returns to the US, but is drawn back to Jamaica to rekindle the smouldering fire; she meets Winston's parents – the mother is not amused – and Winston moves back to San Francisco with her. After the inevitable doubts and resentment over age and money differences, Winton decides he is returning to Jamaica, but there is a reconciliation, and we learn that he could be heading to medical school after all.

The *New York Times* review of the film on 14 August 1998, conceding that this is far from the first Hollywood movie to flaunt the look and attitude of a glitzy travel brochure, opined that 'it may be the first to blatantly portray a tropical paradise as a sexual mecca beckoning tired American businesswomen to shed their clothes and inhibitions and roll around with the local talent.' Here was a repeat of the *Cocktail* scenario, but played out with a local sexual partner instead. The other main difference, however, is the fact that the players are all black, immediately establishing an affinity with Caribbean audiences that a film like *Cocktail* could hardly match.

Another Terry McMillan novel, the best-seller *Waiting to Exhale,* had been immensely popular among African American women, whose difficulty in finding suitable eligible African American men it chronicled. It touched a nerve among middle-class African American women in particular, who readily identified with the book's female characters, and turned out in large numbers to see the film adaptation. McMillan's follow-up novel, *How Stella Got Her Groove Back*, was based on her own experience in Jamaica, and once more women identified with the protagonist, this time because of the way she successfully handled her relationship with a man young enough to be her son. The film adaptation showed this upending of stereotype beautifully, and brought raves of delight from audiences when it was first shown in the US. The *Boston Globe* of 19 August 1998 reported that whoops broke out in the movie theatre when Winston appeared on screen:

> Much to audience delight, the movie ... reverses Hollywood's trend of matching older men with younger women. In a time when Warren Beatty, Robert Redford, and Jack Nicholson – nearly senior citizens – can play strapping men who win the hearts of attractive women in their 20s and 30s, this film may be the first to seriously buck outdated social mores concerning age and gender. According to movie patrons hollering their approval, it's about time.

The fact that the movie adaptation also filmed its location shots in Jamaica gave it an air of authenticity that *Cocktail* lacked. Still, this authenticity of location is not without its flaws, or at least its touches of stereotype.

Despite the presence of black characters, who should conceivably show more affinity to, and interest in the indigenous population, there is the same lack of interaction here that we see in most of the other films shot on location. The dance floor is again the only place where outsider and insider appear to meet. The fact that Stella falls for the son of a middle-class doctor, who is of better breeding, one imagines, than the so-called beach bums who prey on single, fun-seeking tourists, does not completely sugar-coat the harsh reality. Many visits to Caribbean resorts are thinly disguised excursions into unbridled sex, to the extent that such visits are familiarly known for their four S's: sun, sea, sand and sex. But this negative aspect of tourism is offset by the benefit the country derives from the marked increase in arrivals. The *Boston Sunday Globe* of 6 December 1998 reported that as a consequence of the movie many women – American, English, German and Swiss – were flocking to the island's north coast beaches 'to get their groove back':

> Jamaica couldn't have paid for the publicity we're getting, says photographer Ken Ramsay, referring to the scenes of white-sand beaches, turquoise and emerald waters, cloudless skies, and exotic flowers.
>
> Jamaica's Tourist Board has screened the film for US travel agents and aired TV spots promoting the island as a lover's getaway.

Understandably, those responsible for advertisements destined to attract tourists – and with them much-needed hard currency – will easily overlook the few negative images that they did not create in the first place. One such image, for example, is of Winston's father (Glynn Turman). Apart from the fact that such a role could easily have been given to a Jamaican, it is painful to see this actor wasted, appearing as a silent appendage to the scene in which his wife takes Stella to task for virtually stealing her son. The house he shares with his wife shows him to be a successful doctor, that is if material trappings are to be believed. Consequently, his lack of voice is extremely puzzling.

There are other minor points that seem not to have concerned the film-makers, but which come naturally to mind for Caribbean audiences, and which it would have been good to have explained. How does Winston get to the States so easily? Perhaps, given his father's status, the entire family has multiple-entry visitor's visas, but if university study is involved, then the type of visa must be changed. At no time in this film, nor in any of the others we have discussed, is the immigration issue ever raised. It is admittedly not a major issue, but it does add to the reality and authenticity of the way in which life in the Caribbean is presented.

Clara's Heart

Ease of migration is also apparent in *Clara's Heart* (1988), in which hotel maid Clara Mayfield (Whoopi Goldberg) is taken back to America by a visitor. Leona Hart (Kathleen Quinlan) has just lost her baby daughter, and decides to leave her almost adolescent son and her husband home alone, and spend some time by herself at a resort in Jamaica. The location scenes, lasting only about eight minutes, are mainly at a bungalow-type hotel, where Clara is assigned to clean Mrs Hart's rooms. She instantly begins dispensing no-nonsense advice to the visitor (with whom she comes face to face for the first time), and so enthralls her that she is quickly hired to live with the family back in the States. Without any formalities, then, we see her being introduced to husband Bill (Michael Ontkean) and son David (Neil Patrick Harris). The rest of the film revolves around her relationship with the son, especially after the Harts' marriage ends in divorce.

There are a couple of points that give a Caribbean audience pause. Firstly, Clara's forthright, outspoken attitude is somewhat misplaced in the context of the tourist industry in which she clearly works. This does not mean that her job requires her to be self-effacing and sub-servient, especially if it is not her nature to be. But the way in which she bosses this guest she has just met, at the possible risk of a com-plaint being filed against her, does not ring true, or if so, is highly unusual. One suspects that she is more Whoopi Goldberg than Clara Mayfield; the actress no doubt wanted this role to be given more dignity and strength than would ordinarily be the case if she were playing a typical/stereotypical maid. She is the modern version of Dominique, the maid in *Affair in Trinidad*.

Secondly, in view of the growing restrictions imposed on would-be immigrants to the United States, it is more than surprising to see Clara actually accompany Mrs Hart on her return from the hotel resort. It is always possible that she already had the requisite visa clearance, and was only biding her time before leaving the island, but the film is silent on this, as it is on how she managed to be allowed into the US. A few words worked into the dialogue would have clarified this poten-tially important point for Caribbean viewers.

Once Clara gets to the United States, she is a model of support for the Hart family, and specifically for the Hart son. Caribbean viewers can only be proud of the way in which she handles herself. She is a strong woman, who has been through a lot in her time, as we will learn during the course of the film, and the mysterious occurrence that leads to her on-going tussle with a fellow Jamaican seems only to have toughened her. Her outspoken philosophizing seems more natural in the American milieu, where she is the one who eases young David through the pain of his family's break-up.

We hear actors attempting to capture the Jamaican accent, though they at times lapse back into their American way of speaking. Interestingly, even David gets into the act, and shows off how

'Jamaican' he can sound. The Caribbean ear picks up these attempts very easily, and is amused rather than offended by them. They do, however, lead listeners to long for more films in which actual speakers of some Caribbean creole are used. This situation occurs again in films like MGM's *The Mighty Quinn* (1989), where the fictitious island is a carbon copy of Jamaica, and Disney's *Cool Runnings* (1993), the story of the Jamaican bobsled team.

The Mighty Quinn

Of all the movies made on location in the English-speaking Caribbean, *The Mighty Quinn* comes closest to resembling one that could have been made by Caribbean film-makers, even despite the fact that its lead actors are African Americans playing Caribbean characters. Denzel Washington plays police chief Xavier Quinn on an unnamed island that is Jamaica's double. He learns early in the film that a wealthy developer has been murdered at one of the island's resorts, and that his childhood friend Maubee (Robert Townsend), a semi-dreadlocked drifter, is the prime suspect. The ensuing investigation brings to light a cover-up attempt on the part of the island's governor (Norman Beaton) and a visiting entrepreneur (James Fox), whose wife unashamedly tries to seduce the police chief. Quinn and his wife are having marital problems, which she tries to overcome by singing in a reggae trio, so he is free to devote all his time to proving Maubee innocent. In the end, Quinn is reunited with his wife after the bad guys get their just desserts. Roger Ebert calls the film 'a spy thriller, a buddy movie, a musical, a comedy, and a picture that is wise about human nature.'[19]

The Mighty Quinn has all the elements we have seen in previous films: reggae performances from start to finish, including a couple by Rita Marley; a local obeah woman, called a witch in this instance; the governor colluding with outside parties; and scenic location shots, leading the *Washington Post* review of 17 February 1989 to label the film just an excuse to tour Jamaica: 'Neat pastel cottages and polluted juke joints contrast with the antiseptic beauty of the beachside resorts amid the rhythms of reggae.'

There is less of a feeling that outsiders have come to run the show, probably because of the manner in which police chief Quinn deals with those that do appear. Trained by the FBI, he now has the police force firmly under his control, a marked contrast from the police situation we see in earlier films like *Affair in Trinidad* or *Island in the Sun*. Local audiences have no difficulty identifying with a son of the soil who has made good, and who has not forgotten his roots. He is able both to seek information among the stragglers in his village, and to lead an investigation that pits him against highly sophisticated criminals.

The service roles are de-emphasized, so that one never gets the impression that the tourist aspect of the island is being catered to while the rest of the citizens are neglected. The governor does worry about the effect of the murder on the tourist arrivals, and as a result is amenable to cutting corners to avoid adverse publicity. But, all things considered, life in the island is shown to continue in a fairly routine fashion, though some scenes – for example, the country church service, where Quinn goes looking for Isola (Tyra Ferrell), the obeah woman's niece, and the manner in which the obeah woman herself and her surroundings are portrayed – border on the stereotypical. Nevertheless, the *Washington Post* commented that 'Schenkel and company in no way stereotype the islanders, but offer an affectionate portrait of their eccentricities.'[20]

It is refreshing to see islanders outsmart the all-knowing foreigners of former films. Maubee's evading capture by the American pursuer is as it should be, given his naturally superior knowledge of the local terrain. On the other hand, his Samson-like destruction of a ramshackle building in order to slip from the grasp of the police stretches credibility. The only local character who suffers from the actions of an outsider is obeah woman Ubu Pearl (Esther Rolle), who is bound in her wheelchair while her house is set on fire by Miller (Emmet Walsh), the American visitor-turned-villain. Similarly, it is encouraging to see that the police chief is an island citizen, and that he obviously has the respect of his subordinates, all of whom seem to have come through the British system of police training.

The foreigners on the island do not seem interested in its music and arts. There is no scene, for example, showing the American entrepreneur's wife shedding her inhibitions to dance to calypso, reggae or steelband, as stereotype would have led us to expect. The Caribbean is no longer presented as a region that invites possession by quasi-demonic forces that yank visitors onto dance floors in wild abandon, as bystanders stare in wonder. All the dance scenes involve islanders, so there is no shot of an outsider trying to master the correct steps or moves. As a result, Caribbean viewers get the impression that the film is really addressed to them as opposed to non-Caribbean audiences.

Although the island is not identified, it seems already independent, or, at the very least, well on its way to shedding the colonial mantle. There is little mention of the political climate, or of social conditions under which the population is living. The chief's wife makes a snide allusion to waiting for invitations to the governor's parties, leading viewers to conclude that there is a subtle class barrier, since the governor is black. But for all the fictitious nature of the island, Caribbean viewers see and hear Jamaica. The visual identification is even unwittingly encouraged as the title credits are being shown. They are in red, yellow, and green, colours associated with the Rastafarian movement, and are shown over a dreadlocked singer performing the reggae song 'Guess Who's Coming to Dinner'. Aural identification comes from the Jamaican accents we hear from local actors like Carl Bradshaw, Charles Hyatt, and Oliver Samuels. These 'authentic' accents at times contrast rather humorously – but fortunately not annoyingly – with the learned ones we hear from the principal African American actors.

Cool Runnings

African American actors playing actual Jamaicans on location in real-life Jamaica are featured in Walt Disney's *Cool Runnings*. The film is based on the true story of the Jamaica bobsled team that astounded sports watchers worldwide by the sheer unlikeliness of the Caribbean island's participation in the Winter Olympics. As such, we are back to the situation we had in *Clara's Heart*, where Caribbean audiences could judge to what extent the actors really captured the essence of the Jamaica creole.

As can be expected in a Disney movie, there is 'wholesome family entertainment' in this film, with the emphasis being on comedy and providing an inspirational story. Summer Olympic hopeful Derice Bannock (Leon) is unfortunately tripped during the qualifying heats for the games, and loses the opportunity to represent his country. His hope is not dashed completely, however. He finds out that former Olympic bobsled champion Irving Blitzer (John Candy) had earlier approached his father, then a champion sprinter, with a scheme to capitalize on the renowned speed of Jamaican sprinters in a new sport, bobsledding. He also learns that this gentleman is living in Jamaica, and we can almost see the light snap on in Derice's brain.

The recruitment begins. The coach is cajoled into accepting, as are the three other members of the team: Sanka Coffie (Doug E. Doug), the island's pushcart derby champion, along with Junior Bevil (Rawle Lewis) and Yul Brenner (Malik Yoba), the two sprinters who fell with Derice in the ill-fated heat. They train in a makeshift bobsled and confidently fly off to Calgary, where, despite being the butt of snide jokes and remarks, they manage to make it to the qualifying rounds. However, their bobsled flips over, ending their dream of copping a medal at the games. They return to Jamaica as heroes, we are told just before the final credits roll; and 'four years later, they returned to the Olympics as equals.'

The Jamaica shown in the early portion of the film is quite different from the one usually seen in the films set on the island. There is no talk of hotels, or guests, or any such allusion to the tourist industry; nor is there any pointed reference to the political or social climate of the island, though, because of the reconstruction of actual events, both were readily known. It is a Jamaica with which the man in the street can readily identify, although it does seem somewhat cleaned up and sterilized. *Washington Post* critic Richard Harrington commented on 1 October 1993:

> The film's title, *Cool Runnings*, is doubly apt. In Jamaica it's an expression meaning 'peaceful journey' – and that's clearly what director Jon Turteltaub (*3 Ninjas*) has in mind. His Jamaica is family-sitcom clean – no poverty, no ganja, not even a ganja joke.

This apparently bland manner of showing Jamaica and Jamaicans did not appeal to a second *Post* critic, Desson Howe, who on the same day wrote that 'the characters are delineated with thick crayon edges for family-viewing convenience.' The running gag of the athletes' reaction to the bitter Canadian cold is criticized as being tied in with 'those other "jokes", such as blacks' wide-eyed fear of ghosts'. This critic is unhappy with a stereotypical presentation, which Caribbean viewers, considering what they have always heard of Canadian winters, would not find particularly offensive. It is not unlike the way they imagine most white visitors to the islands having difficulty eating spicy foods, or keeping time to island rhythms. Unfortunately, even tame attempts at humour and stereotyping, unavoidable at times, can give offence, as this same critic concedes:

> Thanks to its sun-bleached writing ... this movie would have to work double time to really offend anyone. But the ghost of Stepin Fetchit is hovering in the tropical ether. It's in those wide-eyed double-take faces, the fast-motion (à la *Gods Must Be Crazy*), and the way one of the Jamaican bobsledders tries (unsuccessfully, of course) to hold his overloaded bladder during a particularly bumpy run.

Every constituency, then, could find something offensive if it looked hard enough.

Veteran Jamaican actors Winston Stona and Charles Hyatt appear in roles that do them more justice than the brief walk-on parts with which some local actors end up when films are shot on location. As Whitby Bevil, father of one of the bobsledders, Hyatt captures to perfection the determination of Caribbean parents to see their children do well, often leading them to consider anything non-academic as detracting from this overriding goal. His journeying to Canada to order his son, for whom he had secured a job, to return home smacks of carrying things too far, but it does allow the Disney film-makers to tug at audience heartstrings when the son asserts his independence and opts to remain with the team. It is also one of the few occasions when island people are shown dealing with an emotional issue, and the father's eventual show of support as the games get under way is all in keeping with the family orientation of the film.

The film adequately captures the fever that takes over any of the islands when it is participating in games at the international level. A similar fever was apparent, for example, when Jamaica made it to the finals of the World Cup 1998, the emblem of supremacy in football/soccer, and is also evident when the West Indies cricket team is playing at the test (championship) level. The Disney film-makers openly opt for comedy over drama. The images of Jamaicans glued to television sets are believable, as is the viewers' spontaneous response to the sportscaster's rhetorical question when the team shows great improvement from one day to the next: 'Where did these guys come from?' 'Jamaica,' they shout in unison.

Marked for Death

Coming from Jamaica is not always an easy admission to make, particularly in the United States, the home of nearly all the production companies of the films discussed. As the US government struggled with its drug interdiction programmes, the blame for the increase in drug use was placed on the shoulders of suppliers and distributors from several countries, one of which was Jamaica. The result is that there has developed in the mind of the American public an association of drugs with Jamaicans, and more so with noted gangs, called *posses*. It is admittedly a stereotypical association, but one that is prevalent nonetheless. It is not surprising, therefore, to see in an action film like *Marked for Death* (1990) a running battle between good guy John Hatcher (Steven Seagal) and Jamaican drug-gang members led by Screwface (Basil Wallace).

When Hatcher and his partner go to Kingston in search of Screwface, Director Dwight Little uses the opportunity to correct some of the stereotypes: Jamaica is not all sunshine and bikinis, we hear, nor are all Jamaicans dope-dealing dreads. It is the film's second attempt to soothe an anxious audience, the first coming from the television news-caster who is at the scene of a shoot-out involving one of the posses. She gives us statistics: less than 1 per cent of Jamaican immigrants are involved in these crimes; there have been over 10 000 incidents spread over 20 states, and they have resulted in some 1400 murders over the previous three and a half years; finally, we are told that the posses favour torturing and maiming their victims. Despite both these attempts at balance, the overall picture of Jamaicans is not flattering, a fact that is noted by the *Washington Post* of 8 October 1990. It accuses the director of stressing both racial and ethnic stereotypes, and of engaging in 'some hokum spook'em that is not going to do much for the image of Jamaicans in general, and dreadlocked ones in particular.' It is unfortunate that said stereotypes, so easy to create, are so difficult to eradicate.

As we leave this examination of the manner in which images of the anglophone Caribbean have been presented when filmed on location, it is important to stress the fact that many of these films were not made with Caribbean audiences in mind. The mainstream film indus-try, which usually counts a film's success in millions of dollars, does not depend on revenue from viewers in the islands. It also films on location in many parts of the world, and it would be counter-productive to alienate any region in particular.

Further, even if many of the images were stereotypical, they were not necessarily offensive. Putting the shoe on the other foot, we see numerous stereotypical views of Americans in films that do nothing more harmful than illustrate the American way of life. The Caribbean way of life is its own reality, and the outsider's image of it should not be denigrated simply because it emanated from beyond the region. The Caribbean cannot project itself as a place of sun-drenched tranquility, of carnival, calypso and reggae, of carefree people speaking with lilting accents, and then be annoyed when foreigners zero in on these very images. One would hope that Caribbean viewers do not lose their sense of humour as they view how others see them. By the same token, nonetheless, they must be ever vigilant that the images others have of life in the Caribbean ring true, and be prepared to help correct them when they do not.

Notes

1. Anthony Luengo, 'Patrons of Empire' (1998), n.p.
2. Kennedy Wilson, 'On Location' (1996), 93.

3. Stephen Hunter, *Washington Post*, 13 December 1998.
4. Kennedy Wilson, 'On Location', 93–4.
5. Pauline Kael, in *Microsoft Cinemania 96*. Review on CD.
6. See Louis Nizer, *My Day in Court* (1961) for a full account of the plagiarism case that was fought over the use by the Andrews Sisters of Lord Invader's calypso.
7. Kennedy Wilson, 'On Location', 95.
8. Co-written by Lester Lee, who also wrote 'Trinidad Lady' used in *Affair in Trinidad*.
9. Stephen Bourne, *Black in the British Frame* (1998), 103.
10. Valerie Bloomfield, 'Caribbean Films', (1977), 286.
11. Donald Bogle, *Toms, Coons, Mulattos, Mammies, and Bucks* (1974), 243.
12. Bermudan-born actor Earl Cameron, who had migrated to England in 1939, claimed that he was supposed to get this part, but was turned down by co-producer Harry Saltzmann. See Stephen Bourne, *Black in the British Frame*, 160.
13. Damian Cannon, Internet Review of *Live and Let Die,* Movie Reviews UK, 1977.
14. Roger Ebert, *Microsoft Cinemania 96*. 'Roger Ebert's Video Companion 1985–94', review on CD.
15. Supriya Nair, 'Expressive Countercultures and Postmodern Utopia (1996), 71.
16. *Sunday Express*, 19 May 1996.
17. See *Microsoft Cinemania 96* 'Leonard Maltin's Movie and Video Guide, 1996', © Dulton Signet 1995.
18. Technically, only the independent Commonwealth territories had governors-general, and St Nicholas is not yet independent.
19. Roger Ebert, *Microsoft Cinemania 96.*
20. *Washington Post*, 17 February 1989.

3

Caribbean feature films: joining the big league

It was inevitable that the newly independent nations of the anglophone Caribbean would seek to produce their own feature films. The aim was obvious: to control the image of themselves, and at the same time correct many of the stereotypes that foreign-made films had projected; in short, to tell their own story, especially since they were rapidly acquiring the expertise to do so. A variety of factors, to be examined in a later chapter, would make this undertaking at times exceedingly difficult, but the fact that Caribbean film-makers sought to become part of the international world of film-making – to join the big league – is certainly creditable, and deserves closer examination.

Although national pride would seek to give a total Caribbean identity to the films that were produced in the region, the fact is that in nearly every instance the final product included efforts by people who could have their Caribbeanness questioned. Those who nit-pick the details of production might have asked, for example, how a Greek director could make a Jamaican film, or how an African American or an Indian could make a Trinidadian film. But, given the cosmopolitan nature of many Caribbean societies, and their paucity of technical facilities, it would have been difficult to produce an entire film without input from someone outside the region at some stage. Such a situation, incidentally, is taken for granted in the music industry without giving rise to any questioning of the authenticity of Caribbean music. In this regard, I stand by a definition I have used before, and consider as Caribbean films those which are produced in the region by and with a majority of Caribbean personnel, and whose conception, realization, and flavour present a distinct Caribbean world view.[1]

Harbance Kumar and the first Caribbean films

Harbance Kumar, a native of Bombay, India, directed the first two locally produced feature films in the anglophone Caribbean in 1970.

He had migrated to Trinidad, and had married a Trinidadian a few years earlier. As a result of his close involvement with DeLuxe Films, a successful local company that distributed Indian films, he felt he knew what the public would want to see, and decided to make films with mass appeal. The result was *The Right and the Wrong*, the screenplay for which was done in collaboration with well-known playwright Freddie Kissoon, whose comedies routinely drew large audiences. This was followed shortly thereafter by *The Caribbean Fox*, for which Kumar received sole credit as screenplay writer.

Kumar had difficulty finding actors for his films, and ended up using several rank amateurs, many of whom, like himself, had never imagined they would be involved in a feature film.[2] But he was an ardent promoter, and offered many incentives, including a prize of TT$1000 to anyone composing the best two calypsos that could fit into the story he was about to film. With some TT$75 000 as working capital, he started shooting *The Right and the Wrong*, which ended up costing him TT$102 000 (approximately US$55 000), a very modest sum by international standards. Local press reports in October 1969 had claimed that as much as TT$300 000 would be spent on the two-hour-long movie, but this estimate was apparently overly liberal.

Writing in the *Sunday Guardian*, Carl Jacobs profiled Harbance Kumar after the release of *The Right and the Wrong*, and shortly before the December 1970 premiere of *The Caribbean Fox*. The film-maker was portrayed as very optimistic about the future of the island's film industry, even claiming that he was setting out to make Trinidad 'the Hollywood of the West Indies', complete with its own galaxy of stars. This grandiose claim would be heard time and again over the following decades as spasmodic attempts were made to start a Caribbean film industry. The reporter indicated that Kumar had no doubts or qualms over the success of the film in spite of 'the critical mauling it received and the insults heaped upon his head'. In addition, the new film-maker saw the benefit for the Caribbean of developing the film industry. He was quoted as saying:

> The benefits of such an industry are incalculable. Apart from employment in every sector of movie-making and in allied areas such as catering and transport plus the creation of new technical skills, there is the priceless publicity which Trinidad and the Caribbean will get all over the world. ...
>
> This was the first local picture with all the tremendous difficulties attached, and it seemed that everyone was just waiting to pounce down on it. ...
>
> They missed the most significant thing about *The Right and the Wrong* – and that was the fact that it was actually

made at all. It proved beyond a doubt that movies can be successfully produced in Trinidad.[3]

Kumar later admitted that he had played many scenes purely for laughs because he had deliberately set out to make a film that was not intellectually artistic, and thus one that had mass appeal. Too many artistically superior films, he insisted, were completed but never released.[4] The reported financial success of his effort seemed to justify this practical approach, for the Jacobs article informed readers that *The Right and the Wrong* had 'done splendidly at the Caribbean box office, actually breaking records in some places such as Grenada and Surinam.' It further indicated that the film had won a gold medal at the Atlanta Film Festival,[5] and earned the director a nationwide interview on 'Voice of America'.

If Trinidad, and by extension the Caribbean, was going to join the big league, then it would have to play by the rules of the game. This meant that whereas the film might appeal to local audiences because of the familiarity of the scenes and the actors, when it was viewed by non-Caribbean eyes, accustomed to a stereotypical view of the Caribbean in the first place, then the judgment might be quite harsh. Of course, even some Caribbean eyes would view the film with disfavour, undeterred by the very familiarity that drew some viewers to excuse its imperfections.

One such pair of non-Caribbean eyes belonged to reviewer Richard Combs. Writing in the *Monthly Film Bulletin*, he blasted the film as 'penny dreadful material, whose account of how slaves lose their chains through hard work, meekness and Christian piety would have won the approval of the fiercest Dickensian capitalist.' That conclusion came after the following synopsis:

Shyam and Jojo, slaves of sadistic, white plantation-owner Malcolm, argue with their fellow slaves that non-violence and not rebellion is the only Christian way to change their condition. After a quarrel with his wife Christine about his penchant for taking slave women to bed, Malcolm accedes to her request that he spare Jojo from punishment and allow him to help her in her studio; and when Malcolm decides to add Shyam's sweetheart Chanda to his harem, the increasingly frustrated Christine forces Jojo to make love to her by threatening to harm his sweetheart Didi. When Malcolm attempts to make love to Chanda, she is rescued by Shyam, and the two flee from the plantation to the other side of the river. Jojo is also forced to escape when Malcolm finds him and Christine together, and the three friends return by night to rescue Didi. They overpower Malcolm, take the guns from his guards, and persuade the other slaves to leave with them and establish their own community across the river. Malcolm makes one last attempt to recover his slaves with the help of two traitors among them, the original agitators for rebellion, who return the guns to him only to be shot for their pains. But Malcolm's plans are foiled when he trips fatally over a pitchfork, and his ex-slaves interpret his fate as an act of God.[6]

One does get the impression that the writers included every stock situation they could imagine, and bothered little about plausibility or even authenticity. There were, for example, (East) Indian slaves, a historical inaccuracy no doubt confirming the director's subsequent assertion that he played many scenes for laughs. Be that as it may, one cannot escape asking why the public would support a film that was clearly flawed. Was it because it came at a significant time in the history of the country? Trinidad and Tobago had just lived through the Black Power 'revolution', for many the true start of the nation's independence, the final casting-off of the colonial yoke. It is not inconceivable that the patrons who went to see this movie did so out of a sense of defiance and pride: to show the rest of the world that little Trinidad and Tobago could compete in the area of film-making, that it was time to back talk with action. It was film's ability to help in nation-building that prompted the *Daily Express* to bemoan the fact that this movie's producers had 'stampeded into an area where others have long been reluctant to tread':

> The potential of a local, hopefully a regional film industry is literally mind-bending. The powerful impact of the film media can, if it accepts the task, make a tremendous contribution to development. As with so much else, however, talk is not good enough. And for quite some time all we have had is talk about a film industry. The step beyond the old talk is to make a start. And this is the essential validity of Harbance Kumar and DeLuxe Films Limited's efforts at filmmaking.[7]

While not wanting to 'trespass on the territory of the film critics', the *Express* nonetheless was quite blunt in its opinion of DeLuxe Films. 'The abominably low quality of its product is obvious to everybody.' Still, it conceded, 'people are nevertheless taking it in because it is something with which they hope to identify,' thereby unwittingly providing the reason for the film's initial box office success. So much of what had been seen up to that point had come from elsewhere. Almost anything purporting to show what one's compatriots could do stood a reasonable chance of success. Harbance Kumar understood this, but was taken to task for deciding, in the opinion of the newspaper, to ignore 'genuine potential in pursuit of short-term gain'.

Kumar's second venture into film-making met with the same mixed reception: success at the box office, but a disaster in the eyes of the critics. *The Caribbean Fox* passed muster as far as the technical aspect was concerned, but the script and the acting left a lot to be desired. Richard Combs reviewed this film as well, and summarized its plot:

> A fortune-teller and amateur pickpocket in a Trinidad market place, Ram Singh falls in with Butch, a local gangster who agrees to give him his first chance at real crime. But the enterprise is not a success: Ram Singh is raped by his first hold-up victim, and Butch – after a violent set-to – is forced to conclude a truce with rival gangster Boysie. Butch and Boysie are attracted to Kim and Angela, whose demonstra-tions against the exploitation of women cause both their nightclubs to be wrecked; and when – through a sinister underworld figure called the Caribbean Fox – the two gang-sters become involved in drug trafficking, the girls attempt to put a stop to it by intercepting a shipment which they have learned about from the trusting Ram Singh. Sooner than alienate their girlfriends, the gangsters decide to give up pushing drugs; but the Fox kidnaps Kim and Angela and uses drugs on them in order to force the men to change their minds. The four of them are rescued by the sudden arrival of the girls' liberated colleagues and the dauntless Ram Singh, all brandishing clubs. After the battle, Butch and Boysie abandon their life of crime for the responsibilities of marriage.[8]

The reviewer thought the project – the start of a West Indian film industry – praiseworthy, but 'the meagre commercial ambition of its early product is anything but.' He concluded, pessimistically, that in this film 'there's scarcely a glimmer of talent.' Again, one notes that the screenplay seems overcrowded with the various scenarios that would test even accomplished actors. Sidney Hill, film-maker attached to the Trinidad and Tobago government's film unit, observed that '*The Caribbean Fox* used every dirty ploy there was to keep the audience interested ... it was a dreadful movie.'[9]

Kumar had sought to tempt the calypso-loving Trinidad public by casting the Mighty Sparrow as himself, a surefire draw as patrons

flocked to see the popular 'Birdie' on the screen. Through trick photography, Sparrow was seen playing a woman in addition to himself as
calypsonian, and one of his calypsos was on the Vietnam War.
According to the Carl Jacobs article,[10] Kumar felt he had learned from
his first film, and had produced a superior movie in his second attempt:
pure entertainment and light comedy replacing ponderous drama and
heavy philosophical theme. This view was not shared by his critics,
however.

The *Daily Express* thought the film's script and plot deserved 'a
special prize for crassness and banality', and regretted that potentially
good actors such as Angela Seukeran, Ralph Maraj, Kenneth Boodoo,
and Wilbert Holder, some of whom had acted in Kumar's first film,
were made to struggle with such material. It showed, the editorial concluded, 'the tragedy of the situation which West Indian talent is in
today'.[11]

Harbance Kumar's experience with film distribution paid off for
him and his company. He was able to have the films shown in New
York as a double feature both on Broadway and at the Globe (where
the lobby was decorated with scenes of Caribbean countries and promotional material for British West Indian Airways); they were also
shown in London at the Classic Cinemas in Kilburn and Brixton.[12] The
double feature would be shown intermittently over the years in the
Trinidad, but by the end of the 1990s the films were virtually lost,
though not forgotten. They are remembered as pioneering films that
were interesting to see because of the familiar locations and the recognizable indigenous actors, but they are also dogged by the constant
criticism that they were not of the highest quality.

The Harder They Come

At about the same time that Kumar's two films were being made and
shown, another feature film was in production in Jamaica. Some two
years in the making, *The Harder They Come*, directed by Perry
Henzell, finally premiered in Kingston before an appreciative audience, and in the process wrote itself into the history of Caribbean
cinema and film. Interviewed by Martin Hayman for the London
opening of the film, Henzell related with pride that at the Kingston premiere on 5 June 1972 over 6000 people had invaded the Carib cinema,
with some 3000 more encamped outside. Hayman commented: 'That,
he reckons, is a measure of his people's thirst to see themselves, their
island, and their life on film for the first time. It's also a triumphal vin-
dication of Henzell's belief that people want to see, and will pay to see,

reality and not celluloid fantasy, on the screen.' Predictably, Henzell also expressed the hope that his film would be the starting point for an indigenous black film industry based in the Caribbean.[13]

Valerie Bloomfield shows the complete contrast between the reception of this film and that of the two shot in Trinidad:

> The reviewers praised the film for the sense of national identity, its social realism, its successful combination of revolutionary message with high commitment value, and its effective use of reggae music to express the tone of the whole action. The film was a great success in Jamaica.[14]

Two comments are in order with respect to this observation. Firstly, it says a lot about the Jamaicans' keener sense of national pride as opposed to the Trinidadians'. The Jamaican masses showed the sort of initial support for a home-grown effort that Trinidadian masses did not. Unfortunately, this situation has hardly changed after two decades, and will be examined later. Secondly, it does not acknowledge the fact that there was some uneasiness over the film's subject matter as opposed to its artistic quality. In his review, Gordon Rohlehr wrote that '*The Harder They Come* was received with mixed feelings in Jamaica. Censors ordered the film to be cut in places which one critic thought did some violence to its coherence and continuity.'[15] Social considerations at home, and concern for projection of the right image in the eyes of the international community were interfering with the work of the artist.

One of those not too happy with the theme was Harry Milner, columnist for the *Sunday Gleaner*. He did not totally dismiss the film, and praised it for its fine reggae score, its vital acting, its brilliant direction, and the star personality of its lead, Jimmy Cliff. However, he was put off by the heavy dose of crime and violence, and actually entitled his piece 'Crime In Films':

> I still think it is a pity that the first fictional movie made here for international circulation, and which through its quality, its sensationalism and its novelty is bound to resound abroad should have been this film of murder, violence and crime, which is certainly these days an important part of our life, but in the long run not the most important, nor the most typical, nor the most endearing.[16]

It is ironic that a decade after independence there could still be the latent desire to please the larger countries – hence the reference to 'international circulation' – the very ones that worried precious little about the images exported into the Caribbean in the first place. What was it about *The Harder They Come* that made it so attractive, so appealing, to the point that even its flaws were praised by the said 'international' community?

After his studies in Canada and England, and a stint at the British Broadcasting Company, Perry Henzell, described as a 'conscious' white Jamaican, returned to Jamaica and made a living producing television commercials. His ambition to make feature films led him to collaborate with playwright Trevor Rhone in writing the screenplay for the movie *The Harder They Come*. It might be more accurate to say that they collaborated on the concept of the screenplay, since the shooting schedule never followed a set script, extended as it was over a period of two years, and forced to undergo adjustments as a result of various logistical and financial quirks. Franklyn St Juste, who served as director of photography, has recalled how the crew would have to work around the availability of Jimmy Cliff, with the attendant technical difficulties of recreating the exact lighting of a particular scene shot over a period of months.[17] Similarly, Michael Thelwell, upon agreeing to do the novelization of the film, immediately asked to see the script, only to be told that none existed. 'No complete script existed,' he wrote, 'because, in obedience to the grim economic reality of the Black world, the film had to be shot in fits and starts, piece-meal, with months intervening between shoots, as additional funds were scraped together'.[18]

The plot is relatively simple. A young man, Ivan, played by Jimmy Cliff, leaves the country to seek success in Kingston, convinced that he can make it as a singer. He tries in vain to find a job, and ends up being taken in by a zealous preacher, but that association soon sours, for the newcomer has the audacity to be attracted to the preacher's protégée, Elsa. A fight earns Ivan a caning in his first brush with the law, a humiliating experience that makes him urinate as his bare buttocks absorb the strokes administered by the uniformed prison guard. We subsequently see him on the rebound, trying to eke out a living with Elsa, but ruthlessly exploited as he attempts to earn a reasonable return from his first record. He resorts to selling marijuana to make a living, but, unfortunately, the exploitation continues even in the drug trafficking. He is betrayed into a police trap, leading to his shooting of several policemen, and to his transformation into a folk hero of sorts as he evades capture, and as his record eventually achieves success. He is finally gunned down by government forces after an unsuccessful attempt to escape to Cuba.

The story was based loosely on the exploits of Rhygin, Jamaica's first ghetto gunman of the late 1940s, who was reportedly so obsessed with westerns he saw himself as a cowboy.[19] It was modernized, so to speak, into a tale of contemporary bourgeois insensitivity to the plight of the lower class, and unscrupulous exploitation in an emerging record industry. This latter aspect was a perfect context for the sound-track, for, as Carl Bradshaw, who played Jose, has said, the film was 'musically driven.'[20] In this respect, the film was almost a mirror image of the early career of its lead actor, Jimmy Cliff, whose por-trayal of the exploited would-be reggae singer had an authenticity that must have stemmed from his own experience.

The Harder They Come was a veritable broadside in the face of Jamaican/Caribbean reality. It did not glamorize crime as such, but it could well have, given the sympathetic light in which we see Ivan, and his growing belief, as the movie approaches its climax, in the western's unwritten rule that all scores could be settled with a six-shooter. It was not by accident, then, that there is the subtext of cinema running throughout the film, from Ivan's first outing in Kingston with Jose to his suicidal invitation to his captors to send one man out to face him in his imaginary version of *High Noon* or *Gunfight at the OK Corral*. The splicing of snatches of the Italian-made western, *Django*, and of audi-ence reaction thereto, is a powerful, almost subliminal reinforcement of the role that such images played in the lives of urban moviegoers such as Ivan and his friends. The flight of fantasy taken by the film's hero is thus one with which many of its viewers could identify. The cinema screen became a virtual mirror.

The film manages to be critical of certain aspects of Jamaican society without being condescending or mean-spirited. The sympathy is clearly with the urban Afro-Jamaican youth, with at least one other character seen as making the best of his situation, albeit in a manner that does not engender hostility toward him. The record producer, fre-quently seen in his chariot of power, his Mercedes Benz convertible, represents the greater economic clout wielded by those of fairer com-plexion in these islands. He is depicted as helpful in his own self-serving way, and not at all unlike similar producers of other films depicting that early period – witness his Hollywood counterparts in the movie *Why Do Fools Fall In Love?* (1998) or the earlier *The Five Heartbeats* (1991), both of which depicted stymied attempts by budding artists to earn reasonable royalties from their records. Similarly, the complicity between the drug traffickers and the police is handled in a manner that almost seems to let the upholders of the law off the hook; they are forced into a position of understanding that the drug trade, while not totally desirable, is nonetheless crucial to the livelihood of certain sections of the population. While the hero does die in the last reel, there is no open condemnation of his activity by the director, all of which helps to leave the impression with viewers that their hero had given the system his best shot.

At a time when it might have been politically correct to produce a film in which the language spoken was comprehensible to international ears, leading perhaps to a stilted but 'correct' English that sounded unnatural, *The Harder They Come* was shot uncompromisingly in Jamaican creole, the language of Kingston's streets. 'This gave the actors tremendous self-confidence and power, by releasing energies which might otherwise have been consumed in self-consciousness about speech and accent, for the business of pure acting'.[21] The concession to ears unfamiliar with the creole was to use subtitles, quite an innovation at the time, and not unusual on television nowadays whenever the speakers of English are judged to have thick accents.

The music that accompanies this film is not there simply as 'background.' Like the creole language spoken throughout, the music is the people's, an integral part of the film, and cannot be watered down for international consumption. For example, when Ivan's request for assistance is rejected by the obviously middle-class matron on her verandah after his attempt to find employment in building construction fails, the soundtrack features Jimmy Cliff singing 'Many Rivers to Cross'. This most moving and appropriate song marks a poignant moment in the film, capturing to perfection the mood of despair that overcomes Ivan. Paradoxically, of course, the music did not have to be adulterated, as the international community avidly accepted this new sound, making reggae into one of the most recognizable of Jamaican contributions to world culture. The soundtrack would later be named among *Rolling Stone*'s 100 Most Influential Albums.[22]

If we accept the fact that most films, whether explicitly or implicitly, have something to 'say', what, then, did *The Harder They Come* say to its audiences? Edward Brathwaite seems to provide one of the more telling replies:

> 'For the first time at last' it was the people (the raw material) not the 'critics', who decided the criteria of praise, the measure and ground of qualification; 'for the first time at last', a local face, a native ikon, a nation language voice was hero. In this small corner of our world, a revolution as significant as Emancipation.[23]

What the movie said was that the Caribbean people's time had come, and this was visual, thus undeniable proof. Caribbean people were being seen by their own, not by the outsider, who invariably missed much of what made them tick.

One of the elements that could be missed by viewers unfamiliar with the broader social context of the film was the political atmosphere in which it was shot. Jamaican audiences were aware of the constant rivalry between the ruling Jamaica Labor Party, which seemed out of touch with the masses, and the clearly more popular, more grounded People's National Party, led by the charismatic Michael Manley, which promised better days ahead. It was a rivalry that had led to protests and had often included violence. As such, when the film's opening coincided with Manley's assumption of power, it was seen as a statement on the triumph of the people, and on their hope for the future. It was 'in its way a symbolic commentary on the first ten years of Jamaican independence, and an insight into the tensions of urban society in contemporary Jamaica.'[24]

If what the outside world saw was unexpected, even unsavoury, such was the reality of life in the islands. Beaches could be places to die on as well as to sunbathe. *The Harder They Come* did an excellent job of dispelling the stereotype of the Caribbean as an exclusive tourist playground. In this respect, it foreshadowed *Rue Cases-Nègres*, which the Martiniquan Euzhan Palcy would make some 12 years later. Palcy's film took an unflattering, yet charming look at life in the French-speaking Caribbean, and evoked strong emotions both when it was being filmed, and when it was finally screened. The language of the people, *Creole*, was used with the same effect: to get straight to the heart of the French Caribbean psyche. It is significant to note that this film also gained almost instant popularity upon release and, like *The Harder They Come*, became an illustration of what Caribbean cinema could do when given the right combination of circumstances.

But, as is inevitable in destroying stereotypes, a film can also unwittingly create others, or at least contribute to their propagation. The most glaring of these in *The Harder They Come* were the use of ganja by certain sections of the population, and the preoccupation with reggae music. This latter element is so pervasive that it surfaces in most films made in Jamaica, making many of them seem like distant sequels to this seminal production. Some critics were of the view that *The Harder They Come* was made mainly as a vehicle to promote music, given the involvement of Chris Blackwell and his Island Records.[25]

It has been difficult to obtain data on the financial success of the film. Shot on the proverbial shoestring budget – the figure US$10 000 is often cited – it is reported to have taken six years before investors got their money back. Over the years, the popularity of the film, especially with audiences outside the Caribbean, has been mainly as a cult classic, hence said audiences have typically not been large enough to guarantee a major profit for the film's producers. Its ready availability for purchase or for rent on video-cassette has, however, assured it a well-deserved place in the annals of Caribbean film history.

Periodically, both Perry Henzell and Jimmy Cliff are reported to have different versions of a sequel.[26]

The film's success at festivals in the years immediately following its release – notably at Cork and Venice – was further enhanced when, on its silver anniversary, it was recognized by the Sinbad Film Festival as one of the most influential independent films of all time. It was more than ironic that this festival took place in Trinidad and Tobago, where censors had initially balked at releasing the film. It was nonetheless comforting that the Caribbean was recognizing that it too could play in the big league, and that in *The Harder They Come* it had produced the quintessential Caribbean film.

Bim

The heavy hand of the censor also played a part in delaying the release of Trinidad and Tobago's third venture into feature film-making. In its article on the return engagement, 'practically through a back door', of the movie *Bim*, which the subheading erroneously claims was 'the first local movie', the *Sunday Express* wrote:

> *Bim* became somewhat of an artistic success, winning awards in various film festivals and it became a West Indian cult movie in the genre of the Jamaican movie of the same era, *The Harder They Come*.
>
> But in Trinidad and Tobago, the country of its origin and the setting for the story, the movie never really took hold. Even before *Bim* premiered in Port of Spain, it caused an upset. The film was banned by the censors on the strength of the fact that one of its characters uttered 'oh s..t' and 'mudder a..' once or twice in the two hours it took to unravel the tale.[27]

Common sense, and the law, prevailed. The offensive words were removed, and the film was released, though not without lingering trepidation over its use of the words 'nigger' and 'coolie'. Given the racial mix of the country, such words belied the public relations image of racial harmony.

This bickering in Trinidad and Tobago over words deemed offensive by certain sections of the public would crop up from time to time, and was not restricted to movies. Earl Lovelace saw his novel *The Dragon Can't Dance* almost banned from schools because of the 'f' word; in 1991, Godfrey Sealy's play, *Home Sweet Home*, was stopped by armed policemen, who arrested its actors in mid-performance; and as late as 1998 the Lord Street Theatre Company's production of the play *Jean and Dinah* found the police threatening to arrest its actors for using obscene language.[28]

Trinidad of 1974 experienced a cultural revival of sorts, spearheaded by the production at the Little Carib Theatre of Derek Walcott's *The Joker of Seville*, directed by the playwright himself. The making of *Bim* fell neatly into this pattern of artistic creativity. The film's director, Hugh Robertson, born in America of Jamaican parents, came with impressive credentials: film editor for *Midnight Cowboy* (1969), which had earned him an Oscar nomination, and *Shaft* (1971), and director of *Melinda* (1972). He had previously been in Trinidad filming Walcott's *Dream on Monkey Mountain* for the National Broadcasting Company and, like Harbance Kumar, had ended up marrying a Trinidadian.

Robertson and his wife were instrumental in setting up Sharc Productions, and once again the hope was expressed that this would herald the start of a vibrant local film industry. *Bim* was the company's first venture into film-making, and it drew upon an impressive roster of both experienced and new cast and crew, many of whom, including the lead actor, Ralph Maraj, had appeared in *The Right and the Wrong* and *The Caribbean Fox*. Raoul Pantin wrote the screenplay, which, according to the *Sunday Express*, 'was to have been based on a book on the murders by Boysie Singh written by an English author. However, the author asked too much money for the rights and Raoul offered to write a play from imagination, based on the rich experiences of Trinidad.'[29]

Bim is Bheem Singh, an (East) Indian from the Indo-dominated sugar-cane belt in Central Trinidad, where the inevitability of the end of British colonial rule is causing overall uneasiness and unrest. He is sent to live with an aunt in the capital after the murder of his father during a wedding reception. Once in Port of Spain, Bim has to face the fact that he is nothing but an Indian in the Afro-dominated urban setting, with the resultant prejudice and insults. From his very first day at school, he is subject to indignities and harassment by both teacher and classmates, one of whom he stabs in self-defence, his first act of open rebellion. Bim nonetheless manages to rise above the destructive nature of this situation and the ensuing life of crime, for which he inexplicably never pays the legal consequences. He eventually becomes involved in politics, working for the unity of the Africans and the Indians – his aunt is seen living with an African mate – but declares that 'if Negroes want to live by theyself, Indians accustom to that.' 'Through a series of coincidences and unfortunate accidents his career goes down the drain. Bim eventually implodes; he disintegrates after a crazy night of self-indulgence and self-destruction. The film ends with a long painful scream as he realizes he has blown it all.'[30] Bim has just pumped bullets into the body of the driver of the car that was carrying a couple of thugs who had been rash enough to attempt to violate his girlfriend. Maybe this time there would be no escaping the full weight of the law.

There is a level of gunplay – almost western-like – unusual for the Trinidad of that era, but, as with the crimes that go unpunished, the viewers are led to concentrate on other aspects of the film. There are, for instance, delightful performances by Wilbert Holder as Wabbam, a shady entrepreneur with police connections, and by Hamilton Parris as a ship captain allegedly involved in helping illegal immigrants. The Trinidad shown is very authentic, all the same, particularly the rural scenes, which could easily have been stereotyped, the way the police officers are almost caricatures. Finally, the white police commissioner and the expatriate governor manage to convey colonialism's dying spasm quite effectively.

It is interesting to speculate on what the reception of the film in Trinidad and Tobago would have been had it been released in the mid-1990s after the United National Congress, with the help of the National Alliance for Reconstruction, had formed a slim majority government under East Indian prime minister, Basdeo Panday, who was, like Bim, a union leader. The speculation is all the more intriguing when one considers that the lead actor, Ralph Maraj, was now in the cabinet of the Indian prime minister as Minister of External Affairs, after having served in a similar capacity in the African-dominated party of the previous government, the People's National Movement. The feeling that Indians' time had finally come could easily have given a different tone to the reception of the film, whose racial dimensions, according to the *Sunday Express*, caused it to be banned in Guyana, where, of course, sensitivity to African-Indian relations was quite keen. The sense of alienation that Bim experiences in the face of subtle oppression by the British colonial masters, and overt disdain by the Afro-Trinidadians, who behaved as if Trinidadian culture were their exclusive domain, would surely be viewed more as an observation of the indignities of the past than as an indication of the hopelessness of the future. But even with all the talk of support for the arts emanating from the cabinet of which former lead actor Maraj is a part, and with the added knowledge that the prime minister himself is a trained actor, there is no apparent attempt by his government to revive and re-release *Bim*, a film that clearly had a lot to say to both the African and the Indian population in the late 1990s.

But at the time of the film's release in 1974, many Indo-Trinidadians felt cut off from the mainstream, culturally if not numerically. Consequently, there was some concern about the authenticity of

THE CARIBBEAN FOX

AA

A RIB TICKLING COMEDY,
WITH
SPECIAL GUEST APPEARANCE OF "THE MIGHTY SPARROW"
(Calypso King of the World)
PORTRAYING
"MISS SPARROW'S"
ADVENTURES IN VIET-NAM

Produced
and
Directed
by
HARBANCE
KUMAR

FEAST OF SITAR, MUSIC, STEEL-BAND MUSIC, CALYPSOES, ROMANCE, PASSIONS, VIOLENCE, DRAMA & NON-VIOLENCE

Promotional material from *The Caribbean Fox*
Courtesy Mickey Nivelli (formerly Harbance Kumar)

Jimmy Cliff as Ivan in *The Harder They Come*
Courtesy Perry Henzell, International Films Ltd

Perry Henzell
Courtesy Bruce Paddington

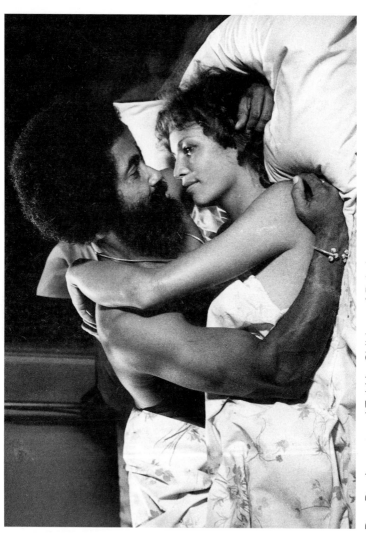

Don Parchment and Tobi in *Children of Babylon*
Courtesy Mediamix Ltd

Horace Ové
Courtesy Bruce Paddington

Lennie Little-White (right)
Courtesy Bruce Paddington

Herbert Norville in *Pressure*
Courtesy Horace Ové

Mark Danvers and Paul Campbell in *Dancehall Queen*
Courtesy Island Jamaica Films

Publicity still from *The Panman*
Courtesy Kamalo Deen

the social milieu presented on screen. In a radio discussion on the film, Denis Solomon held that the film misrepresented 'the mores of the Indian community,' possibly explaining why the chief censor had had reason to be worried about its effect on certain sections of the viewing public: 'I think that there is a fundamental misrepresentation of the conflicts existing in the sugar belt in an Indian rural society and it was a serious error because of the fact that everything else depended on it.'[31] The question of artistic licence – a concept local cinema audiences never seemed to bother about as they viewed foreign films – did not arise for this observer, who felt that Trinidad's history showed that the film's depiction of gang-type conflict for control of a sugar union was something that could not have taken place.

The film, which proudly carried an on-screen reminder that it was filmed entirely on location in Trinidad, did not attract mass audiences to the cinema, perhaps because of the type of problem raised by Denis Solomon; urban middle-class Indians received it coolly, and rural lower-class Indians did not put themselves out to attend the city cinemas where it was shown. The soundtrack, on the other hand, composed by the popular Andre Tanker in collaboration with many accomplished Indian musicians, received ample air play. Like the soundtrack for *The Harder They Come*, it too was released as a separate album, produced on Sharc's own label. The fusion of African-based calypso-style rhythms and East Indian melodies, of early steelband with tassa drumming, was a forerunner of the chutney music mix that would sweep Trinidad and Tobago in the 1990s:

> Tanker says the music of *Bim* itself was very Caribbean. The thing about it is that Mungal Yankeran [sic] had also been hearing other Trinidad music all his life, so *Bim* was more than a fusion. It was something that was familiar to both of them and to the population who would not, could not turn it off.[32]

Tanker used his music quite effectively to illustrate what the film was really all about: fusion and unity. Still, one participant in the above-mentioned radio discussion, when asked to comment on the function of the music, on its obtrusiveness or acceptability, claimed that he was not particularly impressed by it because he 'had this major problem about knowing all the actors.' This admission showed that history was repeating itself. The same problem that had greeted the emergence of indigenous written literature – the inability of readers to accept the familiar as worthy of literary merit – was apparently lurking in the wings for the emerging film industry.

In societies as small as those in the Caribbean, it is tempting to confuse the actor with the character he or she is playing, and the ensuing ironies can be both humorous and devastating. Columnist B. C. Pires, reviewing the reprise of *Bim* for the *Sunday Express* of 20 December 1992 noted the 'particularly delightful sort of dramatic irony which caused the 1992 Minister of External Affairs to confess his unsuitability for the job as early as 1973.' What he was referring to was Bim's admission, when offered a chance to lead a sugar union, that he didn't 'know too much about this politics business.' In all fairness to the Trinidad/Caribbean audience, however, one must concede that mainstream actors – those in soap operas, for example – have been similarly identified with the characters they portrayed.

Also lurking were reviews by critics who normally wrote for the publications that covered the big league productions, and who would be almost merciless on films that did not appear to meet usual international standards. For example, in its issue of 31 March 1976 *Variety* found that the film presented an 'insulting oversimplification of issues' with 'little commercial interest.' The reviewer, who in the same issue praised Trevor Rhone's *Smile Orange*, felt that 'some political sophistication along the lines of Frantz Fanon would have helped Robertson and scripter Raoul Pantin understand the real issues.' Finally, little tolerance was expressed for the 'inane theme song by Andrew Beddoe,' and the fact that the 'actors' dialect is hard to understand in the absence of subtitles.'

There is little evidence to support the assertion in the previously cited *Sunday Express* article that *Bim* became a West Indian cult movie in the genre of *The Harder They Come*. Such a status would require that the film be available with relative ease for showings at cinema clubs, at specialized festivals, or on cable television, if such a cult following is to develop. This has not been the case, though the film was shown in a few festivals in the early years of its release: St Thomas, Virgin Islands (1975), Los Angeles (1976), and Carifesta '76, Jamaica (1976). Given the easy accessibility of the video-cassette format, we can further appreciate the marketing acumen of the producers of *The Harder They Come*, who ensured their film's wide availability on video.

If Trinidad and Tobago was going to have anything remotely resembling a film industry, then one film per company would not suffice. With this in mind, Sharc Productions attempted a second movie, *Avril*, from another Raoul Pantin screenplay. Unfortunately, it was never released in Trinidad and Tobago. Financial problems made it impossible to have the film edited professionally, and the company never managed to shoot another feature. But *Avril* had not disappeared entirely, for a decade or so later, and shortly before Hugh Robertson died, the Black Filmmakers Hall of Fame held a retrospective on the films he had either edited or directed. For this event a copy of *Avril* was completed, but the film now bore the title *Obeah*, and had its world premiere at the York theatre in San Francisco on 24 October 1987. The *San Francisco Chronicle* reviewed the film, and gave the following brief synopsis:

> 'Obeah' – the word in Trinidad for voodoo – is based on the true story of a young couple whose love affair in 1973 was ruined as the result of a spell cast by the boy's aunt, an Obeah priestess. Today he resides in Toronto; the young woman remains in Trinidad.

Toward the end of the review, the writer comes to the conclusion that:

> Robertson treats the beliefs of these African descendants with as much respect as that paid to others who believe that wine and the communion wafer represent the blood and the body of Jesus. In fact, the New Testament is the tool used to fight Avril's hysterical condition.[33]

Ironically, there were those in Trinidad's acting community who seriously felt that the complications Robertson and his company encountered with this film – the *Obeah* version still did not make it to Trinidad screens – and the series of disasters that befell many of those who were associated with it, were due in large part to its subject matter. It was, some thought, as if something unnatural kept hurling obstacles in its path. Be that as it may, the end result was that Sharc Productions ceased operations, thus withdrawing itself from the line-up of those companies wishing to be part of a Caribbean film industry.

Smile Orange

The idea of establishing a corpus of work that would constitute irrefutable proof that anglophone Caribbean film-making had taken its rightful place in the big league seems to have found more currency in Jamaica than in the other territories. After *The Harder They Come* there would have to be some follow-up to show both Jamaicans and the rest of the Caribbean and the world that this first effort was not a fluke. Trevor Rhone answered the call, and with David Ogden wrote the screenplay of *Smile Orange*, an adaptation of his successful play of the same name. He also directed the film, which retained many of the comic touches seen in the play during its record-breaking run of 245 performances when it was first staged in 1971 under the direction of Dennis Scott.[34] The film won a gold medal at the Cork Film Festival in 1975, and was also shown at Filmex in Los Angeles in 1976.

In her book on West Indian theatre, Judy Stone tells us that Molière was a favourite writer of Trevor Rhone's.[35] A viewing of the play *Smile Orange* confirms this affection, for there are many scenes that remind the spectator of the controlled farce of many of the French playwright's comedies: among them, Ringo's hiding in a garbage can while the assistant manager is looking for him; busboy Cyril's clumsily exposing his armpit to the dinner guest he is serving; and Ringo's attempt to teach this country bumpkin to speak without his annoying lisp. In addition, the unsuspecting insertion of biting social commentary in the midst of comic action is also very reminiscent of Molière's use of the French classical stage – as is, incidentally the respect for unity of place, allowing for off-stage activity to be reported from the vantage point of characters on stage.

In view of Jamaica's push into the tourism industry, an important earner of foreign exchange, it would seem somewhat ironic that such a play would be so popular. One would have expected the attitudes expressed in it to come more probably from a country like Trinidad and Tobago, where for years the official response to tourism was one of benign neglect. As it turns out, Rhone was quite prophetic, and much of what is criticized in the play has come to pass in those territories that have aggressively sought to earn money through tourism. As such, the play could easily be set nowadays in Barbados, in the Bahamas, or even in Tobago, which has belatedly become an attraction for the type of tourism that *Smile Orange* satirizes.

Black visitors to Caribbean hotels in countries with major tourist attractions can identify with the play/film's Social Director who was not served in the dining room as readily as the white guests. They can also understand how they could be seen as the very cause of the problem, for the other side of the coin shows them treating black waiters with scant respect. 'If a man don't respect you, you can't respect him back,' Ringo tells his assistant manager. In the midst of all the laughter, then, there is subtle criticism of the cultural prostitution involved in earning the tourist dollar, and of the emasculation of many of those plying the tourist trade, symbolically encapsulated in the significance of the title, a reference to the mistaken belief that the consumption of oranges leads to impotence.

The film version, produced by Knuts Productions Limited in 1975, expands what the audience sees, but is very faithful to the original text of the play, with much of the dialogue kept verbatim. Scenes that the playwright did not show on stage are played out in full, so that we now see the guests, most of whom are shown arriving by Air Jamaica.[36] Most are but caricatures, though, hardly even speaking, and playing set roles – the hen-pecked husband, the nagging wife, the glutton – none of which are very flattering to the tourists. Carl Bradshaw later commented that the film ridiculed white people, possibly explaining why it did not have as wide a distribution as *The Harder They Come.*[37] Trevor Rhone confirmed that, for all the problems with marketing, 'audience response was amazing.'[38]

Bradshaw reprised his stage role as Ringo, and the expanded arena of the film medium gives him ample room to be the consummate trickster, the true Anancy of Caribbean folklore, constantly scheming and living by his wits. The very opening scene of the movie shows him slipping out of bed at the start of a series of adventures that lead to his coming to terms with the fact that he must go with the flow, for, as Ringo observes in both play and film, 'if you is a black man and you can't play a part, you going to starve to death.' Ringo plays many parts: the seducer is able to entice a young woman hitch-hiker into an impromptu sexual encounter, but things go awry when the couple end up scratching themselves all over as a result of their contact with cow itch, and have to run naked into a nearby river for relief from the irritant grass; the charm school teacher shows the hapless busboy how to make the most out of the tourists, and how to mimic the American accent; the con man knows how to secure a loan from the unwilling hands of his assistant manager. The roles succeed one another with great speed. Mervyn Morris notes the importance of this aspect of the play/film:

> Play-acting is a recurrent metaphor. The blacks, including Assistant Manager O'Keefe, are playing roles to which they have been assigned by the tourist industry and the realities of power. The lifeguards are exposed; there is a tragedy. The difficulties for Ringo, Joe and O'Keefe are overcome when they recognize the possibilities of a new performance – Ringo as selfless hero, with supporting cast. A little help from the press, and they can act themselves out of trouble.[39]

It is this busybody quick-wittedness that ultimately keeps the film leaning toward the funny side as opposed to the serious, so that the criticism of the tourist industry, and of the white people who are an integral part of it, is not really taken to heart. There is a tongue-in-cheek quality to the criticism because there can be no doubt that the country needs the jobs and money brought by this industry. 'Exploit the exploiter – God laughs,' is Ringo's rationalization of the potentially devastating situation.

Apart from the opening scenes that show the Jamaican countryside, the film shows very little of the island, with the majority of the location shots showing a typical tourist hotel. The telephone receptionist is portrayed as anxious to leave the island in search of greener pastures in America, with the resultant willingness to exchange her 'pearl' for the opportunity when it presents itself. She is apparently the only one who does not see through the whole sham of her instant relationship with the newly arrived guest, and when we have confirmation that he has taken the plane home, there is a tragi-comic ' I told you so' in the attitude of her telephone gossip partner as well as the other hotel workers.

The assistant manager is shown to be on the losing end of his inter-racial marriage. He is very busy at the hotel, and she has a replacement lover in the black gardener. The film does not dwell on this twist to the story, but places it in the same context as that of the bungling busboy capturing the matronly white visitor on the beach. The scenes are played for comic effect, but Caribbean audiences know exactly what to think when they see them, and are comfortable with their mixture of truth and stereotype.

The film score is not typically Jamaican, in that it is not reggae-dominated. There are traditional 'welcome to Jamaica' songs performed without much gusto, the type one would indeed expect in a hotel that has seen better days, and catering to the tourist idea of local music. Ringo's exploits are often accompanied by a female chorus, telling of the picaresque nature of Ringo Smith's adventures. *Smile Orange* can be viewed on two levels. On one hand, it is a biting commentary on the tourist industry that leaves the viewer in pensive mood; on the other, it is an enjoyable comic romp that celebrates Caribbean humour.

One notes that the Caribbean-made films were not usually promoted as comedies. *If Wishes Were Horses*, made in Guyana in 1976, was billed as 'Guyana's and the Caribbean's First Full-Length Musical Comedy'. The publicity blurb told viewers that

> this exciting musical comedy from the Caribbean is based on the misadventures of a reluctant farmer played by the Caribbean's foremost comedian Habeeb Khan. He escapes from the problems of reality through hilarious fantasies including: dreams of being the dashing D'Artagnan and romantic Romeo.

There are nine original songs and four dances, but these seem more like attempts to give exposure to local artistes than items that were conceived as part of an original screenplay. Poorly shot, and badly in need of editing, the entire film also seems like a collection of Habeeb Khan's stand-up routines and skits, with the barest thread of a story about the benefits of collective farming. To its credit, however, the film tries earnestly to present Guyana from a Guyanese perspective.

Rastafarian trilogy

Where *Smile Orange* looked at the tourist industry, the Jamaican films that followed it over the next five or six years, *Rockers* in 1978, *Children of Babylon* in 1980, and *Countryman* in 1982, would all show varying aspects of the lifestyle of the country's Rastafarians, who were vilified by some and admired by others for their beliefs and strengths. From Jamaica across the Caribbean to Trinidad and beyond, the Rastafarians have attracted hordes of followers sympathetic to their return to the simple life, more in tune with nature; but they have also attracted their share of critics, many of whom have developed a love-hate relationship with the group, enjoying the reggae music it creates, for example, but rejecting many of its other customs and habits. This duality of response to the Rastafarians is not unlike the primitive *versus* civilized dichotomy, a point that is made by Ed Guerero in his article on modes of resistance in *Rockers* and *Countryman*:

> ... the schizophrenic allure of the 'primitive' and his lifestyle are as old as the colonial and industrial imagination itself. The 'civilized' mind is drawn to the seductive appeal of dropping the neurotic trappings of a fragmented, technological society for the uninhibited immersion in nature and the utopian, tribal relations that its systems of material 'progress' have worked so hard to eradicate. Simultaneously though, this same mind deeply fears the loss of definition, power, and privilege that such a letting go would entail. Thus the Western psyche must constantly struggle with the tension between the more historically dominant impulse to discipline, exploit, and control both nature and the exotic 'savage,' usually destroying them both in the process, against the nostalgic, romantic yearning to identify and merge with them.[40]

This *de facto* trilogy of Rasta-friendly films allowed viewers with only a sketchy knowledge of Rasta lore to see for themselves what lay behind the veil of innuendo, false accusations, and mystery that shrouded the Rastafarians in general.

Rockers

Of the three films, *Rockers* is the crudest, and for this reason the one that some observers feel most closely captures the essence of the true Rastafarian lifestyle, anchored as it is in the desire for a pre-technology simplicity. There are times when the camera work resembles amateur home video shoots, and much of the acting is lost in an unscripted babel of Rastaspeak that is not always fully captured by the subtitles. We are back to the theme of exploitation in the music business, and the hotel manager hiring the film's lead to play music for $20 a week sounds uncannily like the record producer in *The Harder They Come* offering Ivan a similar sum for his record.

Rasta reggae drummer Leroy 'Horsemouth' Wallace, playing himself, tries to make a living distributing records. His efforts are hindered when his motorcycle is stolen by the so-called music 'Mafia,' and much of the remaining action revolves around his recovering his property, and exacting revenge for its theft. He and his fellow musicians, a *Who's Who* of Jamaican reggae performers, some of whom have only brief walk-on parts, end up raiding the warehouse where much of the 'Mafia' loot is stashed. The items recovered by this Jamaican Robin Hood – a variety of consumer goods – are left by the roadside for members of his impoverished neighbourhood to help themselves. At the end, Horsemouth prefers to sleep off his tiredness, as he opts not to participate in the redistribution of the wealth, and this despite the urging of his woman.

The point of view of the entire film is Rastafarian, with the result that there is an anti-establishment tone – anti-Babylon in Rastaspeak – that forces the viewer to sympathize with the underdog. Horsemouth, for instance, upon being knocked to the ground by an irate father, who does not want his daughter associating with people of that ilk, does not respond with violence. He uses the occasion to look directly into the camera, shake his locks, beat his chest, and proudly proclaim victory for himself and his brethren, strong in the love of Selassie I, for 'not even the dog that pisses against the wall of Babylon shall escape this judgement.' Audiences accustomed to the stereotype of criminal or other unsociable activity associated with Rasta lifestyle may find this reaction somewhat surprising, but it is all part of the quest for social justice, which 'is achieved not so much by confrontation and struggle with corrupt institutions and bureaucracies as by submission to Jah's will, which is always equalizing and redemptive.'[41]

It is clear, however, that the Rastafarians are caught in a dilemma, for they cannot fully escape all of the very Babylon they reject. Horsemouth's children are shown preparing for school, the same school apparently as the rest of the children of the 'baldheads' There is the intention, later in the film, to have them taught the 'culture', but we do not see the actual teaching, as in *Countryman,* where we see children being taught by the venerable Rastafarian elder, Jahman. Similarly, for all their rejection of the capitalist obsession with money, they are forced to deal with it if they are to coexist peacefully with

Babylon – and in fact, several Rastafarians have become visibly quite wealthy; nor can they reject technology completely since it helps them spread the word and the music. In this respect, the symbolism of the commandeering of a disk jockey booth by Horsemouth and his friend Dirty Harry, because 'rockers music don't play', is striking. While police officers stand by helplessly, Dirty Harry locks himself in the booth from which he has just evicted the rightful disk jockey, and proceeds to play reggae music as opposed to the American-dominated songs that the previous disk jockey was playing. 'This is a take-over,' he shouts into the microphone in celebration of his *coup,* as the soundtrack plays yet another of the lengthy list of reggae numbers that punctuate the action in this film. It was unconscionable that foreign music could have so much exposure at the expense of the indigenous, which when not banned 'received very little broadcast play on the two radio stations, one of which was government-owned and the other independent.'[42] Sebastien Clarke comments on this situation, which, incidentally, had its counterpart in the world of calypso and steelband in Trinidad:

> Of course, middle and upper Jamaica controlled the cultural fate of Jamaica, if only ephemerally. They defended their inferiority complexes by inundating radio with their American heroes, and looked contemptuously on the 'noise' that was being made by local Jamaicans. Since local (and poor ones at that) Jamaicans possessed no example of 'culture' or 'history' it would be an impossibility to accept that they had anything meaningful to say to them.
>
> Middle Jamaica was ashamed of the new strivings for Jamaican cultural identity and viewed the musical expression with ridicule.[43]

What the Rastas want is more airplay for their music, something that technology and good faith on the part of the powers that be could easily make happen. Greek director Theodoros Bafaloukos, an obvious admirer of Rastafarian culture, lets the film make this point quite eloquently at this juncture.

Social commentary is evident in the film once one knows where to look. One notes, for example, the Rastas' less than equitable treatment of their women; or the white visitors who cannot even tell reggae from calypso, but for whom the locals are catering in their quest for the tourist dollar *à la Smile Orange*; or even the exploitative nature of the hotel hiring practices. Still, one cannot escape the impression that what motivated its production was an attempt to capitalize on the emerging popularity of reggae on the international music scene. Much of the action thus seems set up simply to lead to the on-screen performance by known *artistes* such as Burning Spear, Gregory Isaacs or Jacob Miller. Beyond these, the soundtrack, as previously indicated, presents a galaxy of reggae stars, including Peter Tosh, Bunny Wailer, Inner Circle and Third World.

There is also the hint, through Horsemouth's grandmother and her participation in a Revivalist baptism, that this Afro-Christian sect has close affinity with the Rastafarians through their rhythmic chants and dances. While Horsemouth and his spiritual leader Hiram the Healer look admiringly upon the rituals, one can only surmise that members of the more mainstream Christian denominations would view with disfavour this 'connection between old-time religion and reggae'.[44]

The use of subtitles to unravel some of the specialized language of the Rastas seems to indicate that the makers of *Rockers* targeted an international or crossover audience. While the Jamaican audience as a whole would be more comfortable with the language, with or without subtitles, it is not at all certain that it would be equally as comfortable with the film's portrayal of Jamaican life. On the contrary, some will argue, it is the ready acceptance by the international community of Rastafarians and reggae that led to the their being co-opted by the Jamaican establishment for both political and commercial gain. One cannot avoid the nagging feeling, then, that *Rockers* will be viewed and remembered in Jamaica mainly for the music and the inside look at the minority Rasta community. Outside Jamaica it will assume larger proportions, and be seen as an exploration of the tribulations of an under-class, one on which the home audience did not care to focus too much of its attention.

Children of Babylon

Jamaica's ambivalence *vis-à-vis* the Rastafarians and their beliefs is again highlighted in Lennie Little-White's first feature film, *Children of Babylon*, though the film is not exclusively about Rastafarian lifestyle. Its title, though, immediately brings to mind the perspective of the Rastafarians, who consistently refer to the establishment, their main oppressor, as Babylon, and the icon used to advertise it featured a stylized head with dreadlocks. Nonetheless, the historical perspective provided by the film-maker gave the following explanation:

> For some people, Jamaica is the classical example of Babylon. Jamaica is a cultural mosaic which just happens to be the home of the Rastaman, Reggae, Rum and Ganja. There are more elements in the country which do not always

attract the world-view but which continue to determine the lives of those who reside there.[45]

The director himself described it as 'more than just another movie about Jamaica. It is a detailed examination of the conflicts which arise in a society stratified along economic, class and racial lines.'[46] Little-White, on his return to Jamaica from film studies in Canada, was committed to developing an indigenous film industry. His determination led to the founding of his own company, Mediamix, and to the producing of *Children of Babylon*. 'The training I got was in filmmaking,' he said as his company approached its 25th anniversary, 'so I thought it was good to make a movie; it came at a time when Jamaica was going through tough economic times but it broke away from the stigma that Jamaica was a place of ghettos and rude boys.'[47]

'A good story is a good story is a good story' was Little-White's description of what he felt would have international appeal. The following is his synopsis of the film, interesting in its revelation of how the director saw the angle from which he worked:

> The story is about people making love while searching for LOVE. Penny, an attractive university student, is doing research for her doctorate. Her thesis examines the sexual relationships of the working class. While doing research in rural Jamaica, she meets Rick, an artist whose paintings have brought him wealth and fame. Rick is staying in a plantation greathouse while he prepares for another exhibition in New York. He offers Penny a place to stay. The housekeeper is Dorcas, and the farmhand is a 'dreadlocks' named Luke. Luke is moving toward the acceptance of the Rastafari faith.
>
> Penny's left-wing views create a conflict with Rick's bourgeois sentiments. However, this does not stop them from getting into an intimate relationship.
>
> The fairy-tale romance is shattered when Laura, the white American who owns the greathouse and plantation, arrives for a weekend.
>
> A confused Penny soon finds solace in the person of Luke, the dreadlocks, This only creates more conflicts as it leaves Dorcas broken and sad. Penny's social background prevents her from adjusting to the strict doctrinaire philosophy of Luke's religion. The on-going dialectic does not result in a positive resolution.[48]

On the face of it, this scenario is not too complicated, but it does show, especially in the way it ends, that the director was seeking to cause viewers to think seriously about situations in the society. Babylon would have to begin to come to terms with the Rastafarians.

On the whole, the film was well received in Jamaica, where it played for approximately six weeks, slightly longer than *The Harder They Come*. It also had a lengthy run in Toronto, but only brief stays in Boston, Brooklyn and Los Angeles. At the international level, then, the film, obviously made with a crossover audience in mind, was not as enthusiastically received as its maker would have liked. A Jamaican director in a Jamaican film was dealing with a situation that was very serious for the home audience, but did not fit the stereotype of Caribbean lifestyle as far as international viewers were concerned. In this regard, Franklyn St Juste, the film's director of photography, believed that on the whole western audiences took a derogatory view of Jamaican 'films that are too polished looking,' expecting and preferring the 'rough, unpolished finish' they had come to associate with 'Third World' films. According to this film professional, the lukewarm reception given *Children of Babylon*, an extremely polished production, exposed this irony.[49] Large audiences abroad, he felt, were not necessarily a sign of acceptance, but of curiosity.[50]

The film, according to the director's synopsis, is 'spiced with the pulsating rhythm of reggae music which provides a backdrop to the beautiful Jamaican countryside.' This sort of tourist-brochure or travel-agency language seems to confirm that a non-Jamaican market was the most likely target. Director Lennie Little-White wrote the lyrics to the songs composed by Harold Butler, who, according to the company publicity material, 'succeeded in drawing on the rich musical heritage of Jamaica to paint a musical picture that few will forget.'

Countryman

The question of target market is also central to *Countryman*, and the reason certain scenes are presented in this film directed by Dickie Jobson. Early in the film, the hero, after rescuing two young white passengers from their crashed light aircraft, serves them a feast of tropical foods and fruit. This scene elicits the following observation from one critic:

> ... it is obvious from the premise of this opening scene that *Countryman* was made for export to a broad 'crossover' audience in the vast media saturated markets of the U.S. and Europe. For in this opening vignette, the spectator/consumer is positioned to enjoy the stereotypical pleasures of an island paradise offered up by a friendly native *Other* who asks for

no greater reward for his services than the acceptance and satisfaction registered on his guests' faces.[51]

These guests must be captured, or heads will roll in this inadvertent drug caper. Add some obeah to the mix, some army bungling, and some political corruption and election intrigue, and one has the basic plot of this film, 'dedicated to Bob Marley,' whose words and music are acknowledged as its inspiration.

Countryman the hero is played by a Rasta-like mystic fisherman, who is nonetheless seen as a Rasta by critics such as Ed Guerero and Paul Gilroy. He is a curious blend of bucolic James Bond, Indiana Jones and Bruce Lee. It is never fully explained why he would risk life and limb to rescue and then hide the white plane crash survivors, but the entire sequence does allow the director to play with certain notions that clearly stem from the concept of the noble savage. Paul Gilroy sees this as an inversion of the Robinson Crusoe myth, with Friday 'recast in the form of a Rasta hermit-fisherman endowed with magical powers that originated in his total harmony with the natural world.'[52] Countryman innocently provides hospitality and simple first aid, but never seeks to grill his guests about the reason for their downed flight. On the contrary, he takes to lecturing them on the virtues of living close to nature; he admits that he has no clothes save those he is wearing, skimpy as they are, and we see no worldly possessions save his boat, fishing gear, and a few cooking utensils; yet he outsmarts the forces searching for him for the entire length of the film. He is at ease with the obeah – though one can just imagine the international audience calling it voodoo – that unnerves or angers many of the other characters. In a recurring *leitmotif*, he is shown running to get to his destinations, returning in this manner to the most primal of ways of moving around quickly. He is, all told, a Rasta superman, non-violent until pushed to the absolute limit, perfectly in harmony with nature, and effectively showing Jamaica and the rest of the world that there is untold inner and physical strength to be gained from the Rasta lifestyle.

Once again, as in *Rockers*, viewers are able to see close-ups of Rastafarian chant and ganja sessions. It is easy to imagine how such scenes could be viewed with some dismay by the Jamaican upper crust – though not with the same alarm that greeted the prospect seen in *Children of Babylon* that their daughters would choose to associate with Rastas. These rituals were seen as pure glamorizing and romanti-cizing of elements that only served to give Jamaica a bad name in the international community. On the other hand, that very community saw this rare authentic look at dynamic ethnicity in operation as indicative of Jamaica's courage in dealing with its 'underclass life that is the majority experience in the island's population'.[53]

The overall pro-Rasta tone does at times leave the impression that, in the best of all possible worlds, this would be the way to go, though there is no evidence that the Rasta lifestyle would solve all problems. There is abundant hope, however, fuelled by Marley's songs on the soundtrack, and the example that those who betray the Rasta cause, even from within, like Mosman, risk meeting disastrous ends. As the film credits roll, Bob Marley's 'Jah Live' accompanies a beautiful sunset, which, coming after the symbolic resurrection of Jahman, leaves the viewer with a feeling of serenity and triumph.

The language is not as deeply rooted in Rastaspeak as in *Rockers*, with the result that there is really no need for subtitles. There is a veneer to the Rasta characters that makes them less threatening, probably due in part to the camerawork of Dominique Chapuis (who would later shoot *Rue Cases-Nègres* for Euzhan Palcy). The fact that this movie is produced by Chris Blackwell of Island Records, and that it is dedicated to Island's superstar, Bob Marley, is not insignificant. Film would help record sales. Record sales would help film.

Jamaican film-makers clearly decided to capitalize on the growing international popularity of reggae, which could no longer be seen as a fleeting musical fad. In a fitting case of poetic justice, Jamaica adopted reggae as a national symbol, with the result that when it qualified in 1998 for the final round of the World Cup, emblem of football supremacy worldwide, the team was heralded as the 'reggae boys'. Trinidad and Tobago, home of calypso and steelband long before reggae emerged in Jamaica, did not have the same marketing success with its indigenous music, though the latter occasionally featured in some of the films made by this country.

Man From Africa/Girl From India

Harbance Kumar, who had used calypso and the appeal of the Mighty Sparrow in *The Caribbean Fox*, once more tried to cash in on the lure of calypso by making the lead of his 1982 film, *Man From Africa*, a nightclub calypso singer. Kamalo Deen and Pempaleh Productions had made *Bacchanal Time* in 1979, a film that featured a variety of calypsonians (Crazy, Calypso Rose, Shadow, Count Robin *et al.*) performing well-known numbers tailor-made, given the film's title, to attract the fun-loving Trinidad moviegoer. The film enjoyed fair success in Trinidad, and would occasionally be doubled with other films deemed to be of local interest with a view to increasing attendance figures, a ploy that, unfortunately, did not work with Pempaleh's other feature film, *The Panman*, which bombed when it opened in 1997, and to which we will return shortly.

The calypso music that drives *Man From Africa* is by the Mighty Arrow, composer of 'Hot, Hot, Hot,' the soca calypso whose many versions have come to symbolize the Caribbean on both television and movie soundtracks, and Michael Walker as lead lip-syncs to Arrow's voice. The film's promotional material describes it as 'shot in West Indies [sic] with beautiful locales, calypso and steel band music, Indian music and the world famous Trinidad and Tobago Carnival.' What audiences make of this music changes depending on what 'version' of the film they see, for the same footage appears as *Girl From India*, in which case it carries a different soundtrack, and, according to *Variety*, 'is pointed at different ethnic playoff'.[54] Ever attentive to marketing possibilities, Kumar had *Man From Africa* distributed for audiences in Africa, and *Girl From India* for audiences in India. Both titles fit, but the connotation changes depending on whether one is viewing one or the other. For audiences in Trinidad and Tobago, whose African and Indian populations are evenly split, this was tantamount to flirting with controversy.

Almost two and a half hours in length, this movie tells the story of Michael, the nightclub calypso singer of African descent who is a typical macho love-and-leave type, firm in the belief that marriage spoils everything. Girlfriend Margot, forced by Michael to have an abortion, decides to mend her broken heart in New York. Michael is now free to cavort at will with lover after lover, always stopping short of marrying them; but to avoid the constant risk of impregnating his partners, he has a vasectomy. As such, when one lover turns up pregnant 'with a little help from another fellow', he knows she's not bearing his child. Her father and ruffian brother arrange a shotgun wedding, but the bride is left abandoned when Michael sends a jackass in his place, while he escapes to New York. Once there, he reunites with Margot and ends up marrying her.

Alongside this action is the story of the Indians. Michael's bosom friend Shyam, whose parents go to India to choose him a wife, Reena, discovers upon marriage that he is haunted by the demon of sex as sinful, and cannot consummate the union. He nonetheless encourages his wife to go out and enjoy herself, although this is viewed with disapproval by his parents, who think that activities such as listening to calypso, visiting nightclubs, or wearing swim suits on a public beach are signs of the decadence of western culture. Reena meets and has an affair with an artist, and ends up pregnant by him. Shyam accepts the son as his, and for a while the grandparents are thrilled, but they still ostracize Reena because she is seen as the devil incarnate. Shyam is killed, and his father blames Reena for all the trouble that has befallen his household. The solution is to have her killed, just like her lover before her. Matters take the wrong turn and she ends up in court on trial for murder. Michael and Margot are among those in the crowd outside the courtroom protesting her innocence. The entire movie is a flashback, for it had opened with Reena's trial, and ends with a maudlin notice on the screen: 'You judge her. Thank you.' There is no verdict in the film.

There is soap opera written all over this film, and the melodrama confirms this. The director, as he had done in his earlier films, reaches into every bag of cinematic tricks that he can find, as he plays both to the home and the international audience. Michael Walker, who plays the African lead part, is new to acting, but when not forced into too demanding a situation does a creditable job alongside the more experienced Ralph Maraj, by now a veteran of nearly all earlier feature films made in Trinidad. Sanam Suri as the girl/wife from India brings dignity to her role of sacrificial virgin, though the trailer leaves the erroneous impression that she is also one of the women seeking the African's love; and Kabir Bedi, described in the printed promotional material as a Middle East star (but as an international star in the trailer), uses his non-Trinidad accent to highlight the disorientation of the nation's Indian community.

Once again, one is led to speculate on the reaction to this film had it been done a generation later, when the sense of not belonging would not have been so acute. The desperate attempt by Mr Krishna, played with convincing awkwardness by Ralph Maraj, to keep his culture and ethnicity pure seems out of tune with the push for national unity between the Africans and Indians. Michael, Margot, Shyam and Reena do their part to promote inter-racial unity, but the older generation, as represented by the Indian parents, is seen as too rigid – Mr Krishna ends up taking his own life rather than continue to live with all the turmoil swirling around him. In the final analysis, both races suffer from the stereotype presented on screen: the Africans are lovers of music and dancing, time-wasting activities, and not responsible when it comes to dealing with their women; the Indians are clannish, somewhat backward, and unwilling to participate in what has become the national culture.

Michael Walker, a fashion model before he became an actor, plays the role of trickster with ease, and is just another version of the Anancy character that Carl Bradshaw captures so well in *Smile Orange*. He gives the impression that he is thoroughly enjoying being a film star, though beneath the on-screen character lies the ever fun-loving

Trinidadian who does not take himself or the film too seriously. Indeed, some six years later Walker again teamed up with Kumar (who by then had changed his name to Mickey Nivelli) and made *Jealous* in 1988, in which he played the part of an out-of-work actor from the West Indies who concocts a major scam while in the United States. In order to earn money for a movie he and his similarly unemployed actor friend want to make, he decides to join him in pretending they are evangelists, first at street corners, then with their own church. He is now Reverend Anancy, and with his partner in trickery proceeds to indulge in many of the tricks and schemes that had proven to be the downfall of real television evangelists. Religious sensitivity is hardly ruffled, however, in view of the tongue-in-cheek manner in which the film is directed, and the twist at the end when the gullible congregation is told the truth. Predictably, Michael Walker gets the girl he was pursuing.

There is no attempt to pass this movie off as Caribbean. The only connection with the region is that Michael Walker, played by Michael Walker, comes from 'the West Indies' – by the same plane, boarded in the same shot of him running up the gangway used in *Man From Africa* – and does not attempt to disguise his Caribbean accent or mannerisms. When it was shown in Trinidad, the *Daily Express* described it as an entertaining flick, 'Walker's best', with a simple, easy-to-follow plot, though the reviewer did point out several technical short-comings in this film by 'Trinidadian' Nivelli.[55] It is this technical teething problem that further links this movie with the ones done entirely on location in the Caribbean, as opposed to other mainstream American films that used Caribbean actors like Jamaica's Madge Sinclair or Trinidad's Sullivan Walker. As such, *Jealous* is very close to the type of film we will be discussing in a later chapter: made outside the Caribbean, but dealing with the experience of Caribbean people.

'Bad-words' and violence

The Lunatic

How well the Caribbean was dealing with its emerging movie industry's teething problems can be seen in the Island Pictures' 1990 production of *The Lunatic*, a film about a Jamaican situation but made with local actors and a foreign crew, and one in which a subject fraught with possible pitfalls is handled with skill and technical expertise. The question of fantasy in an adult setting is always risky, and this film deals with it from start to finish. The blurb that accompanies the video-tape version is typical of the way movies made in the Caribbean are presented. While mentioning the *de rigueur* 'pulsating reggae beat', this one nevertheless avoids the time-worn and increasingly tiresome reminder that the film was shot 'entirely on location':

> Set to a pulsating reggae beat against the lush tropical landscape of Jamaica, *The Lunatic* is the story of a wild and crazy love affair. When Aloysius, a carefree Jamaican, meets Inga, a lusty German tourist, his simple island life goes totally insane. Uninhibited and sexually insatiable, Inga has no trouble seducing the eager Aloysius. But, their romantic interlude becomes complicated when Inga also seduces Service, the local butcher. With two Jamaican lovers at her side, Inga is in tropical heaven, until her money runs out. Then, a life of lazy love turns into a life of crime, with some very funny, disastrous results.

The implication of the blurb is that the carefree Jamaican's life goes crazy only after he meets the German tourist. In fact, he already seemed crazy from the very first scene. The screenplay is an adaptation by Anthony C. Winkler of his own novel, and stays very close to the original story of a village madman 'tolerated by neighbors but forced to eke out a living doing odd jobs while he uses the hospitable wood-lands for shelter. He is starved of human companionship; instead he has running conversations with trees and plants.'[56] His other quirk is his intoxication with polysyllabic words that he appropriates as his names. Both these oddities are handled with humour and understand-ing, and without any hint of condescension.

If there is caricature, it is in the portrayal of the German visitor, 'more terrorist than tourist', according to the *Washington Post* reviewer.[57] She has come to Jamaica ostensibly to research the flora, the fauna and the language, but is more intent on satisfying her insa-tiable sexual appetite. The camera work makes her copulating with Aloysius seem more like aerobics than love-making, though the smiling madman begins to take her sexual attention for more than it is, and responds by claiming that he now loves the domineering visitor. The trees, bushes, animals and even a cricket ball, to which Aloysius speaks, act as voices of conscience, and steer him along the right path whenever he is on the verge of going astray.

The film has many funny moments: the white upper-class Busha McIntosh worrying about where his last remains will be buried; his wife thwarting his every effort to spend a vast sum on a tomb; widow Dawkins coyly offering to help Aloysius, taking him in after his brush with the law, and reading for him the letter Inga has sent from Europe minus all the parts with the 'nastiness'; Aloysius winning the cricket game for his side; even the voices of the inanimate objects, one of which is chided as a 'born-again bush', although the *Post* review snidely commented: 'You know a film's in trouble when a tree has all the best lines.'[58]

In the midst of all the fun and fantasy, the film manages to prick more than a few consciences, and to provide much food for thought. Firstly, Inga's obsession with sex can be seen as an obsession with black sex, and as such can reopen the entire debate over inter-racial sexuality, over which race secretly desires which one to be totally fulfilled. Secondly, there is the symbolic stripping of vulgarity from so-called bad language. Jamaican words like 'pum-pum' (for the female genitals) and 'bombo' (usually used with 'claat' to mean roughly 'menstrual pad'), normally not used in 'polite company', undergo either a marked devaluation, or become a weapon to be used against island sensitivities:

> In the specific case of 'bad words', there is not only the simple aesthetic pleasure of recognising the familiar as art, but also the thrill of collectively breaking taboos. At the 1990 Carib theatre world premiere of the Island Records movie, *The Lunatic*, ... it was noteworthy how indulgent the predominantly 'up-town' audience was in their liberal refusal to receive as 'slackness' the generous use of bad words. Just like the masses. Much to their amusement, '*bombo!*' becomes the battle cry of the satirised expatriate feminist, Inga, who represents the despotic terror of the rule of foreign *pum-pum*. ... Indeed, these same 'bad words', used in 'Roots Plays' or in popular song, are subject to censure.[59]

Thirdly, there is the irreverent allusion to the Queen and her defecating, which takes more than a light-hearted dig at the whole question of royalty from the perspective of the commoner. The implication, of course, is that all humans, be they royal or common, have the same body functions, a fact that the lower class take as a sobering equalizer.[60] Finally, there is the distinct impression in the end that Aloysius is easily redeemable. All he seems to have lacked is someone to understand him, or to pay him the proper attention. As a result, we are left to wonder about the many other village madmen, in Jamaica and elsewhere in the Caribbean, who end up like Aloysius simply for lack of adequate attention.

The Caribbean seen in *The Lunatic* is basically rural – the lush tropical landscape mentioned in the videotape blurb. Even the beaches are not the ones typically shown with tourists and hotel workers. In an ironic turnaround, the stereotyping is of the foreigner: the autocratic German, the sexually liberated feminist, the over-exuberant anthropologist, although the dancing spectators who celebrate after Aloysius bowls his team to victory make it easy to understand why the West Indies cricket team is noted for playing 'calypso cricket'.

It is reassuring to see established Caribbean actors appearing in repeat starring roles in Caribbean-made films, as opposed to occasional small parts, like for instance Oliver Samuels' role of pillion rider in *Countryman*. Winston Stona, the police detective from *The Harder They Come,* plays the sympathetic barrister who is able to free Aloysius from his legal trouble, and Carl Bradshaw continues his dominance of the Jamaican movie scene with his portrayal of Service, the butcher who completes the *ménage à trois*, and who fares worst in the eyes of the court. This gradual building of a corpus of roles and a cadre of recognized actors is what the budding industry needs if it is to take itself seriously.

Klash

What the industry does not need is dissension among the viewing public, since feature films need supportive audiences to ensure adequate financial returns, which in turn encourage further investment in the industry. An example of the problems facing entrepreneurs investing in the film industry was evident in the large doses of negative response to the film *Klash*, produced by Laurie Broderick and Kingston pictures.

Prior to premiering at the Carib in Kingston on 29 February 1996, this film was shown at the Sundance, Cannes, New York and Los Angeles Pan African film festivals, obviously with an eye on the eventual international market. The film's executive producer compared what he was doing in this movie with what had taken place in Australia:

> Our approach is somewhat similar to the beginnings of the Australian film industry which is now a very profitable source of foreign exchange earnings for the country. Our Jamaican culture, our music and language have grown in popularity, and by bringing the world the experience of Jamaican life and music, we hope to fully utilise and develop local talent as well as strengthen the Jamaican film industry.[61]

Ironically, the executive producer saw no paradox in making a film with the stated aim of showcasing Jamaican culture, music and language, but using as the leads two non-Jamaican actors, Jasmine Guy and Giancarlo Esposito, in addition to an African American director, Bill Parker. Surely there was Jamaican talent aplenty? As such, one can only conclude that if what Mr Broderick said when he went to Trinidad to promote the film is true, namely that he had done it 'to make money', then there still were no surefire box-office Caribbean names some 25 years after *The Harder They Come*.

What was seen as the ticket to success, on the other hand, was the appeal of the new style of Jamaican music, dancehall. 'Basically,' Barbara Blake Hannah of the *Gleaner* wrote on 13 March 1996, '*Klash* does for the dance hall genre of Jamaican music what *The Harder They Come* did for reggae 20 years ago. ... The film is the closest I, and many others, will ever come to dance hall, and it is, therefore, an interesting window into the culture.' The look at the world of dancehall is provided by an impressive list of *artistes* (Shabba Ranks, Patra, Snow, Ninja Man, Carlene *et al.*) performing an equally impressive number of songs – over 40. The film, then, is essentially a 90-minute concert, into or around which is woven a story, 'flimsy but entertaining', according to Howard McGowan, also writing in the *Gleaner*, which gave the following synopsis on 18 February 1996:

> *Klash* opens like a concert documentary, then develops into a dramatic thriller, with a plot that is threaded between the performance on stage. It tells the story of Stoney (Giancarlo Esposito), a North American photographer on assignment to cover a klash concert in Jamaica.
>
> During his stay, Stoney is reunited with this old flame Blossom (Jasmine Guy), a streetwise hustler trying to get free from the power of Lee (Lucien Chen), her boyfriend, who is also a local ganglord. She tells Stoney of the plot by Lee to steal the box office gate from the klash concert in association with some small time hoods, Ragga (Stafford Ashani) and Ultimate (Paul Campbell).
>
> Blossom then invites Stoney to help her double cross Lee and escape with her and the money to a new future together.

The film received a relatively positive review from the *Gleaner:*[62]

> I was surprised at how good it was,' 'especially knowing that there were great technical, legal and financial problems surrounding its making and completion. ... It's not to my taste, but I must applaud another excellent effort from the combined efforts of the Jamaican film industry, and anticipate great overseas success for *Klash*.

Even Jasmine Guy's Jamaican accent passed muster, a minor oddity in return for the international following that her presence promised. But the movie, also released in the United States, did not have anywhere near the success the producers intended, despite the boast by one of the actors, businessman Lucien Chen, that it would not suffer the same fate as *Marijuana Affair.* This film, produced by Chen, had failed to be picked up by a major distributor, and had resulted in a major financial loss for its backers.

As soon as it began its run, *Klash* was dogged by the amount of violence it showed. In Trinidad, where it was criticized as too violent, its executive producer gave the following justification: 'Those who think that the movie is violent do not want to see a true reflection of society. Although we edited a lot of the film, it still represents our present-day society.' He felt that the negative reviews were planned by 'those who have their own agendas. Certain people orchestrated such reviews in Jamaica.'[63] The negativity led to a curtailed run, and the *Jamaica Herald* saw fit to publish an editorial regretting the turn of events:

> The movie *Klash* played in the Corporate Area and is now in Montego Bay. It has been one of the most controversial films to have hit the local movie circuit in recent times, yet few people have actually seen it, and the film appears to be about to have an unceremonious closure.
>
> Something was clearly wrong with either the movie or the movie-going audiences, or both, why this film appears to have bombed here. We need to keep in mind that a great deal of Jamaican talent and treasure went into producing this film.
>
> There is agreement that the film is technically flawed, but where most of the disagreement lies is whether it is a good or a bad film in telling us any truths about ourselves. Individuals need to draw their conclusions about this, but we believe that more Jamaicans need to be given the opportunity to see this film.
>
> The fact that *Klash* has stirred debate both for and against itself suggests that it might have some artistic merit. On that basis, we believe that the swift departure of this film should be delayed.[64]

This same fate – the shortened run that does not allow the public adequate opportunity to view the film – was to befall *The Panman,* made in Trinidad the following year. What is needed, this editorial is saying, is a public that will view the film come what may: either because it is good and deserves to be seen by everyone; or because it is bad, but can serve as an example of where producers went wrong in their attempt to join the big league.

Men of Gray

The label of violence could just as easily be applied to *Men of Gray II: Flight of the Ibis,* a 1996 film shot by JoMox Productions of Trinidad, and one that sought to cash in on the popularity of action films. Such a film, of necessity, had much on-screen violence, but this was all part and parcel of the movie and television industry of the 1990s. Billed as Trinidad and Tobago's first full-length martial arts movie, the original *Men of Gray* had been shot on videotape in 1990, and was meant for television, though it premièred at the DeLuxe cinema in Port of Spain. It was the culminating project for Trinidadian actor and co-producer, Gerard Joseph, in fulfilment of his film school requirements in Los Angeles, and in partial realization of his dream to give a boost to the local film industry. The film, directed by his JoMox business partner, Ric Moxley, had a plot that was typical, almost irrelevant, for the genre where the accent is on the Kung Fu fighting: martial arts instructor and one-time policeman wages a virtual one-man crusade against drug barons of Trinidad.

Men of Gray II: Flight of the Ibis is a continuation of the same, with a healthy dose of fight scenes: a police officer seems to have everything going well until an evil villain starts a smear campaign against him. Director Ric Moxley, one of only two non-Trinidadians in the entire crew, candidly admitted that he was going after a popular audience. When asked how he felt the film would do in festivals, he declared:

> ... let me first say that Gerard and I never wanted to make some artsy-fartsy film that appeals to a narrow band of esoteric snoots. JoMox as a company wants to establish the visually stunning Caribbean location that Trinidad truly is as the backdrop for upbeat, entertaining movies with a big budget Hollywood look. We want to make films that people want to see. So it may never do well at Cannes or at other film competitions, but I believe it will do very well where it counts; at the box office and in the VCR at home.[65]

A quarter of a century after *The Right and the Wrong* we were back to the same stated aim in local film-making: simple entertainment that was not too concerned with intellectual considerations. Suffice it to note also that as the 1990s came to an end, there was still no sign that JoMox Productions had any major film project in the works. The boost that was to be given to the local film industry had not materialized, though two other companies' productions would at least make an effort in this direction – with both of them promising to pave the way for the re-emergence of said industry. One, from Jamaica, gave rise to much hope; the other, from Trinidad, left observers wondering whether it was worth the trouble to pursue the idea of a Caribbean film industry.

Island Jamaica in the big time? Dancehall Queen

With a longer track record in the production of feature films, Island Jamaica Films, the latest version of Chris Blackwell's original film company, made a concerted attempt, in association with Hawk's Nest Productions, to enter the big league with its 1997 film *Dancehall Queen*. Of this low-budget, high-tech production, June Givanni wrote:

> The film was initially conceived for the video market, but the creative team of directors and actors seized the opportunity, put their heart and soul into it and produced a film that claimed its own place on the big screen. The film is one of the first feature films to be shot and post-produced in Dvc format. Shooting on video meant that production costs were very low (cheap stock, small crew, easy to move around); and allowed the filmmakers greater spontaneity and flexibility in capturing the swirl of action inherent in Jamaican cultural life.[66]

With the possible exception of the fact that there was no internationally-known lead, the company pulled out all the stops to ensure that this movie competed on a level playing field: a high profile producer, Carolyn Pfeiffer, whose credits included *Kiss of the Spider Woman*; a director, Don Letts, born in Britain of Jamaica parents, with numerous music videos to his name, an asset for a film on the dancehall phenomenon; a cast that showcased many dancehall giants, such as Beenie Man, alongside seasoned actors such as Paul Campbell and Carl Bradshaw; and wide international distribution and exposure, including screening at the Toronto film festival.

Once again, those involved were optimistic with regard to the film's contribution to the establishment of a film industry. Don Letts was quoted in the *Sunday Herald* of 3 March 1996 as being of the view that Jamaica had the potential to become the next film capital of the world. 'We didn't have to bring in any outside talent, all of the talent we need already exists here. And part of the philosophy behind making *Dancehall Queen* in Jamaica is to begin putting back into Jamaica what so many people have taken out.' Co-producer Carl Bradshaw is also quoted in the same article as saying that 'Jamaica has the most naturally talented people I have come across anywhere in the world. I know the young talent can bring great creativity, exciting energy and immense ability to a new form of filmmaking.'

As its name implies, *Dancehall Queen* is about Jamaica's latest music/dance craze, though, according to the director, 'it doesn't really revolve around the music; there is a very strong story line ... it's a solid story.' Marcia, played by Audrey Reid, is a Kingston street vendor, struggling to make it as a single parent with two children. She receives financial assistance from family friend, 'Uncle' Larry (Carl Davis), who suddenly develops a sexual interest in her 15-year-old daughter, Tanya (Cherine Anderson). When Tanya complains about the unwanted attention, her mother hints that, under their dire financial circumstances, it might be prudent to 'go along with the program', and Larry ends up deflowering the teenager.

Marcia realizes that she must find a way to leave the ghetto exist-ence to which she seems condemned, and toys with the idea of joining the dancehall scene, an unlikely development in the eyes of Tanya, who seems wise beyond her years. She borrows money from a good friend to have a costume made, and when she goes to collect it happens upon Larry, who does not recognize her in her dancehall outfit. He is smitten with this new person, and she decides to milk the situation to her advantage, since she is now able to receive lavish gifts from this admirer.

The subplot has Marcia's brother, Junior (Mark Danvers), on the run and going mad temporarily after he witnesses the knifing of his friend by Priest (Paul Campbell); it turns out that Priest and Larry are involved in a series of shady deals leading to their climactic fight scene in which Priest is stabbed to death. Meanwhile, Marcia enters for and wins the title of Dancehall Queen, though not before a moment of hes-itation, which Tanya convinces her to overcome.

This 'solid' scenario does need audience complicity to succeed. Taken at face value, Marcia's transformation is hardly convincing. The *Sunday Gleaner* called it simply 'unbelievable.' The outlandish wig, skimpy costume, and change of voice provide too little disguise to have fooled someone like Larry, who has been paying Marcia's rent and buying her groceries for years. If this is indeed so, then Larry's determination to seduce Tanya evidently clouds his vision and powers of recognition, and reduces him to a mere animal in search of a mate for the ritual copulation.

On another level, however, the transformation can be seen as more symbolic than actual. In this respect, the movie takes on a whole different tone, for it shows the lengths to which a person will go to escape the curse of poverty. It is equally unconvincing that a mother would sell her daughter, one with so much promise at school, to an unscrupulous family friend, but, unfortunately, such are the realities of the daily struggle of ghetto life. As such, what the audience sees becomes symbolic of the desperate attempts by this lower-class woman to use her wits and dancing talent to escape the prison of economic despair and stringency.

Predictably, the film drew the ire of the *Sunday Gleaner*. In his review on 19 August 1997, Michael Reckord wrote:

> Our latest local motion picture, *Dancehall Queen*, has lots of mass appeal. There were large numbers of ordinary folk at Carib 5 Wednesday night (I'm judging from their dress and speech) and they vociferously enjoyed the movie. This does not mean that the film is good. It's vulgar, both in the sense that it is 'of the common people' and 'tasteless and lewd'.

He did concede in the end that the acting is convincing. 'One is pleased with the naturalness of the experienced performers ... as well as Pauline Stone-Myrie and the singer/deejays Beenie Man, Lady Saw, Anthony B and Chevelle Franklin, and of newcomers like Cherine Anderson.' After commenting on the fuzzy transformation to the large screen of images originally shot on digital video, the review concluded: 'But despite its weaknesses, the movie's strengths – its strong characters, its fine structure which makes for tension and suspense – and the fact that we love to see ourselves on the screen, will ensure that it'll be around for a while.' The reviewer is especially ill at ease with the image of Jamaica that the film presents. If only there weren't all those disturbing dancehall scenes, he implies, because he cannot see any redeeming value in them. They show a Jamaica that is 'violent, ugly, crude and coarse, as well as lascivious.' But the dancehall scene is much more than lewd exhibitionism, and if the international audience does not fully understand why such dancing takes place, and what is happening when it does, the Jamaican audience should at least be more tolerant. Carolyn Cooper explains the significance of this 'lewd' behaviour, popularly referred to as 'slackness':

> In its invariant coupling with Culture, Slackness is potentially a politics of subversion. For Slackness is not mere sexual looseness – though it certainly is that. Slackness is a metaphorical revolt against law and order; an undermining of consensual standards of decency. It is the antithesis of Culture.[67]

Marcia chooses to do battle with life in the arena that best suits her, for 'the dancehall is the social space in which the smell of female power is exuded in the extravagant display of flashy jewelry, expensive clothes, elaborate hairstyles and rigid attendant men that altogether represent substantial wealth.'[68] So, what at first seems implausible, turns out to be perfectly plausible when considered from this perspective.

There were many voices in defence of the film, and the *Gleaner* itself published letters taking the opposite view to Mr Reckord's. On the Sunday following his critique, the newspaper published a response by Glynis Salmon that said in part:

> I went to see *Dancehall Queen* and from the opening scenes to the very end, my attention and my emotions were riveted to the drama unfolding on the screen. I was totally absorbed in a story that of itself was simple enough, but the superb acting and the very real background against which the story unfolds, transformed a five-minute precis of a story into a fantastic, dramatic episode in the lives of people whom persons like Michael Reckord would prefer did not exist. ...
>
> *Dancehall Queen* is to be applauded for its excellent acting, very good casting, honest, true-to-life story-line and the courage of the producers who have dared invest their time and money in a project that does not show the picture-perfect post-card slice of Jamaica that some people would prefer to see. Instead it showed the raw, crude and tattered side that may offend, but is another only-too-real part of the Jamaica that we all share.[69]

Ms Salmon also reminded readers of the point that artists throughout the Caribbean have made for years, namely that what comes from outside the region is judged by different standards from what is produced within it:

> So many celebrated movies have been foisted on us from abroad filled with the grossest kind of expletives, violence and sex. Movies that are plain vulgar, tasteless and lewd and absolutely lascivious. Yet do I hear Mr. Reckord's voice in strong protest and condemnation? No. My bone of contention is that Reckord did not review and critique a film. He criticised a people.

She was incensed that the criticism seemed to go beyond the movie to the very core of what the nation was striving to achieve in the world of film-making. Co-producer Carl Bradshaw, commenting on the *Gleaner* review, felt that the author took that position because he had not seen the film from a film-maker's point of view.[70]

By all accounts, the film was a financial success, apparently recouping the reported US$500 000 production cost, and played well in the Caribbean, in North America, and in the United Kingdom.[71] Twenty-five years after *The Harder They Come* the film-makers felt that they no longer needed to use subtitles. The *Calgary Herald* of 11 July 1998, which called the movie 'a musical sensation trapped in a stale narrative', claimed that 'even after the viewer has become familiar with the accents, great passages of dialogue remain incoherent. This is one case where subtitles would have been greatly appreciated.' In addition, the 'bombo claat' references were noticeably more frequent, but were greeted with less embarrassment.

The failure of The Panman

The formula seemed to be working: human interest story accompanied by strong soundtrack, making most of these films somewhat inter-related. It runs through nearly all the films we have discussed so far, and is again evident in the final film to be treated in this chapter, Pempaleh International Productions's *The Panman*, released in Trinidad in 1997. Unfortunately, what happened with the release of this film was cause for grave concern in some quarters over the future of a Caribbean film industry.

Where Jamaica had successfully co-opted reggae and dancehall, Trinidad and Tobago had calypso, soca and steelband, indigenous musical forms that could potentially achieve the same type of success for the twin-island state. The Caribbean was so readily identified with the steelband that a few chords of pan music would be all that was needed to create a Caribbean atmosphere on the soundtracks of most American-made feature films and television shows. The idea, then, to make a film celebrating the pan, Trinidad and Tobago's 'national instrument', seemed destined to work, at the very least in the nation whose chauvinistic calypsos yearly proclaim how the world is anxious to hear the music created in this novel manner.

Kamalo Deen wrote the screenplay, then produced and directed the film, a low-budget affair typical of so many of the films shot in the Caribbean by local companies. The plot is uncomplicated. Paul Ambrose (Adrian James Reyes) is a young man raised in a middle-class home by his father after the death of his mother. He is bright and multi-talented, and wins a university scholarship, which he turns down because he would rather devote his life to the steelpan he loves. He leaves home, tries to find some direction to his life, and ends up in Tobago, where he meets an old panman, Titus (Carl Puckerin), who has devoted his life to pan. Paul stays with him and his wife Stella (Sheila Warner), learning a lot about the instrument, but leaves after they die in a fire. After more trials and tribulations he ends up a street performer, and is soon invited to join an American touring orchestra. Despite the attractiveness of this offer, Paul decides to return to Tobago and continue the work Titus had begun. The music that accompanies the film is by some of Trinidad's most accomplished artists, including Jit Samaroo, for years a leading arranger of steelband music, and George Victory.

The film finally opened in October 1997, doubled with *Bacchanal Time*, the company's earlier film, as a potentially surefire draw to attract an increased audience. The way it was advertised is of interest. 'Panman is 100% Trini stuff. Feel the Pride! The story of a true Trinbago hero! Sing with him! Laugh and cry with him! Then swell your chest with pride for who we are, from where we came, and where we're going!' The ad copy further promised 'no Hollywood gimmicks' and the 'sweet pulsating sound of "we" pan.' An appeal was made to the sense of national pride in the moviegoing public, but what had worked in Jamaica a quarter of a century earlier failed miserably in Trinidad. Feature film as social commentary apparently did not appeal to mass audiences the way calypso as social commentary did.

The film lasted barely one week at the seven cinemas that premièred it throughout Trinidad. Distributors claimed that they could no longer afford the heavy losses incurred in running it to empty houses, and the word-of-mouth publicity was negative, based largely on technically flawed trailers seen on television. Shot in super 16 and blown up to 35 mm, the film ended up with a disturbing graininess which the director nevertheless felt should not affect the quality of the movie *per se*. In addition, dialogue was not always synchronized with the movement of the actors' lips, a further indication of the lack of money for proper post-production work.

Two months after the opening, another cinema, DeLuxe, tried to revive the film, and the result was equally disheartening. At the first showing, the 'must-see' double drew one patron (who, according to the *Sunday Express* report of 7 December, was refunded his money). To all appearances, the film was unable, at least to a significant degree, to 'tug at the heartstrings of those who advocate more of our images on the screen.'

One of Trinidad and Tobago's four dailies at the time, the *Independent*, in an editorial on 4 October 1997 entitled 'Cultivating Taste', commented on the fact that the failure of the film was 'a blow to all those who have worked to make the local media more cultural relevant.' The problem, the editorial surmised, was both one of taste, which must be developed, and of cost, which made it difficult to produce quality local fare:

> But cinema may not necessarily suffer the same fate. The theme of *The Panman* is similar to that of the most success-ful of Caribbean films, the Jamaican movie *The Harder They Come*, which had considerable international success, despite the fact that the Jamaican dialect on the soundtrack required subtitles. It is true that the principal actor in that film, Jimmy Cliff, was already well-known outside Jamaica, and there is no international star of pan as there is of reggae. But Jamaican Trevor Rhone has made little comedies of high quality and reasonable success. Deen's previous film, *Bacchanal Time*, was well received in this country. Besides, a successful film, unlike a television production, will recover its cost in proportion to its success. So despite the fate of *The Panman*, it may well be in film rather than in television that local producers of drama can best make their mark. At all events, they will continue to try, and must be given every encouragement.

Kamalo Deen did not wait around for the encouragement. He left for the United States, from where he planned a new marketing strategy for the film: private showings to select groups, and short cinema runs in neighbourhoods frequented by Caribbean immigrants. By the end of 1998, barely a year after the disastrous release in Trinidad, the film had been shown in Boston and Brooklyn, and Kamalo Deen had the satis-faction of having audiences tell him how much they enjoyed the film. He remained convinced that the Trinidad and Tobago audience would have reacted in the same manner if only they had given themselves the opportunity to view the film.

Conclusion

There have been other Caribbean feature films that were made but never released, or released and instantly forgotten. Some are irretriev-ably lost; others have been abandoned, or are on hold in varying stages of the production process. For example, the Trinidad production company, Bandit Films, shot *Enter the Black Dragon*, an action film about two families fighting in a world of drugs and guns, and announced that the film would be in the cinemas in early 1998.

Already experiencing delays in its premiere date, it was further set back when one of its stars, Patrick Jackson, was killed in a car crash just as he was about to leave for the United States, reportedly to negotiate the movie's release. It would not be surprising if this film were to end up languishing on the shelves, or having a short run before disappearing into oblivion.

Hollywood's big league players also suffer similar setbacks, and there have been movies that have not been released after millions of dollars were spent. But the infrastructure of that system can more easily absorb such losses than the Caribbean, where there is hardly a system, and only the barest of infrastructure. It is evident that a dozen or so feature films in approximately 30 years do not constitute overwhelming evidence that the Caribbean is ready to join the big league as a full-time member. However, if the playing field is level – and technology is constantly working in the Caribbean's favour in this regard – then the international community of film-makers may be ready to invite the region to play an 'exhibition game' from time to time. In so doing, they will be allowing the Caribbean to present itself as it knows it is, and not as others imagine it to be.

Notes

1. See my chapter, 'Film, Literature, and Identity in the Caribbean', in Mbye Cham (ed.), *Ex-Iles* (1992).
2. Personal communication, Summer 1998.
3. Carl Jacobs, 'Trinidad's Pioneer Movie-Maker' (1970).
4. Personal communication, Summer 1998.
5. The award was for photography.
6. Richard Combs, Review of *The Right and the Wrong* (1971), 225.
7. *Daily Express*, 'Righting the Wrong', 21 December 1970.
8. Richard Combs, Review of *The Caribbean Fox*, *Monthly Film Bulletin* 38 (1971), 217.
9. See Sophia Persad, 'A Look at the Local Film Industry'. (1996), 10.
10. Carl Jacobs, 'Trinidads Pioneer Movie-Maker'.
11. *Daily Express*, 'Righting the Wrong', 21 December 1970.
12. See Valerie Bloomfield, 'Caribbean Films' (1977), 288.
13. Martin Hayman, 'You'll Succeed At Last'. Report of interview with Perry Henzell. *Cinema Rising* 3 (August 1972).
14. Bloomfield, 'Caribbean Films', 288.
15. Gordon Rohlehr, 'Once in a Blue Sun: Review of *The Harder They Come*,' in *My Strangled City and Other Essays* (1992), 99.
16. Harry Milner, 'Crime in Films' (1972).
17. See my 1998 interview with Mr St Juste in Appendix I, page 166.
18. Michael Thelwell, '*The Harder They Come*: From Film to Novel'. In Mbye Cham *Ex-Iles* (1992), 183.

19. See *Daily Gleaner*, 9 October 1948. The Special Edition carried the front page headline 'Rhyging Killed By Police: Gun Battle on Lime Cay This Morning.'
20. See my 1998 interview with Mr Bradshaw in Appendix I, page 162.
21. Rohlehr, 95.
22. Howard Campbell, *Caribbean Daylight*, 13 May 1996.
23. Edward Brathwaite, *History of the Voice* (London: New Beacon Books, 1984), 41.
24. Rohlehr, '*My Strangled City ...*', 96.
25. See Paul Gilroy, '*There Ain't No Black in the Union Jack*' (1987), 169; and Kenneth Harris, 'Sex, Race Commodity and Film Fetishism in *The Harder They Come*', in Mbye Cham *Ex-Iles*, 211.
26. See 'Sequel to Cult Moview Raising, Friction', *Sunday Guardian*, 9 February 1997.
27. Elizabeth Solomon-Armour, '*Bim* Is Back', *Sunday Express*, 13 December 1992. Valerie Bloomfield in 'Caribbean Films (289) reports that the film won a Gold Medal Special Jury Award as 'a film of unusual merit' at the Virgin Island International Film Festival in 1975. Suzanne Robertson, interviewed in 1998, could not recall any other awards.
28. The Theatres and Dance Halls Ordinance of 1934 and the Cinematograph Act of 1936 provided the legal underpinning for these decisions.
29. *Sunday Express*, 13 December 1992. Boysie Singh was a notorious henchman of the 1950s.
30. *Sunday Express*, 13 December 1992.
31. See proceedings of radio programme in *Tapia*, 13 April 1975.
32. *Sunday Express,* 13 December 1992.
33. Judy Stone, 'A Bad Spell for Lovers in "Obeah"', *San Francisco Chronicle*, 23 October 1987. Note that the writer of this review is not the same Judy Stone who writes on theatre out of Trinidad, and who is cited later.
34. Mervyn Morris, 'Introduction,' in Trevor Rhone, *Old Story Time and Other Plays* (Harlow: Longman, (1981), x.
35. Judy Stone, *Theatre* (Studies in West Indian Literature Series) (London: Macmillan Caribbean, 1994), 42.
36. Collectors of movie goofs will note that the Air Jamaica jet with four wing-mounted engines is identified by the airport announcer as a DC9 flight. The DC9 had two rear-mounted engines.
37. See interview with Mr Bradshaw in Appendix I, page 162.
38. Personal communication, Fall 1998.
39. Merilyn Morris, 'Introduction', in Trevor Rhone, ix.
40. Ed Guerero, "Jah No Dead': Modes of Resistance in *Rockers* and *Countryman*,' in Mybe Cham *Ex Iles*, 107.
41. Ibid, 112.
42. Anita M. Waters, *Race, Class, and Political Symbols* (1989), 102.
43. Sebastien Clarke, *Jah Music* (1980), 62–3.
44. See Kenneth Bilby's chapter 'Jamaica' in Peter Manuel *et al.*, *Caribbean Currents* (1995), 170.
45. Text for 'The Historical Perspective', on the web page giving information about Lennie Little-White's company and on *Children of Babylon*.
46. See Victoria M. Marshall, 'Filmmaking in Jamaica: "Likkle But Tallawah"', in Mbye Cham, *Ex-Iles*, 105.
47. Reported by Horace Campbell in the *Sunday Observer* (Kingston), 21 June 1998.
48. Victoria Marshall, 'Filmmaking in Jamaica', 105.
49. Reported by Victoria Marshall, 'Filmmaking in Jamaica', 103.

50. Personal communication, Summer 1998.
51. Guerero, 'Jah no dead', 106–7.
52. Gilroy, *There Ain't No Black in the Union Jack*, 169.
53. Guerero, 'Jah no dead', 109.
54. *Variety*, 19 May 1982.
55. *Daily Express,* 26 November 1988.
56. Back cover blurb from Anthony C. Winkler, *The Lunatic* (Kingston: Kingston Publishers, 1987).
57. *Washington Post*, 28 February 1992.
58. Ibid.
59. Carolyn Cooper, *Noises in the Blood* (1993), 98–9.
60. The censors in Trinidad took a dim view of this reference to the Queen's defecation and restricted viewing to mature audiences.
61. *Jamaica Herald*, 20 February 1996.
62. Barbara Blake Hannah, the *Gleaner*, 13 March 1996. She admitted, however, to having worked on the film.
63. *Sunday Express*, 10 March 1996.
64. *Jamaica Herald*, 18 March 1996.
65. *Sunday Guardian*, *Men of Gray II* Supplement, 7 January 1996.
66. June I. Givanni, 'Les Reines du Dancing' 1997.
67. Cooper, *Noises in the Blood* 141.
68. Ibid., 155.
69. *Sunday Gleaner*, 26 August 1997.
70. See interview, Appendix I, page 162.
71. The Internet Movie Database reported that the film, playing on three screens in the US, made $162 723 between 12 October and 2 November 1997. Carl Bradshaw also confirmed that the film had made money in Trinidad (personal communication).

4 | Caribbean diaspora film-makers and the immigrant experience

Despite enjoying warm weather year-round and a relaxed way of life – key attractions for countless visitors – Caribbean people leave the islands and migrate to other countries. In relatively large numbers, given each territory's population, they have migrated to the metropolitan countries in search of job opportunities and higher education. Some have returned to the islands permanently; many have willingly integrated themselves into the fabric of their host countries; others have simply been forced to remain through circumstances beyond their control. They have all become part of the Caribbean diaspora, and are taken into account when matters concerning Caribbean people are being discussed.

With the already strong connection reinforced by active recruitment on the part of the colonial authorities, it was understandable that in the 1940s anglophone Caribbean residents – West Indians – would go to England. The first large group set sail from the Caribbean on the *Empire Windrush* in 1948, marking the start of full-scale migration to the 'mother country'. Within recent decades, however, there has been migration to the United States and Canada. This occurred especially after Britain enacted measures that black immigrants found unacceptable, even hostile, and after the restriction on migration to America was eased.

The difficulty that Caribbean immigrants met on arrival in their metropolitan host countries has been well documented in the written and oral literature. Samuel Selvon's *The Lonely Londoners*, for example, is a humorous, yet telling account of the problems encountered by a group of Trinidadian immigrants on their arrival in London in the mid-1950s. One is almost tempted to ask why Selvon's immigrants left the Caribbean at all. They now had to contend with winter in addition to the same problems they had back home: no proper job, no adequate housing, no money, no meaningful romantic relationships. Their attempts to keep warm foreshadowed the comic efforts seen in *Cool Runnings* when the Jamaican bobsled team arrived in Canada.

Still, they would agree with calypsonian Lord Kitchener when he sang upon arrival in England: 'London is the place for me.'

After the initial curiosity of seeing black people from the islands wore off, so apparently did the welcome. Blacks in Britain, especially those from the Commonwealth, felt increasingly isolated in a society that should have welcomed them. All the rhetoric about coming to their 'mother country' and being 'citizens of the United Kingdom and colonies' sounded hollow to these disappointed guests. It became very clear, in all the media, that the people of Britain were growing more and more uncomfortable with the blacks in their midst. Similarly, these blacks were more and more disenchanted with the way they were being treated. In such a climate, it was to be expected that mainstream radio and television, controlled by the white establishment, would offer very few programmes dealing with black people. Those that were offered invariably showed the negative side of the black presence.

The situation was much the same with the cinema. At the outset, mainstream films either did not show blacks, or, when they did, showed them in marginal or stereotypical roles. As matters improved, thanks in part to the popularity of Paul Robeson's films, many Caribbean immigrants were hired for small parts in feature films.[1] They worked mainly with writers and directors who were not from the Caribbean, and who had little incentive to make the sort of films Caribbean immigrants – then still an undefined audience – would want to see. But there was no escaping the fact that, as first generation immigrants settled down and began to have children, a budding public was being created. The time was indeed ripe for immigrant film-makers to begin telling the immigrants' story. To this end, the Caribbean film-makers who took up the challenge all had the same aims: to reverse stereotypes, to unmask British hypocrisy, or to celebrate Caribbean heritage and lifestyle. This chapter looks at some of the film-makers and the works they produced as a result of this engagement. It also looks briefly at how the immigrant experience was depicted in North America.

To Sir, With Love

The need to have Caribbean film-makers involved in the telling of the Caribbean immigrant's story was aptly illustrated when Columbia Pictures made *To Sir, With Love* in 1967. Although the film's setting was East London, and the principal character an immigrant from the Commonwealth Caribbean – actually British Guiana, considered Caribbean despite its continental location – the studio did not use an actor who, career-wise, was usually identified as being from the Caribbean. No doubt with an eye on potential box office success, Columbia brought Oscar-winner and Hollywood superstar Sidney Poitier from America.[2] E. R. Brathwaite, author of the autobiographical novel from which the film was made, claimed that Harry Belafonte, more readily identified with the Caribbean through his calypso singing, was interested in the role, but it was felt that he did not possess sufficient stature as an actor.[3]

Stephen Bourne likewise felt that 'Trinidadian actor Errol John would have been perfect for the leading role' and that director James Clavell missed a golden opportunity to make an authentic film: 'Consequently it is a film that avoids the gritty realism of the book, and ends up as little more than a sentimental, overblown soap opera, unfaithful to its source, aimed at the American box office.'[4] He does concede that nothing could prevent the film from becoming one of the year's biggest commercial successes, and propelling Poitier the following year to the number one spot as far as box office attractions were concerned.

The international success of *To Sir, With Love* would seem to belie Stephen Bourne's harsh criticism, and give the impression that writer/director James Clavell did something right. What does seem plausible is that the film was done through the filter of the American civil rights disturbances of the mid-1960s, and as such sought to show a black character in a positive light. Poitier the super-black, who would soothe some more white consciences in *Guess Who's Coming to Dinner*, also made in 1967, was more crusader than struggling immigrant teacher from the Caribbean.

Poitier plays Mark Thackeray, a recent engineering graduate unable to find a job in his field. He decides to accept a teaching position in a school noted for its tough students, and he sets about transforming them, much to the surprise of his principal and colleagues. Meanwhile he keeps applying for jobs, and when he finally lands one, and is about to move on, he is touched by the reaction of his students. He destroys the job offer. The plot, yet another version of the *Blackboard Jungle* scenario, is simple, and the film's success obviously owes a lot to Poitier's almost naïve missionary zeal.

The film's Caribbean roots are played down. We do learn that Mark Thackeray is from British Guiana, but we are also told that he came to England after some years in California. Such a stay would probably explain the American tone to Thackeray's speech patterns, and when he shows the class how he might sound were he to speak the way he did back in the Caribbean, the lone sentence we hear is certainly not spoken with a Guyanese accent. Having Thackeray come from America is one of the liberties that the writer/director took with the story, on which the novel's author was not consulted once the rights were acquired by Columbia. When interviewed about the differences between the novel and the film, E. R. Braithwaite could offer no explanation why the name Mark Thackeray was used instead of his own in this autobiographical work. He also did not know why most of the action was restricted to the schoolroom, whereas the novel covered much more.

Thackeray is never seen associating with other immigrants from the Caribbean. He has at least one student, Seales (Anthony Villaroel), of inter-racial parentage – English mother and black father – but apart from standing by him, along with the rest of the class, when his mother dies, he has little interaction with this young man. This apparent lack of connection to someone to whom the teacher could relate led Stephen Bourne to lament that this 'potentially interesting character … is marginalized.'[5] The one other Caribbean 'connection' comes when a colleague advises Thackeray that he had better brush up on his voodoo if he wished to remain sane.

The problems faced by the novelist as black colonial immigrant in white metropolitan society are transformed in the film to ones of cultural ignorance. The white colleague, with whom the author is romantically involved in the novel, becomes merely a helpful co-worker, no doubt because of the American discomfort with matters of inter-racial romance. As far as the students are concerned, if only one could instil some proper etiquette and down-to-earth philosophy in them, all would be well, and Poitier is the ideal actor to make worldwide audiences believe this facile solution. Those who were agitating to 'Keep Britain White' could hardly be threatened by a film such as this, where even the potentially inflammatory racial slurs – like when Thackeray is cut and one of his students is surprised to see red blood – are handled with Poitier's characteristic genteel smile, and what Pauline Kael termed his 'self-inflicted stereotype of goodness'.[6] The presence of this internationally known actor gave an equally international dimension to the problem at the heart of the film, but in so doing de-emphasized its 'topical' nature as far as Caribbean people were concerned. The budding Caribbean immigrant audience in England would therefore have tended to agree with the Nina Hibbin comment published in the *Morning Star* of 9 September 1967 (and quoted by Stephen Bourne in his book): 'By over-simplifying social and racial attitudes of 17 years ago and attributing them to youngsters who at that time hadn't even been born James Clavell has made a nonsense film.' In all fairness to the film-maker, though, such harsh criticism was not widespread – Leonard Maltin, the well-known film critic, found the film excellent and well acted – and if box office receipts are anything to go by, the weak Caribbean connection did not hurt the movie.

Using *To Sir, With Love* as our yardstick, we can see that the Caribbean immigrant community in England could not depend on mainstream cinema to tell its story. By the same token, there was no real incentive for this cinema to spend time and money on such a small group, no matter how interesting its stories might be. The inevitable outcome of the continual and futile attempt to penetrate this wall of indifference and disinterest on the part of the major studios was the emergence of a new cadre of independent film-makers. Against overwhelming odds, they would make their own low-budget feature films, and also participate in a series of workshops to train future film-makers to carry the torch of cinematic commitment:

> Black filmmaking was not only inventive in its approach to political (racial) themes, but also sensitive to the creative film process itself. It's also worth mentioning in this context that while a number of the filmmakers were trained at the London Film School (now the London International Film School), renowned for its highly motivated students, the majority in fact received no such formal training, but worked in other disciplines like writing and acting. What they all shared in common was an immense enthusiasm for the medium, and a burning desire to extend their creative energies into this otherwise highly expensive art form. Significantly, there was little interest in straightforward documentary forms of filmmaking, and more in feature-length production with a somewhat commercial or entertainment orientation in mind. This did not mean the abandonment of serious social issues, however, but rather a desire to incorporate these kinds of themes into narrative fiction and on a fairly grand ('serious') scale. Interestingly, the Hollywood entertainment films (especially those with Sidney Poitier) and the European 'art movies' both provided useful, albeit contradictory, models.[7]

Pressure

The orientation toward feature-length productions had its concrete manifestation in 1975 with Horace Ové's *Pressure*, the first British-made feature film by a black director, which was funded by the British Film Institute Production Board.

Ové had always wanted to be involved in film-making. Interviewed in 1995, he admitted as much to June Givanni: 'I came from Trinidad where I was influenced by cinema and television, so I was a real cinema bug. From the age of nine I wanted to be a filmmaker, something that I never told anybody in Trinidad about because at that time they would have laughed at me.'[8] When he completed his studies at what later became the London International Film School, and wanted to start a career as a film-maker, he encountered many of the very problems that would surface in his first feature, a fact he revealed in the same interview:

> It was not easy being a West Indian wanting to direct films as there were none of us making films in Britain at that time. When I went for my first appointment at the BBC, the commissioning editor there had a shock because he wasn't expecting a West Indian and he didn't know what to do or say. I always remember telling him not to worry, next summer he would have a tan, and we got along.
>
> It was difficult at the time to get jobs and to convince people that a Caribbean person had the ability to make a film.

Having been part of the typical Caribbean immigrant experience himself, Ové would have no difficulty capturing it on film. His aptly titled first feature, co-written with compatriot Samuel Selvon, thus pulls no punches in its portrayal of the subtle, and sometimes not-so-subtle, 'pressure' exerted on immigrants, be they Caribbean or not, as they try to make a living in a society hostile to their presence.

In essence, *Pressure* tells the story of English-born Tony (Herbert Norville), whose mother, Bopsie (Lucita Lijertwood), and father, Lucas (Frank Singuineau), have migrated from Trinidad. Although the father now runs a greengrocer's shop, back in Trinidad he was an accountant. He does not want his son to make the same sort of sacrifice, and would like him to find a job worthy of his qualifications. Tony is dejected when he cannot find a job, and begins to associate more with his black friends, all unemployed. He has a narrow escape from the police when he and his friends attempt to steal from a supermarket. As a result, John begins to listen more attentively to his politically active, Trinidadian-born older brother Colin (Oscar James), who had accused him of forsaking his black identity. While at a meeting that Colin and a friend, Sister Louise (Sheila Scott-Wilkinson), have helped organize, Tony and his brother are arrested on suspicion of possessing drugs. Tony is released, and returns home to find his house ransacked by the police, and his parents very upset. He decides to leave home and work toward getting Colin released.

Woven into this narrative are microcosms of the many problems that bestrew the immigrant's path in this society. As one reviewer put it: '*Pressure* is interesting not least for the way it has attempted to assimilate its wider concerns within the immediacy of its narrative format.'[9] He further shows how various clips can be labelled:

> Tony has no money, so the white girl buys him chips (social embarrassment); Tony reminds the girl of the geography teacher who used to wonder why he didn't know more about Jamaica (identity problem); the girl's landlady refuses to let him in (racism); and as he makes his way home he sees another black being picked up by the police (police harassment of blacks). The wonder is that such overloading doesn't seriously unbalance the film; the fact that it does not is partly because of the judicious overlay of elements of West Indian culture (the reggae music, persistent but not self-justificatory; the language patterns of West Indian speech, both defiantly 'indigenous' and inventively adapted to urban English), and because Ové has leavened the overt comment with what looks like spontaneous humour.

All of those situations are familiar to black immigrants, as is the generation gap between Tony and his parents. It is as difficult for them to understand what motivates Tony as it is for him to understand, for example, how someone could leave a job as accountant for one as greengrocer, a scenario played many times over during the height of the immigration explosion of the 1950s. In this respect, the film both caters to stereotype and inveighs against it.

On the one hand, the parents are typical of their generation; they have been brought up to believe that British is best, and, all told, being in England is the culmination of a dream that started in the textbooks they read in elementary school. Consequently, for them, Tony should become the consummate Englishman and make their sacrifice worthwhile. On the other hand, brother Colin, with his political awareness and militancy, drives an ideological wedge between Tony and his parents. But in this same vein, he also serves to highlight the incongruity of a black Britain, leading Jim Pines to conclude that:

> In this respect, certain aspects of the film can be 'read' as a critique of the race relations 'industry,' which of course has been instrumental in 'professionalising' race relations, and of (British) society's failure to progress even in the light of a new generation of British-born Black people who are patently not 'immigrants' in the stereotypical race-relations sense.[10]

Ové himself has spoken of the film in the following terms:

> *Pressure* is about a family; it's based on an older brother who
> comes to live here, and it's based on parents who come to set
> up their lives, leaving the Caribbean for the first time to live
> in England. It's their struggle. It's the struggle of how the
> brother who grew up in the Caribbean deals with life in
> England during the Black Power period. It's the struggle of
> that first generation of black kids that were born and grew up
> here with West Indian parents, who went to school here from
> a very early stage in their lives, and how their lives are
> different to that of the older brother's life in the film. The
> environment is the trap; how they deal with those situations
> is what is interesting.[11]

His use of the image of the trap is significant, for it lends a semi-tragic
aura to the whole process, a certain inevitability that the well-known
Caribbean sense of humour could not mask completely.

By the time Ové made *Pressure* he had already shot an impressive number of shorter, documentary-type films, and the technique of
the fact-based genre is apparent in this film as well. It is probably this
matter-of-fact approach to some of the action that led some observers
to criticize his treatment of women in the film, in particular his portrayal of Tony's mother. David Wilson found her performance
'overblown', and 'an overstatement of black subservience to white
values'.[12] Similarly, Jim Pines felt that the film's representation of
women left much to be desired, 'particularly the image of the "mis-
guided" mother figure who is identified as the cause of the family's
"failure to make it in Britain".'[13] It is unlikely, however, that
Caribbean women would see these criticisms in the same light, for the
mother does recall many a middle-class Caribbean parent in her
anxiety to be like the colonizer. The portrayal may seem odd to the
younger, more militant generation, but island Bopsies were not all that
uncommon.

Kobena Mercer noted another possible effect of Ové's documen-
tary-style approach to feature film-making: the lack of a clear-cut 'solution' that a fictional narrative might have imagined at the end of the
movie:

> Narrative closure, the tying up of the threads that make up a
> fictional text, is regarded as characteristic of cinematic
> realism; but the symptomatic irresolution of the story told in
> *Pressure* suggests some of the limitations of documentary
> realism in the attempt to re-code the race-relations narrative.[14]

This view seems to echo that of David Wilson, who thought that *Pressure* does not clarify whether the parents' position is 'specifically a symptom of white racism, discreet or otherwise, or generally a condition of the social and political system under which they happen to live, and which equally affects the majority of whites.'[15] But, in fairness to the director, the foregoing criticism is not as serious an indictment as it first appears. The so-called lack of closure is precisely what makes the situation in the film mirror what Caribbean immigrants found upon arrival in England. On any given day, they could not tell whether they were ostracized because they were black, or because they were immigrants, or both, since 'immigrant' became the code word for 'black'.

Pressure was shown at film festivals – notably the London Film Festival of 1975, and the Toronto Film of 1976 – and in communities with a heavy Caribbean population, but all was not smooth sailing. Ové reports that:

> There was some difficulty even in the BFI which didn't want to release the film because of a few scenes about police raids and black power, and the film was actually banned for about three years. A few journalists who liked it started to write about it and sort of attacked the BFI, and then it came out and got a release.[16]

Black Joy

The ensuing positive reaction to *Pressure* could not attract sufficient crossover patronage to justify wide distribution at the dominant cinema level. The studios still would not touch films of this nature, and were slow to make others with lighter fare that showed the Caribbean comic spirit in action. Such a film was *Black Joy* (1977), based on Jamal Ali's play *Dark Days and Light Nights*, from which, according to lead actor Norman Beaton, 'the political thrust ... was more or less jettisoned'[17] to conform with director Anthony Simmons's non-Caribbean-oriented view of what he wanted to say in the film.

Black Joy shows that Caribbean people in whatever element they have come to call theirs, in this case London's Brixton, can be engagingly funny. There is almost a calypso and caricature-like flavour to this story of Ben (Trevor Thomas), a recently arrived immigrant from Guyana, who is immediately relieved of his wallet by a young thief. He meets Dave (Norman Beaton), the con man *par excellence* and an English version of the Anancy-influenced trickster. This encounter signals the start of a dizzying number of misadventures, but it also signals the start of a genuine friendship between the two. In this light, Dave almost considers it his duty to con Ben, if only to show him how to take care of himself amidst all those tricky West Indians in Brixton. Many aspects of this movie seem like an updated film adaptation of Samuel Selvon's *The Lonely Londoners*, and Norman Beaton's performance as Dave earned him the Variety Club of Great Britain award for Best Film Actor of 1977.

The film was quite popular when it was shown in London. English-born Paul Medford, who played the young thief, later said in an interview:

> I didn't realise how important the film was, or how much effect it had, until I began to notice the publicity on the buses. There were lots of pictures everywhere and the whole black population around where I lived, realising I was in the film, went to see it and really enjoyed it.[18]

This reaction on the part of the clearly Caribbean immigrant public would seem to justify the de-emphasizing of the film's political aspect. Since they expected a political message in films, few as they were, depicting the black experience in England, some observers decried the fact that *Black Joy* 'merely provides an hour of good, dirty fun.' But, as Akua Rugg correctly reminded readers in *Race Today* of January 1978, 'a film which, in the main, depicts blacks as making the best of a bad job, rather than seeking alternatives, is a political statement in itself.' Here are Caribbean immigrants staking their claim for the piece of English turf to which they feel they have a right; they invest it with their bright tropical colours, and bathe it in non-stop reggae music. Ten years after its first release, the film was shown in America, and critic Roger Ebert, writing in the *Chicago Sun-Times* on 25 September 1987, observed that 'essentially this is a slice-of-life film, a film that knows exactly what the streets of Brixton look and sound like, and wants to share the knowledge.'

Burning an Illusion

In 1981, the British Film Institute funded its second black feature, *Burning an Illusion*. Barbadian-born Menelik Shabazz, the film's director, was a graduate of the London International Film School, having completed his studies a decade or so after Horace Ové. He also made documentaries before completing his first feature, for which he wrote the screenplay. There were touches to *Burning an Illusion* that recalled *Pressure*: among them, the brush with the law;

the political awakening; and the search for black identity in white British society.

The film's heroine, Pat (Cassie McFarlane), lives on her own, and works as a secretary. She meets Del (Victor Romero), who has just been kicked out by his father. She lets him move in with her, having at the back of her mind the possibility of marriage and a family, but Del loses his job, and subsequently stays home playing cards with his friends while Pat continues working. Del's macho aggression and his continued lazing around with his friends finally infuriate Pat, and she throws him out. She then goes through a period of trying to find herself. She is reunited with Del just as he is involved in a fracas that leads to his being beaten while in police custody, and then to his imprisonment. She visits him in jail, and sends him books on black consciousness, some of which she reads herself, and this leads to her finally discovering her true identity as a black woman. This new state is manifested in her decision to change her style of clothes from Western to African, and to feed her romance novelettes to her building's incinerator – thus burning her illusion. Upon recovering after being shot in the leg in a racist attack, she is all the more resolved to pursue her militancy.

Pat and Del, who speaks with a thick 'Jamaican' accent, are clearly part of the Caribbean immigrant community, though it is not clear whether they were born in England, or migrated from the islands. It is within this community that we see them functioning, without bothering too much about their place in the British order of things, thus about their Britishness:

> It has no real relevance in the context of the film's representation of Black experiences. Consequently, racial victimization – i.e., the image of Blacks as 'victims,' a familiar motif in race-relations discourse – is not a major concern here, despite its appearance at key moments in the story. Rather, it functions as a plot device which drives the narrative along, and nothing more.[19]

Such an attitude does not mean that they operate at the fringe of the host society. It does mean, on the contrary, that they, unlike their parents, have come to expect that British society owes them a rightful place.

The criticism levelled at Horace Ové, that his treatment of women left something to be desired, could hardly be repeated in this film. Pat's evolution and awakening are so exemplary that women have left showings of the film applauding her resolve to proclaim her independence. The director is of the view that it was his intended treatment of the woman as main character that helped him secure funding for the project.[20] Pat is the perfect foil to a character like Chamberlain (Malcolm Fredericks), whose Caribbean-style male chauvinism – which has him, for instance, advising Del to put Pat in her place – seems inappropriate. This sort of advice might have worked were they back in the Caribbean, where others in the society would have colluded in its dispensing, but in the new milieu with new thinking on the part of the woman, it is unacceptable. Still, there would be some who saw Pat's *prise de conscience* as triggered essentially by Del's experience as opposed to her own:

> Because the woman's transformation is narratively motivated
> by her boyfriend's encounter with police and then prison,
> *Illusion* has been criticised for presenting what is really a
> male-oriented idea of black women's experiences as the female
> protagonist is at all times *dependent* upon the 'politicising'
> role of the male character.[21]

It is a point well taken, but does not really change the overall positive portrayal of the protagonist. *Burning an Illusion* deserves the credit as 'the first British film to give a black woman a voice of any kind',[22] as does its lead Cassie McFarlane for receiving the 1982 *Evening Standard* British Film Award for Most Promising Newcomer. Shabazz did not make a second feature film, but his involvement with the Caribbean diaspora community and with the world of film-making did not end.[23]

Playing Away

Of the Caribbean film-makers involved in making feature films, only Horace Ové has so far followed his first with a second. In 1986, he made *Playing Away* 'about cricket', according to Ové:

> It's about a little Brixton team where most of the characters
> struggle and work hard or steal, or ponce or do whatever
> they do to survive, but who have never really left the area to
> go beyond Brixton. Then suddenly somebody in Suffolk in
> some upper-class English village decides that for their Third
> World Week they will invite a cricket team from Brixton for
> a weekend game, and it's how these two sets of people come
> together, and how they cope with each other, the embarrass-
> ment and the traps. They're trapped in relationships, they're
> trapped in their own kind of little environments, each of

which is quite different; one is black and working class, one
is white and upper class, and in bringing these two sets of
people together that interests me a lot with *Playing Away*.
Because they're trapped, and they have to get on somehow
in this dilemma of a multi-cultural Britain.[24]

To Ové's short synopsis can be added the following details: the Brixton
team is naturally made up of Caribbean immigrant players – or
English-born Caribbeans, since the film does dwell on this information
– captained by Wille Boy (Norman Beaton). They travel to the Suffolk
village of Sneddington by mini-van, get lost along the way, but still
arrive in time for a formal reception at which they present the village
with a Jamaican pennant. They spend the evening in various activities,
attend church the following morning, then proceed to the game, wondering if Willie Boy will make it in time. He does, having been rescued
from drunken stupour in a churchyard, and taken home for breakfast
by prominent citizen Godfrey (Robert Urquhart), who is also the
game's umpire. Sneddington bats first, and soon has Brixton in serious
trouble when half the fielding team walks off after a disputed decision;
Wille Boy goads his team to an easy victory over the depleted home
team, and the activities end with the traditional speeches and good
wishes.

From the Caribbean perspective, the atmosphere is pure fete
match, a time when fun and frolic win out over hard and fast rules and
regimentation. But in the matter of cricket, the symbolism of the
Caribbean (ex-colonials) beating the English (ex-colonial masters)
cannot be overlooked. Calypsonians and scholars alike have commented on the many match-ups between England and her former
colonies, to which she taught the game in the first place. Speaking of
what motivated him to make this film, Ové acknowledged:

When Caryl Phillips came to me with the idea for *Playing
Away*, I was immediately interested in the way he was using
cricket as a metaphor of relations between West Indians and
the English. As you well know, cricket is the one game that
West Indians are very proud of and very good at, and it's the
one game that they know they can beat the old masters at. So
Caryl and I talked about it and researched the subject and
travelled to various places. I particularly liked the idea of
pointing up the ridiculousness of racism, on both sides, and
exploring how it enters into people's lives, and what takes
place. But I also wanted to make the film funny, not in the
television sitcom sense but funny in a real way... .

Playing Away was also dealing with a serious subject, but I wanted to do it in a less intense, more humorous way. One of our strengths as West Indians is that when we get into the worst kind of situations and experiences, we still have the ability to look back and laugh at it. We can tell the most terrible jokes about ourselves and really laugh. I wanted to capture that same idea in *Playing Away*, where both black and white could look at themselves and laugh at themselves. I think it worked. I know a lot of people enjoyed it, and the film had good reviews in England, the USA and Australia.[25]

The funding for this film – Channel Four through the Film Four series – was much greater than for *Pressure*, and increased technical sophistication was the result of this, in particular in the latter moments when the game is being played. But beyond the skill of camera work, there is the view of the English countryside that the Caribbean eye sees. The sense of first-time bewilderment as the Brixton residents venture into the heart of English gentility is reminiscent of the many stories Caribbean schoolchildren read about life in the mother country.

Also captured in this film is the Caribbean tendency to mask problems under levity – to laugh at themselves, according to Ové. Norman Beaton's Willie Boy is excellent at this, and his scene in which he ends up drunk borders on the pathetic. His 'problem that is not really a problem' is the same one facing countless Caribbean immigrants at one time or another: trying to decide at what stage to return to the Caribbean. In this respect, there is an underlying sense of sadness in the film's humour, one with which most Caribbean immigrants can identify. Surely, if their financial and other affairs were in better shape, many of them would instantly trade the gloomy English weather for sunnier climes in their true homelands.

Two Gentlemen Sharing and Young Soul Rebels

Inevitably, as immigrants integrate themselves into the host society, they have to deal with problems that cannot be handled purely from the immigrant perspective. Such a situation is seen in the films by second-generation Caribbean immigrants, such as Isaac Julien, that deal with issues – homosexuality, for example – not strictly tied to the immigrant experience. One of the earlier depictions of black homosexuality on the British screen was *Two Gentlemen Sharing* (1969), based on the 1963 novel by David Stuart Leslie, and adapted for the cinema by the

Jamaican-born writer Evan Jones. This film was not released in Britain, though it was shown in the Caribbean. Paramount balked at releasing it because it felt that the finished product did not correspond to the film script as financed.

The film's gay character, Marcus, is played by Guyanese actor Ram John Holder, and is shown as a predatory prostitute willing to seduce the main character, Roddy, one of the two gentlemen sharing a flat. The other is Andrew (Hal Frederick), an Oxford-educated Jamaican law student, who has problems adjusting to the integrated environment around him. Of Marcus and Andrew, Stephen Bourne has written:

> Marcus is a nasty character, and one of the worst examples of a particular kind of gay movie stereotype: the predatory queen. However, in *Two Gentlemen Sharing*, Andrew is an intriguing character, far removed from the 'noble' image being projected by Sidney Poitier in Hollywood at that time … . But the film suffers from explicit homophobia and racism.[26]

The lack of tolerance with regard to homosexuality exhibited by Caribbean people at the time the film was shown led audiences to hoot at Marcus, and to cheer Roddy when he punched him on the face at the end of the movie.

Attitudes were certainly changed by the time Isaac Julien made *Young Soul Rebels* in 1991, to the point where this film could be touted as the first British feature film made by a black gay director. The emphasis is definitely on the whole question of gay identity and black masculinity as opposed to immigrant difficulty with the host society. The director's Caribbean heritage was hardly mentioned when the film was discussed, marking in a way a step forward in the development of the artist, who would be judged in his own right, and not as a member of a particular ethnic group. Of course, it was always possible that critics were concentrating on Julien's other association, namely that with the gay community.

Much is made of the fact that the movie is set in 1977, the year of the Queen's Silver Jubilee. Julien himself explains:

> *Young Soul Rebels* is set in London in 1977, a time when questions of national identity came to the forefront of British consciousness because it was the Queen's Silver Jubilee year. And there was a counternarrative postulated by the Sex Pistol's 'God Save the Queen.' There's an interesting quote from Johnny Rotten's single: 'There is no future in England's

dream. Don't be told what you want. Don't be told what you need.' I think that needs to be repeated at this moment.

The other reason *Young Soul Rebels* is set in 1977 is because I was a soul boy at that time and Nadine Marsh-Edwards, the producer, was a soul girl. And we were interested in 1977 as the moment in black British culture when you witnessed black style becoming a social force – a kind of resistance through style, if you like. You can recognise those things much more in black music coming from Britain today – Soul II Soul and Neneh Cherry – and the way those things have been culturally exported to the U.S. [27]

It seems clear from the foregoing that Julien had an agenda, and the plot of the movie – a murder mystery of sorts – is almost incidental:

Young Soul Rebels focuses on the friendship between Caz, who is black and gay, and Chris, who is half black/half white and heterosexual. Buddies since childhood, the two run a pirate radio station that plays black import records. Caz's sexual involvement with a white Socialist Workers' Party punk and Chris' desire to break into mainstream broadcasting and his sexual relationship with Tracy threaten both friendship and work.

The Chris/Caz story is framed within a police investigation of a murder. During the first minutes of the film, TJ, a young black male friend of Caz, is murdered by a white man during a sexual encounter in a park. Intent on finding a black suspect, the police try to pin the murder on Chris. Chris, however, finds a tape in TJ's boom box that reveals the identity of the murderer. The climax of the film takes place during the Jubilee day 'Stuff the Jubilee' concert. Pursued by both the police and the killer, Chris broadcasts the truth about the murder to an audience of thousands. The pirate station survives, as do the romances and friendships, and everyone gets together for a song-and-dance finale.[28]

The film, produced by the British Film Institute for some £1.2 million, stirred mixed emotions when released, and won the Critic's Prize at Cannes. Roger Ebert, in the *Chicago Sun-Times* of 6 December 1991, felt that Julien cared more about validating his characters than having them do much of anything, while Stephen Bourne found the film seductive, engaging and challenging. 'Isaac's exploration of sexual and racial identities is unselfconscious and liberating.'[29]

Babymother

The Caribbean connection is underplayed in *Young Soul Rebels*, but resurfaces in *Babymother* (1998), the final British-produced film to be discussed in this chapter, and the most recent feature by a Caribbean diaspora film-maker working out of England, Julian Henriques. The connection is once more reggae music, now recognized as typical of Jamaica and the rest of the Caribbean. Henriques defended what began to look like a pattern in Caribbean films, making *Babymother*, with its emphasis on reggae music, a distant cousin to *The Harder They Come* and *Dancehall Queen:*

> One can only do films one feels for, and there is a place for all kinds of films. Music is our greatest asset, the most highly articulated form we have from the Caribbean. Turn your back on the music, and you turn your back on the strength in the culture. I know we'll be accused of falling for stereotype, but some stereotypes can be positive, and do not exclude other positive things.[30]

The film is called a reggae musical, featuring music by Beres Hammond, Carroll Thompson and Cinderella. According to the film's promotional kit, put out by Film Four Distributors:

> The musical score covers a whole range of reggae inspired and related styles such as Ragga, Dancehall, Lovers Rock, Street Soul, Jungle, Drum and Bass, so the film can truly reflect the mix that fills the streets and estates of west London. How different these styles can be is highlighted by the alternative sounds used for Anita's musical numbers and for those of Don Byron.

Anita (Anjela Lauren Smith) is the film's heroine, an unmarried 'baby-mother' bringing up two children alone in a London neighbourhood, and harbouring dreams of being a deejay queen. Don Byron (Wil Johnson) is her 'babyfather' and a local reggae star. She is soon drawn into an intense rivalry with him, and before the inevitable showdown she forms a group – Neeta, Sweeta and Nastie – then loses the person she thought was her mother, finds out that her sister is her real mother, and endures Byron's running off to perform abroad. She wins the eventual clash upon his return, however, pulling off a veritable coup.

There is a dreamlike quality to *Babymother*, with an ending not unlike the one in *Dancehall Queen*. The underdog struggle pays off for the protagonist, leading viewers to conclude that all is not lost even in circumstances that are far from ideal – in this case the ghetto-like atmosphere of Harlesden, in northwest London. In this neighbourhood, described by the film's producers as having codes of honour and behaviour, as being awash with colour and energy, and as a place whose heart is the dancehall and whose beat is reggae music, the baby-mother and her friends must deal with life as best they can, and survive either without men or in spite of them.

Interestingly, the film's producers also explained the significance of the title in their promotional material:

> 'Babymother' is a term that, depending on where you are, can have both positive or negative connotations. In Jamaica, it is a term of respect that a woman will command as mother and head of the household. In the UK, however, its meaning is more ambiguous. From a woman's point of view, it can mean that she is in control. But for men, it often signifies that they have the power. Having and supporting numerous Babymothers can even be a status symbol, like driving a flash car, and in this context it is an insult.

Director Henriques hoped that the film would encourage a positive interpretation. 'I called the film "Babymother" because it contains two very strong, warm and emotional words. I hope that the film will change the negative understanding of the term and make being a Babymother something to be proud of.' From a Caribbean perspective, this hope is not entirely unfounded.

The film was financed by Channel Four, causing some to day-dream of a repeat of this organization's success with *Four Weddings and a Funeral* (1994) and *The Full Monty* (1997). It's North American premiere was at the Planet Africa section of the Toronto Film Festival, and by then distribution was already assured for Trinidad and Tobago. With its driving soundtrack, and its similarity to previous films that highlighted Caribbean people, *Babymother* came closest to bridging the gap between the actual Caribbean region and its diaspora recre-ation, allowing Caribbean immigrant audiences in Britain to make a spiritual journey back to the islands.

Diaspora film-making in North America

Why similar diaspora experiences did not elicit similar responses and films in the United States defies explanation. One would have expected the acknowledged film capital of the world to have produced films telling the story of the Caribbean immigrants, who are not only numer-ous but also very influential in all walks of US life. Further, important film actors and like Sidney Poitier and Harry Belafonte have a strong Caribbean connection, and have established a body of work that would lend credibility to their efforts. Unfortunately, whether by choice or by accident, the American film industry did not turn its attention to the Caribbean immigrant experience in any appreciable way.[31] One would have thought, for example, that the charismatic Marcus Garvey, born in Jamaica, would have stirred great interest in film-makers, as Malcolm X did for Spike Lee and his associates; the life of the late Trinidadian-born Kwame Ture, the former Stokely Carmichael, certainly rates attention for his role in the Black Power movement, as does that of Jamaican-born Claude McKay for his role in the Harlem Renaissance. In other words, there is no shortage of material, or of Caribbean connections to important contemporary personalities (Colin Powell, Louis Farrakhan, *et al.*) and events, all of which could easily justify funding relevant feature films. The Caribbean immigrant story in the United States is simply waiting to be portrayed on screen.

In Canada, on the other hand, there have been feature films made by Caribbean diaspora film-makers, particularly independents, although they have not all looked at problems specific to the Caribbean immigrant community. Clement Virgo's *Rude* (1996), for example, features a Jamaican-Canadian disc jockey addressing listeners in a mixture of creole and standard English. Jamaican-born Virgo does not spend any time analysing the Jamaican community in Toronto, leading the *Washington Post* review of 12 April 1996 to conclude that 'while one senses the effects of race in some situations, the challenges faced by his protagonists are universal.' His subsequent collaboration with another Caribbean diaspora writer and critic, Cameron Bailey, on the screenplay for *The Planet of Junior Brown* resulted in what Bruce Kirkland in the *Toronto Sun* of 5 September 1997 termed 'a complex Toronto film about the friendship between a 400-plus-pound misfit named Junior [played by Trinidadian-born Martin Villafana] and a skinny street kid named Buddy.' Like *Rude*, however, this film does not linger on the Caribbean connection, and its only concession to this link is in the (apparently) Jamaican creole of some of its characters. Still, it is encouraging to know that Caribbean-born film-makers can operate successfully in the fiercely competitive market of North American film-making. In another Canadian-made film, *Mustard Bath* (1993), Director Darrell Wasyk tells the story of a white medical student, Matthew Linden (Michael Riley), who tries to discover himself by returning to his birthplace, Guyana, after the death of his parents. Most of the film is shot on location in Guyana, which is portrayed quite authentically. Popular singer-composer Eddy Grant plays a priest, Rasta Fad'dah, but since the emphasis is on telling Matthew's story, only one Guyanese character, Mindy (Alissa Trotz) receives more than symbolic treatment.

The Caribbean immigrant experience is however treated in a couple of feature films. The time-worn experience of making sacrifices for the improvement of one's lot is highlighted in *Milk and Honey* (1989), which was financed by Canadians with the help of Robert Redford's Sundance Institute. The screenplay, written by Trevor Rhone from an idea developed by Rebecca Yates and Glen Salzman, tells the story of Joanna (Josette Simon), an unwed mother who leaves her son behind in Jamaica with his grandmother, and goes to Canada to work. She hopes that this sacrifice will be worth the effort, and that she will be able to have a better life for her son in the long run. Unfortunately, she hasn't counted on the exploitation encountered at the hands of the Canadian family that sponsored her – a kind of indentured servitude, according to the *Washington Post* review on 19 September 1989. Her constant struggle to stave off the country's immigration authorities leads her to a life that is far from ideal, and certainly much worse in the long run than the one she led in Jamaica. The film portrays a situation that is all too common in North America, but which has so far escaped full-scale treatment in feature films. The critique of the deliberate exploitation of immigrants in situations such as Joanna's gives *Milk and Honey* a documentary feel, and causes the artistic side to suffer somewhat – the *Post* found it 'honorable but instantly forgettable, too earnest to be effective, but too bland to hate.' Caribbean viewers would probably not share this view, because the situation portrayed in this film provides a reminder of a reality to which many of them can attest.

Stephen Williams's *Soul Survivor* (1995), produced, like *Rude*, with the assistance of Telefilm Canada, which has a Feature Film Fund, and the Ontario Film Development Corporation, provides an intimate look at some aspects of Toronto's Jamaican community. Tyrone (Peter Williams) quits his job in a beauty salon and becomes a debt collector for a local money-lender, Winston (George Harris), whom some would consider a successful businessman. As it turns out, one of those indebted to Winston is Tyrone's cousin Reuben (David Smith), a Rastafarian who sells handicraft and spouts the usual anti-establishment rhetoric about Babylon and what it is doing to make his life miserable. Tyrone tries his best to manage the split loyalties that this situation involves, but cannot prevent Reuben from being shot as time apparently runs out on his debt repayment schedule.

For the most part, the people we see are first- or second-generation Jamaican immigrants settled into their new life in Canada, and are determined to make the best of it. As his health worsens, the hero's grandfather (Ardon Bess) begins to fear not so much dying, but dying in this 'land of strangers', far away from his real home. The grandfather finds solace in drink and cigarettes, while the grandmother (Leonie Forbes) pins her hope on religion and lottery tickets, leading grandson Tyrone to hurl the accusation right back at her when she accuses him of being a dreamer. It is a scene reminiscent of Ivan's conversation with Elsa in *The Harder They Come*. She too had accused Ivan of being a dreamer, and his response was that it was she, on the contrary, who was always talking about milk and honey in the sky. He wanted his due here on earth. Tyrone has the same request, but events work against him. The final scene of the movie is played out under Bob Marley's 'Redemption Song', a poignant evocation of the hero's need to 'emancipate himself from mental slavery'.

Williams uses small details to reinforce the link with the Caribbean and its culture. One of these links is cricket, and we see part of a match on television, with commentary by Tony Cozier, the well-known Barbadian broadcaster, on the performance of star batsman Vivian Richards. Another link is the familiar longing for island food; when Tyrone and Reuben raid their grandmother's refrigerator, they drool over her Jamaican dishes, and for a while Canada recedes in this reverse colonization by taste. These small links, added to the obvious larger ones – reggae music and Jamaican creole – conspire to show that the Caribbean diaspora is alive and lively.

If we take the British and Canadian developments as indicative of what is in store for Caribbean diaspora film-makers, then it is reasonable to expect that it is the independent ones who will be more likely to deal with issues relevant to the Caribbean community as a whole. Unless there is a significant shift of focus, the major studios, with their emphasis on commercial viability for their films, will continue to treat this community as marginal, its box-office power being understandably weak at the national level. This, as far as members of this community are concerned, is no reason why their story should not be told to all and sundry.

Notes

1. For a full account of the black presence in British films, see Stephen Bourne, *Black in the British Frame* (1998).
2. Poitier was born in Miami of Bahamian parents who were visiting the US. He spent his childhood in Nassau, and migrated to America at the age of 15.
3. Personal communication with novelist.
4. Stephen Bourne, *Black in the British Frame*, 228.
5. Ibid.

6. Pauline Kael, in *Microsoft Cinemania 96*.
7. Jim Pines, 'The Cultural Context of Black British Cinema,' (1988), 30.
8. 'Horace Ové: Reflections' (1996), 16.
9. David Wilson, 'Review of *Pressure*,' (1978), 68.
10. Jim Pines, 'The Cultural Context', 31.
11. 'Horace Ové: Reflections', 18.
12. David Wilson, 'Review of *Pressure*'.
13. Jim Pines, 'The Culural Context', 32.
14. Kobena Mercer, *Black Film, British Cinema* (1988), 9.
15. David Wilson, 'Review of *Pressure*'.
16. Interview with Stephen Bourne in Jim Pines (ed.), *Black and White in Colour* (1992), 124.
17. Norman Beaton, *Beaton but Unbowed* (1986), 199.
18. Interview in Jim Pines, *Black and White in Colour*, 200.
19. Jim Pines, 'The Cultural Context', 33.
20. See my interview with Menelik Shabazz in Appendix 1 page 173.
21. Kobena Mercer, *Black Film, British Cinema*, 10.
22. Stephen Bourne, *Black in the British Frame*, 235.
23. See his reflections on this development in the interview in Appendix 1, page 176.
24. 'Horace Ové: Reflections', 18.
25. Jim Pines, *Black and White in Colour*, 128.
26. Stephen Bourne, *Black in the British Frame*, 180.
27. 'Soul to Soul. Isaac Julien talks to Amy Taubin about *Young Soul Rebels*', *Sight and Sound* 1, 4 (NS), 15.
28. 'Soul to Soul,' 14.
29. Stephen Bourne, *Black in the British Frame*, 188.
30. Personal communication from Julian Henriques, Summer 1998.
31. See my discussion of *Clara's Heart* in Chapter 2.

5 | Coming attractions: towards a Caribbean cinema industry

'We need to find the Caribbean way of doing things, including the way we make films.'

Franklyn St Juste

The cinema-loving Caribbean public portrayed in the opening chapter still exists, though, as is to be expected, tastes have shifted dramatically. This shift has as much to do with the type and availability of movies as it does with the viewers' likes and dislikes. The fascination with westerns has dwindled along with Hollywood's quasi-abandonment of this genre. The most likely replacement, the action movie with actors like Bruce Lee, Sylvester Stallone, Arnold Schwarznegger and Bruce Willis, has attracted its own set of *aficionados*, making cinema attendance still a fairly popular activity in the anglophone Caribbean. The traditional pit audience that was so involved in the action on screen that it spoke back to the images, or even threw objects at some of the two-dimensional villains, has evolved somewhat by force of circumstance. In many cinemas, there is no longer the pit section, putting an end to the sacrosanct milieu of some cinema patrons, but not an end to their quick reaction to situations that involve the Caribbean and its people. The lack of free time due to the hustle and bustle of modern living, and the scarcity of money in some circles for leisure activities are also factors in the shift in moviegoer habits, making video productions an appealing alternative, as we shall see at the end of this chapter.

Anglophone Caribbean audiences have not had much that is regionally produced to which to react over the years. They have seen instead a series of films that were shot on location by foreign filmmakers who did not really have the Caribbean region at heart. While the occasional shot of a Kingston market or a Barbados beach for backdrop may say little in the hands of the non-Caribbean film-maker, the same shot for a Caribbean film-maker can say much more, and Caribbean audiences immediately see and appreciate the difference. Why, then, are there not more films made by anglophone Caribbean film-makers, who have a few seminal successes to point the way?

Why, in short, is there no cinema industry to rival the region's music industry?

Problems, potential, and possibilities

There can be no argument that most of the high-grossing films shown worldwide are made in America. The *Washington Post* of 26 October 1998 reported that US distributors took in $5.8 billion at the foreign box office in 1997, and that experts estimated an annual growth rate of 6 to 7 per cent. The *Post* went on to state that this phenomenal growth was achieved despite the fact that foreign distributors have almost no interest in movies with African American or other minority casts and themes, a decidedly small segment of the market. If this is indeed the case, there is little reason to expect US film-makers to shoot many films with a so-called ethnic bias – precisely the type likely to appeal to Caribbean audiences in addition to the array of films they already see on a regular basis. In fact, these film-makers will point to the relatively dismal domestic performance of films like *Amistad* (1997) and *Beloved* (1998) as proof that the ethnic market isn't sufficiently strong to justify major investments.

If anglophone Caribbean cinema – so minuscule internationally that it is hardly ever listed separately in studies of world cinema – cannot depend on mainstream cinema for ethnic movies, the label too readily given to Caribbean films, then it must make them on its own. It must also be courageous enough to produce films and not gauge their success in Hollywood terms. This is admittedly an enterprise fraught with frustration and disappointment for the small Caribbean nations, in view of the high cost and increasing sophistication of quality film-making. On the one hand, there is no shortage of talent to make feature movies in the anglophone Caribbean, and the results, though sparse, have been noteworthy. On the other hand, there is also no dearth of factors to thwart the development of a vibrant cinema industry.

Derek Walcott, interviewed in the *Sunday Express* of 4 September 1983 about his work on *The Rig*, his made-for-television movie, observed: 'There is an inside, classic West Indian acting, and I have seen it in film... . Theater is so expensive, the West Indian future may be in film.' It is difficult to fathom exactly what Walcott meant when he opposed film to theatre, for there is no guarantee that the former was less costly than the latter. The poet/playwright does state in the same interview that 'it's almost simpler to do a film and spend the money there instead of putting it into a production to which nobody comes.' One is led to conclude that the financial difficulty that attends a film production pales by comparison with the difficulty that attends a theatrical production, of which Walcott above all is very aware. That is simply not the case, nor is audience support certain for a finished movie. More to the point may be the fact that Walcott seems to be speaking about films on video – he was, after all about to shoot *The Rig* – if we are to judge from low sums of money (even in TT$) used in his examples: 'Ticket prices are high and budgets for plays are $30,000 and $40,000, but the audience cannot see where the money is spent. If $30,000 is put into a film, there could be a quality product for large audiences to show for it.'

Although masterpieces have on occasion been made on shoestring budgets, consistently obtaining a quality product for such paltry sums hardly seems plausible. Budgets of the sort mentioned by Walcott would doom film-makers to artistic and financial ruin, even if they were to benefit from another of his suggestions: 'It is part of the function of the state to provide amenities for culture as it does for roads and water.' The problem, however, in countries struggling with high unemployment and other economic woes, is one of priority for sparse resources. Unfortunately for artists, support for their work has traditionally been relegated to the lower half of the priority scale.

Walcott's venture into the world of film did not turn him from the theatre. *The Rig* was completed and shown on Trinidad television, but the response was lukewarm. In addition, it was poorly scheduled by the sole station in operation at that time, causing the *Sunday Express* of 8 January 1984 to remark that the relatively small number of viewers 'saw a show with just enough drawbacks to divert them from its many pluses':

> The first-class footage of the locations, both interior and exterior; the essentially Trinidadian roots of the characters and situation (the impact of oil money on a rural community and on different personalities within the local setting); the fascinating original background music; the generally fine use of cameras and lighting; the extremely high quality of the dialogue; and many other details that must be painstakingly put together to make good television, need to be considered and evaluated by the viewing public.

The drawbacks stemmed mainly from the difficulty viewers had following the thread of the narrative, as well as from the lack of clarity concerning certain inter-relationships. By and large, these were minor problems for an accomplished playwright and director like Derek Walcott, but what is significant is that he did not pursue the idea of branching out to feature film in a significant manner. The idea seemed so workable in theory, but the practical implementation proved difficult to realize. There has been talk over the years of film scripts based on his plays *Ti-Jean and his Brothers, In a Fine Castle, Pantomime,* and *Steel,* with Horace Ové in the director's chair, but as the 1990s drew to a close these projects still languished without funding.

The importance of adequate funding is brought home in another made-for-television movie directed by Ové. In 1991, he shot *The Orchid House,* based on the novel by Dominican-born Phyllis Shand Allfrey. Filming was done in Dominica, the setting of the novel, with funding from Britain's Channel Four, a factor that no doubt ensured a wider distribution network for the finished product. Annabelle Alcazar wrote that:

> This was the first costume drama to be made in the Caribbean by British television; set between the wars, it is the story of a crumbling white family told from the nanny's point of view. The production employed hundreds of people as extras, as well as carpenters, painters, drivers and assistants. The series was extremely successful and sold worldwide, prompting other film companies and commercials to use Dominica as a location. One enterprising local travel company even started to offer Orchid House Tours to all the locations used in the film.[1]

The finished product made such good use of the Caribbean location that one was left to wonder why similar productions had not been made before, or why they could not be made on a continuing basis. One could envisage, for instance, an entire series of adaptations of Caribbean masterpieces – from the works of Naipaul, Walcott, Lamming, Selvon, Lovelace, Mais, Reid, *et al.* – done on video and available, after their initial release and airing, to educational establishments as teaching tools. The problem is clearly not a lack of material, or of talent.

Channel Four chose St Lucia as the location of another production, *The Final Passage* (1996), written by Caryl Phillips, who was born in St Kitts but has lived most of his adult life in England. Annabelle Alcazar's article gave the following information on the project:

> Set in the 1950s on a small Caribbean island, it told the story of a young couple's unsatisfactory life and their dream of going to England, their journey, and their subsequent disillusionment. It provided a wonderful opportunity for actor Michael Cherrie, who won the lead role and who had never

left the Caribbean. After filming the second part of the story in London, [Sir Peter] Hall offered him a place in the Royal Shakespeare Company (sadly, English Equity, the actor's union, refused to grant him membership).[2]

It is difficult to assess whether this refusal stemmed from zealous protectionism or from racial insensitivity. The 'official' reason given was that there were enough talented black actors in Britain who should have been considered before a foreigner. It did nonetheless bring home the fact that the Caribbean had little clout when dealing with players in the big league, since such an argument did not prevent Sidney Poitier from making *To Sir, With Love* in England; nor did it prevent Denzel Washington, Robert Townsend or Jasmine Guy from working on feature films in Jamaica.

The attraction of video and television also led Jamaica's Lennie Little-White to abandon feature film-making after *Children of Babylon*, and to turn his efforts to producing television programmes. 'We analysed TV and cable as easier to penetrate capital; it's not as risky,' he is reported to have said, as his company celebrated its 25th anniversary.[3] He had returned to Jamaica full of hope for the future of film-making, but potential collaborators, including the state-owned Jamaica Broadcasting Company, did not offer him much encouragement. He decided to go it alone, and his eventual television series 'Royal Palm Estate' proved successful. It went into its 11th year in 1998, the longest run of any locally produced programme, but nonetheless left its producer unhappy that foreigners were still being brought into Jamaica to do what locals could do.

The foregoing examples underscore the fact that there is abundant film-making talent in the Caribbean; that there is an audience for quality productions as well as interest in seeing the Caribbean story told on film; and that there is, above all, a need for adequate funding of projects.

The question of funding is the most basic, but the most problematic. For the time being, Derek Walcott's vision of low-cost films for television, while admirable, is unrealistic, since even modest television productions can be quite costly. Ironically, theatre productions have continued with encouraging regularity, though with varying degrees of success, while made-for-television films have not kept pace. In addition, it is not improbable that advancing technology will soon provide a very low-cost way to capture high-quality images.

It is now axiomatic to say that film-making is expensive. Apart from American blockbusters and the occasional surprise success – like Britain's *The Full Monty* (1997) – profits on investments in films are the exception rather than the rule. Shooting on location, while improving authenticity, does not lessen the expense of production. Consequently, it is vital that funding be obtained for film projects, since in most instances, film-makers cannot come up with the money needed for their work.

Feature film producers have consistently complained that financiers do not understand what is involved in their projects. From one end of the anglophone Caribbean to the other, the complaint is essentially the same. 'In Jamaica,' Carl Bradshaw said in an interview,[4] 'there were entrepreneurs who were visual conceptualizers, who needed to see their investments in a visual sense. You couldn't go to one of them with a two-page proposal for a film. This meant that the necessary financial backing did not come.' Similarly, in Trinidad, Horace Ové conceded that 'finding finance here is not easy. The money men see film as a high-risk venture and prefer to stay safe with real estate or insurance. What they don't realize is that there are so many sources of return now in addition to cinema tickets.'[5] In this light, Walcott's ideal of having the state provide amenities for culture begins to make a lot of sense.

The type of funding available from organizations like Channel Four in England, or Telefilm Canada, is unfortunately not available from equivalent organizations in the anglophone Caribbean. There are no private foundations to underwrite projects of independent film-makers, nor are there major locally based film companies concentrating on feature film production, apart possibly from Island Jamaica Films, still small by international standards. As we have seen, a company like Mediamix in Jamaica has de-emphasized the production of feature films; and Trinidad and Tobago's Banyan, while involved in many pilot projects and treatments for feature films, has not produced a commercially viable feature length movie.

The example of the United Kingdom, where a percentage of money raised from the national lottery has been used to help stimulate the ailing film industry, has yet to be emulated in the Caribbean. The taxes on cinema tickets in Jamaica and Trinidad and Tobago do not go into a pool which indigenous film-makers can tap. Further, the ministries of culture, perceived as the mainstays of funding in the humanities in the former Commonwealth colonies, have simply indicated that financing feature films is not in their purview.

Several of the laws and regulations that colonial administrations first instituted have survived well into the post-independence era, and their sometimes outdated nature have made for situations inimical to the fostering of creativity. In Trinidad and Tobago, for example, the licensing and operating of cinemas is still subject to the Cinematograph

Act of 1936. Certain sections can only be viewed with amusement in the light of recent developments in the world of cinema and film. One reads in the *Laws of Trinidad and Tobago*:

> 44. (1)   For the purposes of sections 18 and 19 of the Act, the proportions and quotas of British films to be exhibited in each theater shall be in accordance with this regulation.
>
> (2)   In the case of films other than news films, the proportion of British films to be exhibited to the public on payment, during each half year in which any films other than news films are exhibited to the public on payment in the theater, shall be at least fifteen percent, and if the films so exhibited include feature films (being films, other than news films, of not less than 5,000 feet in length) there shall, in addition, be maintained in relation to the feature films the same proportion of British films.
>
> (3)   In the case of news films, the quota of British films to be exhibited to the public on payment, during each complete month in which films are exhibited to the public on payment in the theater, shall be at least 8,000 feet.[6]

If cinema operators were to follow the letter of the law, they would be forced out of business, for the British quota is simply impossible to fill.

There are also any number of customs duties, taxes and other regulations that have made the importation of movie equipment extremely burdensome, causing would-be film-makers to abandon projects in frustration. Trinidad and Tobago, unlike Jamaica, seems not to have paid any heed to the fact that the presence of a foreign movie crew on location means a substantial flow of money to the nation's economy.

Jamaica has set up, as part of its marketing arm Jampro, a Film, Music and Entertainment Commission, with the express mandate to foster growth and development in the island's film industry. In order to pursue these goals, the Commission focuses on strategic initiatives designed to position Jamaica as a key player in the global film industry, and to promote the island as an ideal, strategic location for filming through locations marketing.[7] Jampro and the Commission work with the various local government agencies to solve many of the problems that would normally be encountered by outsiders unfamiliar with administration requirements.

The British Virgin Islands government has also set up a film commission, and 'is busy luring film crews to its 40 largely undeveloped isles and offshore cays.' The hope is that 'a professional infrastructure, proximity to the U.S., and the islands' status as a British dependency will bring the B.V.I. a film industry – and another source of income.'[8]

But there is still the complaint that all these efforts are geared more to helping the outsider than to encouraging the indigenous film-maker, who would rather receive help in securing financing for feature film projects. For this reason, no doubt, the film commission's permit requirements boldly state that it is a matter of policy 'to encourage the utilization of all equipment, human and other resources that are available in the British Virgin Islands before other options are utilized.'

There has been little concerted attempt to capitalize on efforts at feature film-making, or to build on previous successes. From the first indigenous productions back in the early 1970s up to the latest contemporary ones, each attempt has been heralded as the start of a Caribbean film industry. It happened, for example, with the establishment of Sharc Productions and the eventual making of *Bim*. The press trumpeted Sharc and its location as the start of a Caribbean Hollywood, and the government granted a few concessions through the Trinidad and Tobago Development Corporation for the purchase of equipment. It should be noted that DeLuxe Films also sought concessions from the government, but were turned down. Principals of that company then complained that the interest was not in developing the film industry in Trinidad and Tobago as such, but in granting favours to well-connected individuals.

It is also difficult for newcomers to the world of anglophone Caribbean film-making to see the work that preceded them, for there are no official film archives or film commissions ensuring that early works are available for viewing. Films that were made prior to the widespread use of videotape were not always converted to this medium, especially if they were not particularly successful when first released. While this has not been a problem in mainstream cinema, with a ready market for videotapes of just about any film it has made, the lack of interest in ethnic films has meant that the barest minimum of such films has been converted. Consequently, films like *The Right and the Wrong, The Caribbean Fox,* and *Bim* are virtually lost to viewers, for even specialized collections of Third World films do not hold copies. Those that do exist on film are kept in labs, some of which move or go out of existence without informing film-makers of the fate of their negatives.

Audience, action and reaction

The desire of a people to see its story told is ably illustrated in the great interest (East) Indians in Trinidad and Tobago and Guyana show in movies from India, thus constituting a special market for non-mainstream films. Descendants of indentured labourers who first arrived in the Caribbean in the 1840s make up a significant section of the population, and proportionately of the movie-going audience, in these two countries. In Jamaica, on the other hand, the percentage of Indian inhabitants does not seem to justify screening Indian films. Palace Amusements, which operates the majority of cinemas in that country, has however acknowledged helping at least one other distributor from Montego Bay to show such movies.[9] The films from India provided a much needed look at an ancestral land and culture that could easily have been erased from their consciousness:

> This ignorance of what life actually was in India was soon to come to a partial end with the advent of Indian films. East Indian immigrants were to be awakened and enlightened to ways of life, cultural and religious, of their forefathers. And with their first exposure to an Indian film, their appetite was whetted for more knowledge of their diverse culture which they could emulate and adopt to their own ways of life here. Consequently, when we speak of the re-awakened and sustained interest of our people here in the affairs (cultural and otherwise) of their 'Mother Country' it shall have to be ascribed in some measure to the introduction of Indian films in this country.[10]

As a result, certain distributors, like Indian Overseas Limited, handle exclusively Indian movies, catering to viewers eager to maintain the link with their ancestral language and culture.

It is interesting to observe that there is no contradiction in this duality of loyalty: to their current country, and to the home of their forefathers. It surfaces every time the Indian cricket team visits Trinidad and Tobago and Guyana. In this regard, descendants of Africans have been at a greater disadvantage in that African films are not routinely shown in the anglophone Caribbean. Even if they were, they probably would not be viewed with the same admiration, in the light of the legacy of colonial prejudice against things African on the whole. The familiarity with which sections of the East Indian audience view films from India cannot be duplicated among Africans when it comes to African films.

Earl Lovelace's *The Dragon Can't Dance* provides a sympathetic look at the role that Indian cinema played in the lives of many of Trinidad's East Indian inhabitants. His Indian character Pariag, upon first arriving in Port of Spain, works alongside Balliram, who was the one hawking aloud their trade in bottles:

> Balliram's ambition was to be an announcer for one of the movie houses promoting East Indian pictures; and whenever

the van was passing through a place where there were no houses he would practise his announcing: 'Tha Princess Cenemar proudly presents-ah for your-ah weekend-ah entertainment-ah, that wonderful-ah, tha marvellous-ah, tha magnificent, that colossal-ah motion picture. Winnah of five academy awards-ah: Choti Baheen-ah, starring the masterful Dilip Kumar and the exciting-ah Ramjanee Roy with-ah dances by Helen-ah.' Balliram was really serious about his announcing.[11]

Later, we see Pariag struggling to fit into the new urban environment with his wife, and using Indian films as a source of comfort and stability:

'You want to go and see an Indian picture? He asked her one night, while they were lying in their separate sleeplessness. And just like that she had turned and buried her face in his chest and cried.

'Hey! What happen to you? What happen?' But she didn't say anything, just went on crying silently, and then he realized that this was the first place he had asked her to go to, and he found that he had water in his eyes too. And he smoothened her hair and he didn't know what to say, and he held her close, and she held him, and he said: 'That is town for you!'

That same week they went to San Juan to see an Indian picture.

'You like it?' he asked when they came out.

She smiled, delighted, her teeth jutting out. She didn't even tell him it was the first time she had been inside a cinema. But even so, the picture left them feeling very alone, for, for a moment it had plunged them into the fantastic and colourful world of India, bringing about in Pariag a longing for family, for home, for New Lands playground, playing all fours with Seenath, Ramjohn and Bali, for the smell of home, of saffron and green grass and cow dung steaming after a midday rain, and the sight of sugarcane, and the sound of keskidees and nanny-goats and the wind signalling an evening rain.[12]

The on-screen India thus provides a powerful link not only with the ancestral land, but also with the rural Trinidad that he knew prior to coming to the capital.

Bala Joban was the first Indian feature film to be shown in Trinidad in 1935. It reportedly had great impact on the Indian population, and triggered 'a powerful Indian cultural revival in the country'.[13] 'Thousands of Indians lined the streets, pushed, rushed, and abused each other to gain entrance into the cinema for this experience. Almost every local Indian for whom it was possible to do so went to see this "pioneering" movie.'[14] Indian movies did for Indian moviegoers what, ideally, African movies could have done for African viewers. But African cinema developed much later, by which time the pro-West bias would have militated against the sort of adulation Indians showed for Indian films.

Indian viewers continued to patronize Indian films to the extent that there were, by the 1970s, some 13 full-time Indian movie houses in Trinidad.[15] There followed a decline in the 1980s, attributed to the popularity of VCRs, as well as to the overall state of the island's economy, a situation that obviously also affected non-Indian films.[16] The 1990s saw a marked improvement, helped along by better films coming from India, by a decline in video rentals, and by added assistance from radio and television programmes that brought heightened awareness of Indian culture.

The 1995 ascent to political power of an Indian prime minister in Trinidad and Tobago, along with a majority Indian cabinet, gave the Indians the feeling that their time had come. The result was that all aspects of Indian culture underwent a renaissance, and movies were naturally part of the rebirth.

Although by the end of the 1990s the number of cinemas in Trinidad and Tobago had fallen to 28, there had been at one time – mid-1970s – as many as 70 cinemas (including four drive-ins).[17] Many of these cinemas were, and still are, owned by Indians:

> It is a well-known fact that more that ninety percent of the cinema facilities in Trinidad are owned and operated by local Indians. The 'pioneers' in this field of cinema ownership have all come from the more progressive and well-to-do Indian families. Some of those 'pioneers' who built more than one cinema in those early days – some of which, to this day, rank among the outstanding ones and still serve as 'first-run houses,' were: Timothy Roodal ... Sarran Teelucksingh ... Nur Gokool ... and Harry Teelucksingh.[18]

Indeed, in V. S. Naipaul's *A House for Mr. Biswas*, we read that the domineering Indian matriarch Mrs Tulsi, when looking for a daughter for one of her sons, searches among 'the cinema families', equating them with other apparently successful business operators in soft drinks, ice, transport, and filling stations.[19] It is noticeable that Indians also dominate the film distribution companies, leading one to speculate that Indian movies could conceivably dominate in cinemas as well. But the African section of the population, ardent moviegoers, would hardly provide the financial support necessary for that likelihood to become a reality.

One would have thought that some of these same Indian business-men who made money distributing Indian films would have capitalized on the ready market of Indian viewers to produce feature films geared to this specialized audience. Even Harbance Kumar, who made the feature films *The Right and the Wrong* and *The Caribbean Fox,* did not orient those films to such an audience. Later *Bim*, with an Indian as its hero, depended on mixed reactions as opposed to ethnic support from the Indian section. Interestingly, the reaction of Indians in rural Trinidad was different from that of Indians in the urban areas, many of whom were middle class. The local businessmen seem content to earn money in cinema ownership or in film distribution, which is seen as easier and certainly less risky than production. In all of the reported projects likely to foster development of a local film industry, there is nothing to indicate that films specially tailored to Trinidad and Tobago's and Guyana's Indian viewers are even being considered.

The indigenous feature film and the foreign feature film are on a par in at least one area: their treatment at the hands of the censors. As we saw earlier, many of the rules and regulations laid down during the colonial administration are still in effect. This has led to inevitable clashes between the liberalization in foreign feature films and the con-servative nature of the local board of censors. In Trinidad and Tobago, the Board of Censors is authorized by the previously cited 1936 Cinematograph Ordinance, Chapter 20:10, wherein its duties are out-lined in section 13:

> (1) It shall be the duty of the censor or censors deputed for the purpose by the Chairman of the Board to examine every cinematograph film and every film-poster submitted to the Board for approval, and to report thereon to the Chairman.
> (2) The Board's approval shall not be given in the case of any film or any poster which in the opinion of the Board depicts any matter that is against public order and decency, or the exhibition of which for any other reason is in the opinion of the Board undesirable in the public interest.

At intervals, the Board has further drawn up a series of principles for the guidance of the censors. These were intended to help the Board keep abreast of changing moral values, since the basic ordinance remained unchanged:

> Some of the changes reflect a changed political climate. Gone in 1970 and 1973 are the obsolete injunctions against disrespecting British and Allied uniforms, the monarchy, the sentiment of the British Commonwealth, and against all pictures and dialogues obviously intended as anti-British propaganda, or themes likely to be offensive to nationals of friendly nations.[20]

The thorny subject of sexuality was handled in detail:

> In 1970, the principles warned against scenes depicting the sex act, frontal view of the genitals unless for educational purposes, and scenes of sex outrage, including lesbianism, homosexuality, and 'acts of perversion.' In 1973, masturbation is added to lesbianism and homosexuality, and the curious clause 'other acts of perversion' replaces the earlier 'acts of perversion,' the implication being that masturbation, homosexuality, and lesbianism *are* acts of perversion. There is no reference to the growing body of legal and medical opinion that see these as psychological or physiological problems. In the 1973 code, not only is there a ban against depicting 'the private parts of a female and a male' (except for educational purposes) there is also an added restraint against 'erotic exposure of the female breasts.' The liberated female may wonder why there is no similar clause against exposure of the male breast; the artist may ask the censor to define what he considers 'erotic exposure,' and challenge this definition successfully in court.[21]

Such niceties of interpretation only went to show how tricky the question of legislating morality could be. This matter proved even trickier when the small Caribbean societies tried to break away from what had been imposed on them by metropolitan tastes.

The difficulty of having hard-and-fast regulations was seen when television was introduced. It was further exacerbated with the widespread availability of films on cable systems, technology drastically diminishing the clout of the censor:

> As acknowledged in a memorandum submitted by the Customs and Excise Division to the Ordinance Review Committee, films for television enter and leave the country very rapidly; they also enter in great quantity. In addition, the

Ordinance makes no provision for the censorship of films on television. When, in 1978, Trinidad and Tobago Television was prosecuted for exhibiting uncensored films contrary to the Certificate of Approval, the case was dismissed because the law did not provide for censorship of videotape cassettes. Most modern television features are in fact shipped on videocassette, which makes any attempt to censor television material somewhat futile under the existing Ordinance. The profusion of home videocassette recorders, and the ease of access to films on cassette which have not been censored locally also begins to make the work of the Board rather meaningless.[22]

In like manner, with cable and satellite television delivering films directly into the homes of consumers, it is absurd to attempt to ban material that is readily viewable on cable. The implication of this easy, technologically assisted way around local censorship is that what the American censor passes is what the Caribbean viewer sees.

There have been some celebrated disagreements over matters of censorship. Trinidad and Tobago's *Bim*, we have already seen, was almost torpedoed before release by a decision of the censors. In a more recent case in Jamaica, the Cinematograph Authority adjusted its original rating at the request of certain government officials. The film in question, *Amistad*, had been rated A 18 – for adults 18 years and over – primarily because of some of the early graphic scenes. The Ministry of Education felt that the film had sufficient educational value to warrant its being shown to school children, and after representation to the appropriate authorities, the rating was changed to PG 14. Jampress, the government news agency, issued a release stating that the new rating 'would provide the opportunity for young persons to better understand and appreciate this peaceful story.' Steven Spielberg, having heard of the controversy, had asked that the film be returned rather than be cut.

Innovation is not limited to what is shown on the screen, nor to the way what is shown makes its way to the screen. There is innovation in the very milieu in which feature films are viewed. The traditional partitioning of the cinema that led to pit, house, and balcony sections is slowly giving way to uniform seating in multiplex configurations. In 1997 Palace Amusements of Jamaica rebuilt its burnt-out Carib cinema in the new multiplex style, claiming that this arrangement affords a better choice of movies. The *Daily Gleaner* of 17 January 1997 reported Douglas Graham, the managing director of Palace Amusements, as explaining:

When the cinema had one screen the concentration was on 45 pictures each year, but when there are five screens there will be 200 pictures per year. Hence more pictures will be shown and movement will be beyond the blockbusters into pictures of limited appeal; and in so doing address different tastes of the Jamaica population.

One casualty of the switch to the multiplex format is likely to be the double feature. Already, even without the new arrangement, some distributors in Trinidad and Tobago are mandating that cinemas showing their films start showing single features. The move is being opposed in the rural areas, however, where poorer patrons would feel cheated paying twice what they normally paid in order to see two movies.

Cinemas in the anglophone Caribbean have also had to face increasing competition from VCR ownership, videotape rentals, direct satellite transmissions, and cable television hook-ups with service at reduced rates to capture viewer fidelity.[23] Piracy has continued to dog distributors, hurting first-run attendance and attendant profits. Some Trinidad distributors, who handle films for all of the southern Caribbean, report that by the time they send some films to Guyana, audiences have already seen versions that were recorded either off satellite transmission or from other sources that remain undisclosed to the distributors.

The problem of increased crime has also emerged as a factor in assessing popularity and profitability. In areas where patrons have been discouraged from attending the cinema through fear for their safety, operators have been forced to advertise that they provide a secure environment for moviegoers. Some distributors feel that the problem is not as serious as first thought, and that good films will bring patrons in spite of their awareness of the crime situation in a particular territory. By and large, however, the continued success of the exhibition phase of the cinema industry in America will ensure the copy-cat success of its counterpart in the anglophone Caribbean, with a few adjustments for local conditions. For the foreseeable future, Hollywood will continue to dominate, and by extension to dictate, and to send its creations to the Caribbean.

With Hollywood releasing dozens of films per month, and the anglophone Caribbean producing a dozen or so films in approximately three decades, it is clear that an industry with such a small output is destined to be marginal at the international level. There is a glimmer of hope in the specialization of ethnic or Third World markets, but big league players easily overlook anything that is not mainstream.

The fascination of the former Caribbean colonies with what comes from outside the region continues to hurt 'local' productions. This is especially so in a country like Trinidad and Tobago, as the failure of *The Panman* in 1997 plainly showed. The emphasis the producers placed on pointing out the local connections and input backfired, and viewers stayed away from the film's screenings. One Trinidad and Tobago film-maker, Anthony Maharaj, who has made several non-Caribbean features – among them, *Naked Vengeance* (1986), *Final Mission* (1986), *Not Another Mistake* (1988), *Mission Terminate* (1987) , and *The Fighter (1987)* – claims that he frequently removes his name from the credits when his films are shown in his home country. It is his way of avoiding the stigma of 'local' that would be associated with his involvement.[24] Paradoxically at times, the local label does not automatically mean a negative response, as can be seen from the popularity of the television series 'Turn of the Tide' in Trinidad, and 'Royal Palm Estate' in Jamaica. However, when Horace Wilson's *Turn of the Tide* (1988), the movie based on the television series, was shown in Trinidad, small-screen popularity did not translate to the large screen, and it failed miserably.

There are, nonetheless, several Caribbean feature film projects being undertaken at any given time; but they invariably languish unfunded, underfunded or unreleased. In Trinidad and Tobago, for example, Banyan and Pan Trinbago have shot a pilot of a feature film, *Walk Like a Dragon*, produced by Christopher Laird and Tony Hall. Described in promotional material as the spiritual odyssey of a panman, 'a story of liberation through creation', this film promises to make a major contribution to the corpus of anglophone Caribbean films. On 3 January 1997 the *Daily Express* wrote of this project: 'The full-length version of this film will be important, and not merely for the oft-quoted reason of preserving history and restoring to the panman and woman some semblance of dignity and historic position.' Yet while the project seems likely to be of interest to the many lovers of the steelband in Trinidad and Tobago and the rest of the Caribbean, this does not guarantee that adequate funding will be available. Banyan is also involved in producing a series of Caribbean dramas set around the choices faced by the youth of the region. The series, *Uprising*, is produced with the assistance of UNESCO, and one film has already been shot – *Entry Denied*, a film by Christopher Browne, starring Paul Campbell as a Jamaican inner-city youth awarded a scholarship to the USA, but denied a visa to enter the country. This film, along with treatments of another five films from around the Caribbean, will be used to raise funds to produce the whole series of six films for international cinema and television distribution. Unfortunately, despite the financial assistance from UNESCO for the pilot, and the intention to solicit funds from international, regional and local television stations, corporations and art organizations to complete the rest, these are not regular feature films. As such, if they are ever completed, it is very possible that they would not be shown in general release.[25]

Andrew Millington has written, directed and produced what is believed to be the first feature-length by a Barbadian about Barbados. Shot in super 16 mm, *Guttaperc* (1998) – the word refers to a locally made slingshot – was made with the proverbial tight budget of grant money and personal savings that independent film-makers know only too well. It is the story of young Erik (Richard Weekes), narrated in retrospect by an adult Erik (John Phillips), who is sent to live in the Barbadian countryside with his Grandpa (Clairmonte Taitt), a successful businessman. Erik witnesses the transformation in the family and the village when they receive news of a tourism resort project that threatens to displace many of the villagers. Hovering throughout the entire movie is Sister Pam (Leonie Forbes), a combination of obeah woman and griot, who makes sure that the Barbadians do not forget their roots, and with whom the young hero becomes utterly fascinated.

Millington is of the school of committed cinema, a fact that shows in the manner the film was shot. There is a *cinéma nouveau* feel to the scenes of nature, with the camera lingering on images of the sea washing the shore. The haunting soundtrack is somewhat surprising to the average Caribbean viewer, accustomed to reggae and calypso as the standard identifiers of the region. The Barbados depicted in this film is the antithesis of the tourist-oriented playground; indeed, there are no hotels, uniformed waiters, or cruise ships in sight. 'We don't have our own image which is determined by ourselves,' Millington said prior to the film's premiere in Barbados, 'and this is what most of the feature is going to examine.'[26] His intention was to present the film at several festivals in North America and Europe, with the hope of picking up a distributor.

Another feature film released in 1999 is *Angel in a Cage* by Mary-Jane Gomes, who was born in Trinidad but raised in Canada. She based her feature on the story of her family, who were originally wine-makers from Madeira. The film, according to Bruce Paddington in his *Trinidad Guardian* review of 23 June 1999, 'is the first full length feature film made by a woman from the English-speaking Caribbean, that has the Caribbean as its setting and focuses on a Caribbean theme with a Caribbean sensitivity.[27] Location filming was done in Trinidad, in Tobago, and in Canada, with funding from Telefilm Canada and the Canadian Cable Production Fund. However, typical problems – lack of funds and adequate staff, editing, transfer to

35 mm, titling, and so on – pushed the completion and release of the film far beyond the dates announced. The shoestring budget did not permit reshooting certain scenes. The *Sunday Express* of 20 April 1997 reported how the crew had to make do as they filmed in Trinidad:

> In Manzanilla they shot a scene involving a donkey cart, an unbroken donkey and the water buffalo, all of whom behaved so impeccably that they only needed one take. There were still problems to be solved, but Gomes said: "If this were a big-budget movie, we'd have spent six hours on that scene. But we came up with an immediate solution. Nothing happened the way we thought it would, but we managed to adjust."

It is, all told, the same scenario throughout the anglophone Caribbean film-making world: makeshift solutions, improvisations, disappointment, depleted funds and frustrating delays before the fleeting pleasure of the film's premiere and subsequent distribution. Artistic integrity is bound to suffer under such trying circumstances, but such is the price one has to pay for being outside the mainstream, outside the big league. When it opened in Port of Spain in June 1999, *Angel in a Cage* had a short run, falling victim to harsh reviews, including criticism about the actors' accents and inaccurate historical details. Judy Raymond commented in the *Sunday Guardian's* magazine of 13 June 1999: '*Angel in a Cage* leaves one feeling sad, not for Carmina, but for those who put so much into this film, and for all of us who are left still waiting for the Great Trinidadian Movie.'

Quo Vadis?

The urge to be creative will naturally ensure that film-makers in the anglophone Caribbean will not entirely abandon the idea of making feature films. Not all of them will follow the example of Jamaica's Mediamix and leave features alone in order to concentrate on television programmes. Some will want to emulate new companies like Trinidad and Tobago's Ringbellion Multimedia Works, which ambitiously proclaimed in the *Express* of 24 May 1998 that 'the first thing we are going to do is to hold some courses in writing and acting for screen and pop-culture media.' According to the *Express*, 'the courses were designed to take participants behind the scenes in contemporary film and television, with emphasis placed on hands-on experience in the different media.' There is the inevitable feeling of *déjà vu* in such pronouncements, but, fortunately, also a feeling of hope for the future of feature films in the anglophone Caribbean.

One surefire way to arouse and sustain interest in feature films is to present them at well-known film festivals. Those at Cannes, Venice, New York, London and other metropolitan centres have often been the launching pad for unexpected masterpieces. Mindful of this fact, organizers in the Caribbean have also attempted to mount festivals to highlight regional creations. In the anglophone territories, Jamaica, St Lucia, Bermuda and Trinidad and Tobago have held festivals, though not with the same regularity as the one held in Havana. The Carifesta arts festival has included feature films, but in recent times the tendency has been for the Commonwealth Caribbean to concentrate on Caricom and fixing economic woes, to the detriment of regional funding in the arts and humanities.

For a while, it appeared that the biennial *Images Caraïbes* Film Festival held in Martinique would become the major festival at which the anglophone Caribbean, in the absence of other established festivals, would showcase its new feature films. It was out of this festival that there emerged in 1990 the idea of a Federation of Caribbean Audiovisual Professionals, with the following manifesto:

> We, producers, filmmakers, screenwriters, technicians and actors of the second *Images Caraïbes* Festival 1990, being aware of the need to further develop the space within the Caribbean for professional workers in film and video, reflecting our special needs, and after having made a deep analysis of our reality, acknowledging the importance of film, TV, and video, decided to give ourselves the means in order to obtain the conditions necessary for the realization of the expression of the professionals working in film and video.

But the festival fell on hard times, and there was a hiatus, leaving filmmakers without what promised to be an established outlet for their work.

In December 1998 Guadeloupe put on the third edition of the film festival *Noir Tout Couleurs* (All Colours of Black). Promoted as an opportunity to view the best movies made by Caribbean, Afro-American and African film-makers, this festival showed works by Spike Lee (*Get on the Bus*), Mario Van Peebles (*Panther*), Marc Levin (*Slam*), but also Cuba's *Guantanamera*, and Jamaica's *Dancehall Queen*. This festival, according to its director, Lydia René-Corail, 'has been a deliberate attempt both to promote interest in cinema and to establish filmmaking as a viable activity in Guadeloupe'.[28] Only time will tell if this festival, like *Images Caraïbes,* will be around long enough to fulfil the ambitious promises we have come to expect from

such enterprises. St. Barthelemy also began hosting an annual film festival in 1996.
In the best of all possible worlds, artists would work under ideal conditions to create their works. Unfortunately, such conditions are not universal, and artists, film-makers among them, remain subject to the vagaries of several agencies and organizations. It would help immensely if the following suggestions, or variations thereof, could be implemented across the entire Caribbean, thus encompassing all the languages and cultures:

1 Set up a Pan Caribbean Film Commission.
2 Establish a joint funding venture for feature films. The private sector could give its contribution through a percentage of annual profits, and governments could realize funds from taxes on cinema tickets or lotteries where such exist.
3 Support an annual or biennial film festival, with a prestigious prize for feature film award winners. Ensure wide distribution of winning feature.
4 Found a feature film archive as a depository for all Caribbean-made films. This facility could also house an electronic cross-referenced database.
5 Offer tax incentives and other exemptions (e.g. import duty on equipment) for local film companies.
6 Support Caribbean film-makers who have distinguished themselves outside the Caribbean, so they can return and train other Caribbean nationals.
7 Seek partnerships with mainstream studios, some of which might consider exchanging technical expertise for assistance with location filming.
8 Develop an on-going series of adaptations of Caribbean literary masterpieces. Initially, outstanding Caribbean directors could be commissioned to direct these films, which could use, where appropriate, Caribbean screenplay writers.
9 Produce a series of films on the lives of great historical figures of the Caribbean (such as Toussaint L'Ouverture, Marcus Garvey, C. L. R. James, Aimé Césaire).
10 Establish a Film School to train film-makers. Funding could be solicited through international organizations, the private sector, or member governments.

There is a growing consensus that there is a niche to be filled with video productions, a transition already made by Cuban film-makers. It is all too obvious that the Caribbean cannot keep pace with the major film-producing countries; it is outpaced, outmatched, and outdone at nearly every level. Thus, a case can be made for the region to develop its own style of film-making, helped along by the vast improvements in technology. Bruce Paddington, co-founder and director of the Trinidad and Tobago production company Banyan, sees technology, especially video, 'being used to counter, if not conquer, foreign domination of the airwaves and to actively assert and project a unique independent Caribbean culture.'[29] In this regard, it would seem plausible for the Caribbean to make feature films on video (in its most sophisticated format), and in this way to establish a body of work, the best of which could then be transferred if needed to 35 mm for wider distribution. These films could be shown in small, multiplex-style cinemas, building audiences gradually, as opposed to striving for the Hollywood-style blockbuster that draws sellout crowds to each showing. In this manner, the Caribbean could conceivably come up with a system that would be unique, and that other marginal film industries would want to emulate.

Notes

1. Annabelle Alcazar, 'Wanted. Investors with Imagination', (1998), 51.
2. Ibid.
3. *Sunday Observer,* 21 June 1978.
4. Full interview is in Appendix 1, page 162.
5. Quoted in Alcazar, 'Wanted'.
6. *Laws of Trinidad and Tobago*, Port of Spain, Government of Trinidad and Tobago, 1980, Ch. 20; 10.
7. I am grateful to Jampro for sharing this information through its 1998/99 Film Marketing Outline.
8. Kennedy Wilson, 'On Location' (1996), 96.
9. Personal communication with Melanie Graham of Palace Amusements, Kingston, June 1998.
10. Asha Hingoo, 'The Impact of Indian Films on Trinidadians', (1975), 3.
11. Earl Lovelace, *The Dragon Can't Dance* (1986), 95–6.
12. Lovelace, *TDCD*, 157–8.
13. Amrita Basdeo, 'Indian Cinema in Trinidad (1997), 3.
14. Hingoo, 'Impact of Indian Films'.
15. Basdeo, 'Indian Cinema', 4.
16. Ibid, 5.
17. See Indra Ramnarine, 'The Cinema' (1977), Appendix 2.
18. Hingoo, 'Impact of Indian Films', 8.
19. V. S. Naipaul, *A House for Mr. Biswas,* 230.
20. Kenneth Jaikaransingh, 'Film Censorship in Trinidad and Tobago' (1992), 60–1.
21. Ibid, 63.
22. Ibid, 70.
23. Unlike in America, the source of over 90 per cent of cable material, so-called Premium channels like HBO and Cinemax were usually included in the monthly rental for no additional charge.
24. Personal communication from Mr Maharaj, Fall 1997.

25. I am grateful to Banyan for sharing its promotional material, which provided the information for this paragraph.

26. Andrew Millington, quoted in *Sunday Advocate*, 22 November 1998.

27. Trinidadian-born Frances-Anne Solomon, based in London, has also directed a full-length feature film, *Peggy Sue*, but that is about a Chinese family living in Liverpool.

28. Reported by Simon Lee in *Sunday Guardian Magazine,* 17 January 1999.

29. Bruce Paddington, 'Television and Video Production in the Caribbean,' in Mbye Cham, *Ex-Iles* (1992), 378.

Appendix 1 | Interviews

Interview with Carl Bradshaw (Jamaica, June 1998)

Actor and producer. Has appeared in *The Harder They Come, Smile Orange, Countryman, The Lunatic, The Mighty Quinn, Dancehall Queen* and *Third World Cop.*

KQW: Can you begin by telling me about your involvement with film-making, or about film-making in general in Jamaica?

CB: Film-making in Jamaica and the rest of the Caribbean was born out of the region being tropical for one, and it was done mainly for its location potential. None of the films done here before *The Harder They Come* had Jamaica as its primary location. Jamaica was just a by-pass to that whole technology. *The Harder They Come* created a new mindset as far as what we could do as a people in the area of film-making, and it served two purposes, because the film, being musically driven (and the Caribbean is noted for its music) generated curiosity that took the music to a different level because of the quality of the soundtrack, and also because of the visual aspect, the colour and texture of the Jamaica location.

The film was successful because of the speed with which the story was told. From our point of view, there were no clear-cut categories into which to put the film, so we went into the marketplace trying to find a situation that would stir the mind of the outside viewer not too familiar with the language, with the culture. We therefore started out trying to put both worlds together, trying to compromise the language with colour, scenery, location, and characters. Most of the actors were amateurs. No one really had the necessary background. *The Harder They Come* came out of curiosity. Perry Henzell, who was trained in England, saw that we had a good Jamaican base. I don't think the movie was thought of as any sort of blockbuster outside of the Caribbean; it was thought of as being for Jamaica in the first instance, then the rest of the Caribbean, and to a minor degree the communities outside of the Caribbean where there were large numbers of Caribbean immigrants.

Also, what started to happen was a following of curiosity-seekers developed – people who just wanted to be hip, to be able to say they understood the dialect, the psyche of the Jamaicans. Caribbean culture, in a subtle way, was becoming very popular. Calypso and steelband became dominant. In Jamaica, the jazz/blues influence gave way to ska and other popular forms, whence the reggae; *The Harder They Come* was responsible for that kind of interest.

Then, because of the overnight success of what we had imagined as a 'mackerel and banana'[1] type of effort, but which turned out to be a five-course meal, our interest was awoken, and we began to ask ourselves where we could go with films. The big setback, of course, was the cost of making films, for unlike music, where US$100 000 can give you the best LP, when you have US$5 million you're talking low-budget. At that time, we were thinking about spending US$1.5 million to 1.7 million per film, so we were really into what could be called the minor league. But because of the colour of the Caribbean, the facial expressions of the people, the natural talent, something started to happen. In Jamaica, there were entrepreneurs who were visual conceptualizers, who needed to see their investments in a visual sense. You couldn't go to one of them with a two-page proposal for a film. This meant that the necessary financial backing did not come, and things went into a slump.

Jamaica, then, was considered only as a location spot, and not as a place where one could find intermediary actors, not really your main league but at the same time not really your basic extra. No one was cast in major roles in those big films, unless like a Madge Sinclair or a Shirley Ralph, or a Calvin Lockhart or Sydney Poitier from that side who actually live within the system although they are Caribbean people. We therefore didn't get the chance to evolve as film-makers at the pace we would have liked.

Then came the second piece, *Smile Orange*, a film version of a very successful stage play that had had a run of some three years. We had taken a chance before with a film called *No Place Like Home*, but a fire at MGM destroyed the film, and that production was lost. Afterwards, Jamaica began to be looked at as a place where you could find extras with small speaking parts. Money was still hard to come by, though, and when it came it was largely from overseas, with the implication of artistic control that that entailed.

KQW: One would think that with the success of *The Harder They Come*, you could go to financiers and use that film's success to help you get funding.

CB: Yes, but they still wanted to see the visual. They wanted to see concrete proof of their success in the form of a bank, or a building, etc.

This could only result in a depression in the world of film-making, given the nature of what we did. We came ghetto, yard style, hard core, and a lot of the contemporary middle class didn't want to become part of that visual scenario, didn't want to acknowledge their roots, so to speak.

There was still a hard core in Jamaica determined to make this thing work. People like Perry Henzell, Trevor Rhone and myself saw this as our future. We could really develop a local industry, drawing in elements from the rest of the Caribbean, both from a scenic point of view, and from a cultural point of view. We saw where if we had the guts to stick it out, then the future would hold something. I stuck it out, working in film and music. We came up with *Smile Orange*, which, because of the nature of the film, didn't take off like *The Harder They Come*. It actually ridiculed white people, and so couldn't be played in the theatres the way *The Harder They Come* could.

We went on to do *Countryman* and *The Lunatic*, and what started to happen was the big US companies began to focus more on Jamaica. They came with *The Mighty Quinn,* one of the first films shot with some 80–90 per cent foreign backing. I got a part, and because of the strength I gave the character, became one of the secondary actors as far as credit is concerned. Then there was *Club Paradise* in which Jimmy Cliff starred. It had a style similar to *The Harder They Come* in that it was also musically driven, and brought in other big names, like Adolph Caesar. Thus, as time went by there was a whole lot of interest in coming to Jamaica, but still not in a big mega way. The films were still low-budget from an American point of view, although for us it would be a big project. Then these companies could do things here that they could not do in the States because of union restrictions. Jamaica was now a location where these companies could be comfortable with a US$5 million budget, a mere pre-production amount in America.

KQW: What were you doing in the meantime?

CB: Being the sort of person I am, I thought that we must do something as a follow-up to *The Harder They Come*. A couple of films came out: Lennie Little-White's *Children of Babylon*, and *Rockers*, and *Klash*, but I don't think they got the kind of response *The Harder They Come* did, probably because they were trying to cross over, and brought in foreign directors and foreign actors for the leads, people like Jasmine Guy. I said to myself that I must do something that impinged on the Caribbean psyche, but then I might run into the problem of being too 'street'. I came up with *Dancehall Queen*, a sort of modern-day *The Harder They Come* from a female point of view. Whereas the hero in *The Harder They Come* ended up a villain who loses his life, I made the new character into a winner. She started out from the same socio-cultural milieu, with various disadvantages, yet ends up on top at the end of the day. She wasn't even a part of the whole dancehall scene; her thing was outside the dancehall. She sold her knickknacks at the gate. So her knowledge of the inside wasn't as great as her knowledge of the outside; when she entered the dancehall, it marked quite a transition because she wasn't that liberal. I took the female liberalness to a different height, where it wasn't sex or looseness or lewdness that made her into a dancehall character. It was more an awareness of her physical structure and that one could show off one's physique.

KQW: I see that Michael Reckord panned the film in his review in the *Gleaner*.

CB: Well, I can see how some people would see the film as lewd, but I saw the dancehall as liberating. The dancehall was much more – it was a place for fashion, a place for gossip, a place to copy, a place to learn, because if the older elements in the society came to the dancehall they would expose themselves as different from the masses. I think the reviewer saw it from a middle ground, not as a film-maker, not bothering to examine why the dialogue is structured in a certain way, why the scenes are constructed in a certain way, because negativity is one of our fortes. There is a problem with anything that is new and not middle class.

KQW: In Trinidad, our problem word is 'local'. Initially, did you have reactions like Reckord's to *The Harder They Come*?

CB: It was worse. The 'wagonists'[2] as we call them did not come on board until about four years after when the film went to Cannes and won all the awards. They then came on so strong that it was they who wanted us to push it. It was like your carnival and steelband. That was when I was convinced that we were on to something. The criticism by the middle class was farcical, based on a superficial look at the film.

I know that with the new digital technology film-making is in our future. I am hoping to do three films this year, and I'm also going to be putting on film most of the local stage plays. I want to get to a phase where, even if we're not making a feature, we're still working, so we can build up a library of Jamaican action. I plan to use Horace Ové to bridge the gap between things Jamaican and the rest of the Caribbean. I also want to get into Martinique – I did five years of television in Martinique.

KQW: Was this a series in French?

CB: It was done in French and English and was called *Runaway Bay*, and was for European consumption.

KQW: Are your films shown on television here?

CB: Yes, especially on international television, and there were many copies off cable.

KQW: So the average Jamaica child could look forward to seeing these films?

CB: Yes.

KQW: And that augurs well for the future?

CB: Yes. *Dancehall Queen* was the biggest movie ever in Jamaica. We made some $30 million in eight weeks. And there are still the festivals – we just sent it down to Brazil.

KQW: What is the relationship between yourself and the distributors?

CB: The distributor probably gets about 80 per cent of the money. What you have to do is release in a lot of theatres all over the world.

KQW: This is probably a silly question, but wouldn't it be in the interest of the distributor to plough some of this money back into film-making?

CB: They don't see it that way. They can get films from anywhere. They recognize the risk in film-making, and can just wait for others to take the risk and produce the film for them to show. They'll be the last ones to enter film-making, especially a Jamaican film.

KQW: This has been very helpful. Thank you.

Interview with Franklyn St Juste (Jamaica, June 1998)

Director of Photography for *The Harder They Come*, and *Children of Babylon*.

KQW: Can you tell me about your involvement with films and film-making in Jamaica?

FSJ: We first have to look at the tradition of film-making and where it began. The Colonial Office in England (the Central Office of Information) provided all the film material (by way of documentaries) to the colonies for viewing. They found it was a very expensive affair to go all around the colonies and far-flung territories, including the Caribbean, and decided to shut down the Colonial Film Unit. The decision was taken to train colonies in the making of films, resulting in the setting up of film schools all over, including one in the Caribbean around 1950. People from Jamaica, Trinidad, Barbados, and Guyana were trained at Mona to make essentially documentaries. The Caribbean film-making industry had that as its genesis, with film units being established in those territories. Through the Jamaica Film Unit, films were made mainly in black and white (in 35 mm) dealing with matters of health and population well-being as opposed to socio-economic issues e.g. *Too Late* dealing with how one should raise one's family, and *Builders of the Nation* designed to motivate teachers to stay on the job and struggle despite the harsh conditions.

While the other territories' film units eventually suffered a lack of support, the JFU grew and ended up making a number of films, and with the advent of television in 1963 started to film in 16 mm for viewing on television (the 35 mm films were shown in the cinemas whenever possible – a one-reeler might be shown along with a feature). About that time, more private companies started getting involved in advertising, and we started seeing commercials. One such company, Vista Productions run by BBC-trained Perry Henzell, who had wanted to set up a major television company but found that this was done by the government instead, did quite a lot of work. Henzell decided that he wanted to do a feature film, and after toying with the idea for some time, did *The Harder They Come* in 1972. I was one of the directors of photography. I don't think we need to talk about *The Harder They Come* because it's a good film – one that can stand analysis. It has everything, all the conditions that govern analysis.

KQW: I've always been curious. When the film was shown here, did it have subtitles?

FSJ: What happened was this. The film was shot in 16 mm – actually Super 16, which was very new at the time – which was to be blown up to 35 mm for exhibition in the cinemas. It was felt that we should do a print that would serve both the Caribbean and the overseas markets, so Perry Henzell was advised that he should do subtitles for some of the films because in pre-testing there was a little problem in understanding the local language.

The film really works ... I don't want to say miraculously ... but it did not start out structured like that. They shot first, then they put it down, and they shot again, and then they put it together and found that it lacked definition. Characters had no motivation, situations were not resolved, and so on. So they shot again, and it was then that they started bringing in the atmosphere, all the colour, all the feeling, the ambience of the story came out then. So it evolved into a totally different thing by the time it was released, and it worked very well. I always say it was miraculous because I never saw a script, not a sheet of paper.

KQW: I realized that when I saw what Michael Thelwell wrote concerning how he came to write the novel. He says that one of the first things he asked for when he was contacted was the script, only to be told that there was none.

FSJ: I understand there was supposed to be a script by Trevor Rhone and Perry Henzell, but I never saw it. I would go out on location and ask what we were supposed to be doing, and would be told 'I don't know'. But we'd shoot some scenes and build a sequence. There were lots of little things like that, due to inexperience, and in addition, it was done on a real shoe-string budget. Sometimes we didn't have Jimmy Cliff here, so we had to use a double, when we were shooting a fight scene.' It was really very difficult, because you had to be shooting over the shoulder of this double. We'd shoot in a particular location, and two months later Jimmy would turn up, and we'd say 'Let's shoot the close-up now to go with the fight scene,' but we're in a different location, different lighting, but we had to shoot because, next thing you know, Jimmy is off again.

KQW: I saw on the internet a couple of stories about a possible sequel to that film?

FSJ: There are two projects. Perry is talking about a sequel. Jimmy Cliff is talking about a sequel. I don't know what is going to be the position on that. After *The Harder They Come* everybody got fired up and thought we could do it, but for a long while nothing happened. Then a few things took place. A group of people did *Marijuana Affair* – Lucien Chen was the producer, and he brought down a black American director, William Greaves, who's really a documentary film-maker. I don't think it was very successful at the box office.

KQW: Where can one find such a film?

FSJ: You'll have to check with Lucien Chen to find out. There were many local people in it, but it was shot by a foreign crew. Then Calvin Lockhart came down and did a kind of documentary called *Every Nigger Is a Star.* And in 1979, Lennie Little-White, who had started a production house, really to make commercials and so, came up with *Children of Babylon,* which I shot for him.

But before that, Trevor Rhone had ventured into production again. This time, he said he'd do it himself, and he directed *Smile Orange*, which was based on one of his plays. That was all right, though it didn't have the kind of success that *The Harder They Come* had. *Children of Babylon* ran for six weeks, longer than *The Harder They Come.* It did quite well in town. I don't know what it did outside. Little-White controls the box office for overseas, so I don't know how well it did, because it ran in Canada at one of the Eaton cineplexes.

There followed a quiet period for some time, and the government was thinking that we have a film industry – let's see how we can develop it, but they developed it as a short-term thing where you could make quick, hard currency, and we were short of foreign currency at the time. What they did was to offer Jamaica as available for location filming. Of course, the Caribbean had always been used for location filming: *Heaven Knows, Mr. Allison, Fire Down Below, Sea Wife, Dr. Dolittle, Papillon, The Tamarind Seed,* etc. Some of these, like *Papillon* and *Dr. No*, were shot almost entirely out here.

KQW: What I am looking at is not so much the fact that James Bond arrives in Jamaica, but that he could be just about anywhere. In other words, there is very little interaction with the locals *per se*.

FSJ: You see, at that time, Jamaica used to be 'an island in the South Pacific', or 'an island in the tropics', or 'Santa Ana'. We became all sorts of names.

KQW: I'm also looking at the fact that your top actors got very minor parts in these movies, and got little or no credit. I'm interested in seeing what happens when we turn from being the consumer of what others put out to being the producer, and the controller of the image.

FSJ: Yes. Those efforts I've been speaking about were efforts to see if we could control the image, although we were using a foreign sub-carrier, an American-style story structure. But to return to the evolution. After another long period, there was *Countryman*, done by Chris Blackwell's company, and directed by Dickie Jobson, who had never directed a film in his life, not even a commercial. Again a foreign crew was brought down – the cinematographer was from France, Dominique Chapuis.[3] They did a fairly good job. That took us to around the mid-80s. After that, we have been hanging loose; what we have been doing is performing in movies made by other people, either in a Jamaican setting, or some other setting. Sometimes we spend a lot of time on location, only to find that we end up on the cutting room floor. People like Leonie Forbes end up going to the premiere and they do not see themselves in the movie.

The latest thing is *Dancehall Queen*. It is directed by Don Letts, who has done many music videos. I have a lot of quarrels with *Dancehall Queen* in terms of its structure, in terms of its story, the narrative progression, the resolution in the scenes, the character development – there's a lot wrong with it. But people are keeping their eye on the box office, and not keeping their eye on the story, because if you concentrate on telling a good story, and you can tell a story good, certainly it can do something at the box office. They are putting in elements they think the box office will like. But it apparently worked, not in terms of the film, but in terms of crowd appeal.

KQW: In Trinidad, the story I hear is quite different. As soon as a film bears the label 'local', no one wants to go to see it. This happened to *The Panman* recently. People wouldn't even go to see it so they could criticize it. It bombed horribly. I am told by some distributors that the draw now in Trinidad is whatever comes from Jamaica, because of the music, or from Hong Kong, the so-called 'kick-up' movies that draw their own following.

FSJ: That's unfortunate, because they did things like *Operation Makonaima, Caribbean Fox* and the like – really bad movies, though.

KQW: But my point is that even if these movies are awful, my son and grandchildren should be able to see them, if only to see how not to make a certain type of film. For example, the American Film Institute has just put out a list of the top 100 movies, and *Birth of a Nation* is on it. Now, however much we may hate that movie, we cannot deny it its place in history. And of course, we have no real archives in Trinidad.

FSJ: Same here. We have no archives. And the thing is that when the government realized that it could capitalize on Jamaica as a location, they formed Jampro, but it has not done anything to encourage local production. The government can do that in a number of ways: by entering into a partnership with potential producers, by providing funds.

KQW: I was told at Jampro's office that *Dancehall Queen* has done very well, to which I said that this should mean that new scripts must be flooding production companies.

FSJ: Island Jamaica Films, which made *Dancehall Queen*, is working on a script now, but what happens is that they have adopted a policy of only doing a certain type of movie, and that is very sad, because when you look at what Euzhan Palcy was able to do with *Rue Cases-Nègres,* what she did with *Siméon*, you will see what she has attempted to do with the folk culture. But this brings me to an important point, namely how we see ourselves. I'm not talking about a world view, because when you talk a world view, the world sees us as living in little hovels, dusty streets, climbing trees, so there is the feeling that all movies that come out of the Caribbean should be like *The Harder They Come*. What we really need to do is examine ourselves and discover what is our philosophy of life, what it is that motivates us, that drives us to do whatever it is that we do. We have a lot of instances that we can draw from in our folk culture; it doesn't have to be Anancy each time, but the figure of Anancy represents a particular condition. We have in Jamaica Anancy, the trickster, a theme we can use over and over to show how people use their brain not brawn.

KQW: I'm with you on that point, but wonder how you see that happening in the overpowering presence of cable television in the homes of Caribbean people.

FSJ: You have to produce and show it.

KQW: Speaking of showing, is *The Harder They Come* shown periodically on Jamaican television?

FSJ: It wasn't shown here for the 25th anniversary, but it has been shown on several cable channels in the US. There is a lack of foresight. We can't see the marketing possibilities.

KQW: But didn't you say *Dancehall Queen* has been successful? Where do you go from there?

FSJ: Now, we have the opportunity to arrive at some sort of thematic or plot configuration in *Dancehall Queen* without destroying whatever it is that attracted the people to come to the cinema. The thing is, it is written by some foreign woman; the original story is by a Jamaican and some foreign woman comes now and says she's going to make it marketable.

KQW: I hear the word stereotype coming.

FSJ: Well, I suppose she'll say it has been a success in the market place, but I don't think that that is it, because I don't think the thing is marketable, and if you do another one like it, I don't think it will be successful. That is what happens with these things. We keep saying that when we make a film here we have to sell it in America. That is the objective. But they don't want it there, so you can't get it sold.

KQW: You're in the folk category.

FSJ: Not only that. You end up going to some little art house or cineclub, with two dozen people going to see the movie, and they come out raving about it.

KQW: And what about distribution here in Jamaica?

FSJ: Well, that is crucial. Ninety-nine percent of the movies we see come from the US. We don't get to see European or Chinese or African movies. Does the US care about our local market? It does. For instance, a film like *Waterworld* may not do good business in the States, but probably will pick up on distribution in other countries; it will probably pick up on sales of videotapes and so on.

Recently, Mosely Ellis was here from Trinidad to speak to Douglas Graham about possibilities of a triangular arrangement for distribution in which prints would be shared between Panama, Trinidad, and Jamaica.

KQW: Is there a tax on cinema tickets here?

FSJ: There is supposed to be a tax. I was suggesting that 10¢ on every ticket go to a fund that would help potential film-makers. In meetings, people like the idea but no one wants to go against Douglas Graham (who controls distribution in this country). You see, they wear two hats down there: as distributor and as exhibitor. They are really exhibitors because they own most of the cinemas. There was a time when there were little pockets of distributors; it is very difficult for independents to spring up because they will be stifled by the monopoly. There has been a decline in the cinema over the years. People used to leave Kingston and drive all the way to a town in the west like Mandeville to go to a cinema where they were showing some classic films. But when independent cinema operators came up, they ended up being starved for films. One cinema in Mona Heights is now a church, and a large one in Half Way Tree (the Premier) is now a bank.

There has been a slight resurgence in cinema attendance. The Grahams of Palace Amusements replaced their burnt-out 1700-seat Carib cinema with a five-screen complex . Then they built two more screens in Sovereign plaza, and people are going to those. They also took over a large auditorium and turned it into a cinema.

KQW: Did Jamaica have double features?

FSJ: Years ago there were double features. Only some cinemas out in the country still run double features. Cinema houses have their own culture here. There has to be an intermission, so the concession stand can sell all sorts of things. At the Carib cinema on a Sunday night you always had to go dressed. That's all changed now, and people are going in all stages of undress, mostly the women.

There has been a concentration on video, film being very difficult to work with, and video being very easy and immediate.

KQW: Are there cineclubs here?

FSJ: No, but there are video clubs, and these have two sets of following: the major one is for the latest movies, and the smaller set is looking for the classier foreign movies. But there is hardly anything prior to 1991, the one company that specialized in those films having shut down. The foreign movies – Chinese, etc. – are usually recorded off premium cable channels. On a point of interest, we can learn a lot from the Chinese, because they make their films and deal with their way of life and what it is that makes them Chinese, and they don't care what other people think.

KQW: If you had an ideal situation at your disposition, what would it be?

FSJ: There are some people who say that the solution is funding. I say the real solution is good stories. I don't think *Dancehall Queen* has a good story. It had potential, but it wasn't good story-telling. If you have good stories, you can sell. Then there's financing, and let's not forget distribution. It's relatively easy to make a film; it's much harder to distribute it. With barely five million people in the English-speaking Caribbean, the market is not large enough to support major productions. We can then make low-budget films. We don't have to have explosions and special effects and such, but we could tell good stories that people would be interested in.

KQW: Would it help if governments played a greater role? Isn't that the situation in Africa?

FSJ: Initially, yes. Ghana and Nigeria set up film units, but they evolved into different things, like in Burkina Faso. In my proposal, I advocated that governments invest no more that 25 per cent in any film, so that it would not have the final say with respect to the artistic rendering of the product.

KQW: By the way, what was the initial reaction to *The Harder They Come*?

FSJ: Like everything else, a lot of people overseas were upset. I don't think the government was upset – in fact, Henzell later received a national award from the government.

KQW: Any final thoughts as we close?

FSJ: We may have to re-invent the very idea of how we do things. For example, we are busy copying the Americans. How do they denote the passage of time? They can do so by showing the shift from snow to falling leaves of blooming buds, etc. Why don't we look for our own symbols? There are fundamental principles involved in production, and you can't change that; but the French make movies a particular way, the Germans make movies a particular way, the British make movies a particular way. The Americans used Rambo to defeat the Russians. It is a continuation of the western, a crucial element in the understanding of the American way of life. We need to find the Caribbean way of doing things, including the way we make films.

KQW: Thank you very much for your time and your willingness to share your ideas.

Interview with Menelik Shabazz (London, July 1998)

Writer/director of *Burning an Illusion*. Editor and Publisher of *Black Filmmaker*.

KQW: Can you talk about your experience with cinema and film?

MS: In the Caribbean, my experience was with mobile cinemas, which we had in the village, but clearly I didn't ever think of myself as being involved in film, and that only happened through chance. I was actually supposed to go to art school, but ended up applying to the London International Film School. I was accepted, and from there the buzz of being around other people interested in film confirmed in my mind that I wanted to make films in a very serious way. Because at the same time I was involved as an activist, and because I had always understood the politics of film, the importance of images, that was what was making me want to express myself in a way that would have an effect on my people's consciousness. Film became that tool.

Out of film school (75/76), I got into making documentaries. I made *Step Forward Youth*, and that opened many doors for me to work in commercial television. I did a documentary for ATV, quite an event at that time for there were no black film-makers working in mainstream. I was lucky. A commissioner had seen my work and wanted me to do something for them. It was a documentary on the use of the 'sus' law,[4] and the conspiracy law, which was used particularly against black youth at that time. That programme was censored by the broadcasting authorities, which insisted that a disclaimer should be appended to the front of the film. This created a lot of problems. The documentary sought to redress the imbalance in the reporting of young black people and the police, but the Independent Broadcasting Authority felt that the programme had to be balanced, and because it was imbalanced according to their eyes, they insisted on the disclaimer. It was something like: 'This film was made by a black director.' Now, this was a film that had been researched by the staff of ATV, and as far as I know, this kind of disclaimer had never been done before for anybody else's film. That episode immediately confirmed in my mind that I could not function in the commercial arena. I could only function if I was willing to censor myself, and accommodate the changes that I would need to do internally to exist in that environment, and I couldn't do that. So I realized immediately that I would have to be an independent film-maker, and that is where my strength is.

After that experience, I developed an idea for a short drama, which ended up being a feature film. It was about a woman before a camera reminiscing about things, and it developed and developed, and I was able to get some finance from the British Film Institute at the time. I suspect it was funded because it was a woman who was the main character. Had it been a man, it would have been quite different. A story constructed around a male character that doesn't mess up, that doesn't create problems for himself, that comes out of it intact, will mean that you'll have problems. This is what I've been experiencing ever since, but *Burning an Illusion* was funded by the BFI to the tune of some £80 000. It was shot in 16 mm, and was the third film produced by the BFI that was black (after Lionel N'gakane's *Jemima and Johnny* and Horace Ové's *Pressure*), so the BFI was in the forefront as far as financing independent black film-makers was concerned – they would later do *Young Soul Rebels*. The films they did were sort of quirky, and not expected to command a large audience; they dealt with films that had obscure themes. *Burning an Illusion* went against the grain, for, from the start, my concern was to reach my audience, for whom I made the film, which was the first made by BFI to get the proper distribution.

KQW: Who handled the distribution?

MS: BFI, but I had a heavy hand in it because they had no idea who to market the film to, since it wasn't part of their tradition. I was looking for a very different audience from their traditionally high-brow, obscure set. Julian Henriques is having the same situation with his current film, *Babymother*, having to play a big role in how it's marketed.

The film dealt with a woman who is into the Mills & Boon books' idealism of love and romance, a false image in other words. I wanted to challenge that, so the story is of her looking for Mr Right, trying to find a man that fits into her idealism. She finds Del: it's a boy meets girl, boy loses girl sort of scenario, but I wanted to subvert that theme a bit and take her just beyond the resolution of their relationship, which turns on the reality of black living. He ends up in prison, and she has to decide about the path her life is going to take. Must she go back to the vision she once held, or decide to look at things differently? In the end, things begin to rub off on her, and she goes through a transformation, leading to recognition and great awareness of self in the context of the society in which she's living.

KQW: And since that you've not made another feature film?

MS: No, and not for want of trying. I've had a number of commissions of scripts, but it never gets any further. What we see is a kind of pattern, in that there is no commitment in this country for black film-makers to develop their craft and their skills. Black film-makers end up in a dead-end situation, unable to accumulate a body of work. We all think that we have done the hardest part – making the film – and that would put us in good stead to develop our career. What happens – and it did to Horace – is that, basically, your career doesn't go anywhere. It's happened to Isaac Julien as well. You are sidestepped once you produce a feature film, and they go on to the next person, so there is not a body of work by a black director that is matured and developed to the point where it can take off and go to another level. You're always at the first film level, and we see that as a consistent cycle here.

KQW: So what do you do? Live off past glory? Turn to other projects?

MS: For me, I set up a film/video workshop called Ceddo, financed by Channel 4, BFI and others, to produce films in a workshop environment, which had a different ethos. The workshop was about collective working; everybody was paid the same kind of wage to produce documentaries and provide training. Our agenda was to empower the people interested in media who don't have the finance to be able to go through the regular routes. We also showed films; we had guests (Spike Lee, Euzhan Palcy and Cuban directors, for example). Unfortunately, that came to an end when the funding stopped, which was the weakness of that whole movement.

I worked on several script projects but they all came to naught. I decided I couldn't continue spending time and money only to hear that further funding is not forthcoming because somebody thinks there is no major audience for that type of film – they think you're making a film only for people in Brixton. I decided, therefore, to produce a magazine, *Black Filmmaker*. It's a way for me to keep my hand in the industry, and to be able to pass on some of the experiences I have gained over the years; it's a way around the isolation that is so easy to set in. In this country they recognize the power of the written word, so in producing a magazine, I knew we would be able to address certain issues, and that would empower us to take it further into different sectors of the industry.

Like Horace, I'm still eager and bursting at the seams to produce another feature film. We're looking at new technology that could make it possible to do that without having to go through the same structures as in the past, where you're waiting for replies from Channel 4, where you might, at best, get development money. So that's where I am right now.

KQW: What has been the continued critical reception of *Burning an Illusion*?

MS: It's still being shown around the world. At the time, the lead actress won an award; it has won prizes in France and America. It was the first black film to get major distribution in this country: at least four theatres in London and some up north showed it. The film, to this day, has a following, and it's a film that people in the community remember because of the love story, which is enduring. The film has allowed me to travel around the world.

KQW: Was it shown in the Caribbean?

MS: Yes. I think it ran in Guyana for about six months, and Harbance Kumar paired it with his film *Man From Africa* in Trinidad. (I have an ad from *The Nation* showing this pairing, but I'm not sure which country's *Nation* it's from.)

KQW: I thank you for your time.

Interview with Anthony King (Trinidad, August, 1998)

Managing Director, United International Pictures, film distributor.

KQW: I'm told that the public likes certain movies – the so-called kick-up movies, for example. I'm wondering if this isn't a case of which comes first, the chicken or the egg. In other words, the public likes what it sees because that's all the distributors show.

AK: The simplest way to respond to that is to say that the Trinidadian public today is still the Trinidadian public. They are with you today, and tomorrow they are totally against you, and that's exactly how we have to think of film taste. There was a time when we could safely say that Trinidad was an action-oriented market. If you wanted to make big money, it had to be an action film. We've seen, since probably 1995, that there's been a bit of a fall-off in that. We had a film called *Sudden Death* (1995) with Jean-Claude Van Damme, which we thought was money in the bank, but which failed. We're seeing a bit of a resurgence of family-type movies, comedies and the like, so that we're at the point where we can't actually say that the market is heading in a particular direction; if they see something they like they'll go for it, but they may see something they like today and heap scorn on it tomorrow.

KQW: I was told earlier this year that, surprisingly, certain big films did not make money here. *Independence Day* was quoted as an example.

AK: I'm inclined to believe that your source attempted to mislead you. *Independence Day* was a major success in Trinidad. In terms of distributors, there's a big difference of opinion on what constitutes a 'big' film. Is it one that has a $100 million budget? Is it one that has a major star? Is it one with special effects? Trinidadians go for star power. There was no star in *Lost World*, and it is still one of UIP's biggest films; the same goes for *Jurassic Park*, with its digitally-created dinosaurs. There weren't any stars in *The Lion King*, and it is still the highest-grossing animated film ever shown in Trinidad. From this, you can see that there's a lot of chopping and changing in terms of people's taste.

KQW: In America, when a film is released, you can track how well it is doing at the box office on a weekly basis. When American films come to Trinidad, is our take part of that weekly calculation? Do you have to send part of the money you make back to the US?

AK: You have to look at what we do as a different operation. This is United International Pictures, essentially Universal, Paramount, MGM, and United Artists getting together to market their films internationally. Now, each one of these studios operates independently in the US, competes fiercely with one another in fact. When you see figures being tracked in the US, you are dealing with domestic figures. The closest to us would be probably those from Puerto Rico, which are considered domestic.

KQW: So when you go for a film, do you arrange ahead of time how much you are going to pay the studio, or do you operate on a percentage basis?

AK: There are distributors who do outright buys. We operate on a distribution agreement. The studios produce the film, send it to us, and we distribute. They pay us a distribution fee, and we send them the rest of the money. That's pretty much it.

KQW: In Jamaica, there was an interesting situation with *Amistad*, where censors passed it for a particular age group, over 18, I believe. The Minister of Education intervened, and the rating was changed to allow 14-year-olds to see the film. Do we have the same kind of situation in Trinidad?

AK: We do have a government-appointed board of censors. There have been times when we did not agree with the rating given a particular film, and it's as simple as making an appeal to the Board, to the chairman, stating that we are in disagreement. I think the last time we had a major disagreement was with the film *The Last Temptation of Christ*. The film was passed, but after the Catholic archdiocese objected, the Prime Minister stepped in and decided that the film should not be shown. We had already done all our advertising, and were set to go, but had to forfeit the release. I don't think we've had any political problems of censorship since then. I must say that the Board in the last couple of years has been rather understanding, co-operative, and more open.

KQW: One would hope so, since some of the very films that are targeted for censorship are readily available on videocassette and on cable television.

AK: Precisely. That's an issue we have raised over the years with regard to the whole issue of censorship. We have asked what is the point of cutting pieces of a film, when the entire film can easily be seen in another medium because of piracy etc.

KQW: I'd like to get back to the question of distribution, more specifically the scope of distribution. I was told that many of the other anglophone Caribbean islands get their films from Trinidad. Is this so?

AK: Basically, at UIP we cover Trinidad and Tobago, Barbados, Guyana, Surinam, St Lucia (which unfortunately doesn't have any screens yet, but that will be rectified shortly), St Vincent, Dominica, and Grenada.

KQW: Do you have a list of screens per territory?

AK: I don't have a list because there aren't that many, and I can list them from the top of my head.

KQW: I was just in Barbados, and I saw that there's Vista, and there's Globe.

AK: And the Olympic. There was once the Empire and a couple others but they're now down to three.

KQW: And there are islands without screens?

AK: St Lucia has none, though there are plans for a two or three-screen complex sometime later this year. I forgot Antigua, which has one screen right now, with plans to convert to a three-screen complex.

KQW: Well, here in Trinidad, we no longer have cinemas like Roxy, Royal, Empire, Olympic, and Astor, just in Port of Spain alone. What does that do to your market?

AK: You've lost screens, yes, but admission prices have increased. Hollywood has also increased its output, so that you gain in quality and quantity what you lost with the screens. When we had all those cinemas in Trinidad, and not as many releases from Hollywood, we weren't able to release films the way we do now. We are able to release a film in Port of Spain, and do so simultaneously in seven other cinemas across the island. Back then, the other areas would have to wait for the end of the Port of Spain run. We don't have to wait as long to make money on a film. We're at the stage where we can release in Trinidad and Tobago, Barbados, and St Vincent at the same time. We cannot wait too long to release a film because everyone already knows, via cable television and other technological advances, that the movie is out in the US, and is anxious to see it.

KQW: Are you aware of any drop in viewership because of the crime situation? I notice, for example, that some cinemas have taken to advertising that they provide security for their patrons.

AK: Security has become a major issue. Yes, there will be a drop-off in the box-office receipts, but there was a drop-off with the advent of the Lotto and Play Whe.[5] I believe there has been a drop-off also because cinema operators have not kept pace with infrastructure development. If you look at the fast food outlets, you'll see that they are constantly upgrading their facilities to face the increased competition. The same cannot be said of the cinemas. There are so many other distractions for the population that if you are to viably compete within this vast entertainment industry you have to do everything possible to attract and keep the consumer.

KQW: My study is really not dealing with all of the cinema industry. It's not a history of the cinema *per se*, though I will have to look at some of it. I'm looking at what we do when we see ourselves on screen. How do we see ourselves etc? Given what your firm represents, that would automatically exclude the Caribbean, wouldn't it?

AK: The closest we've come to a Caribbean film was with *The Mighty Quinn* and *Cool Runnings*, but we've not distributed a locally produced film.

KQW: I take it that you are exclusively in distribution, that you have little to do with production. Is there any interaction with local film-makers?

AK: Hardly, and it's not that we don't want to interact, but for one reason or the other I think that local film-makers see UIP as a rather aloof company that will not get involved with production. That's not entirely true, because in Mexico there is collaboration with producers.

KQW: The tax that is collected on each cinema ticket, who controls that?

AK: That goes to the government. We see no part of it. The sequence is: you pay for the ticket, there's a tax on the ticket that the cinema owner must turn over to the government; I charge the cinema owner rent plus VAT, which I then pay the government. All that information should be available. We prepare a box office return on a daily basis. The problem is that we do not as a country have a good track record in keeping statistics, so you might have difficulty finding what you need in any one office. I have started asking my staff to prepare not only revenue, but also attendance figures so that at the end of the year I can say to my people that I have, say, 2.5 million people who came to the cinema. But that is still not an accurate figure because I would only be tracking people who came to see UIP's films. I wouldn't be tracking Fox's, for example.

KQW: You speak of our country's track record in keeping statistics, what do you think of our archives in general? And film archives in particular?

AK: It's sad that we don't have some place where we keep our locally made films. We need to see even the horrible ones so that we can know what we're improving on. How do you improve on nothing?

KQW: I couldn't agree with you more. Do you ever show 'arty' movies?

AK: The chance for survival of the 'arty' movie is too close to the lower end of the scale as far as my company is concerned, so they decided simply not to send such movies. The best performing 'art' type film we've had was *Evita. The English Patient* also did fairly well, and survived mainly because of the appeal of its academy awards. *Sense and Sensibility* was not shown because we felt that it wouldn't do well in this market.

KQW: So I see we're back to the chicken and egg analogy with which we started. You don't expose the public to a film because you feel the public won't like it.

AK: Unfortunately, that's the nature of our business. We have to stay ahead of the public sometimes. It's either that, or we go out of business.

KQW: Thank you very much for sharing your thoughts with me.

Notes

1. Hence, down-to-earth, grass-roots, or simple.
2. People who jump on the bandwagon when things appear to be working.
3. Dominique Chapuis was also the director of photography for *Rue Cases-Nègres*.
4. The reference is to the unpopular law that allowed the police to stop and search 'suspected persons' during the 1980s.
5. State-run games of chance.

Appendix 2

Distribution of population and screens in independent anglophone Caribbean

Territory *(Yr of independence)*	Population *(est. 1998)*	Screens *(1998)*
Jamaica (1962)	2 635 000	14
Trinidad and Tobago (1962)	1 117 000	28
Barbados (1966)	259 000	3
Guyana (1966)	708 000	27
Bahamas (1973)	280 000	9
Grenada (1974)	96 000	3
Dominica (1978)	66 000	2
St Lucia (1979)	152 000	0
St Vincent & Grenadines (1979)	120 000	5
Antigua & Barbuda (1981)	64 000	1
Belize (1981)	230 000	0
St Kitts & Nevis (1983)	42 000	1

<table>
<tr><td>Appendix 3</td><td>Shot on location:
A selection of feature films
made entirely or partially in
the anglophone Caribbean</td></tr>
</table>

Antigua: *Circle of Two*, 1980.

Bahamas: *20,000 Leagues Under the Sea*, 1954; *Speed Week*, 1957; *Help*, 1965; *Thunderball*, 1965; *The Spy Who Loved Me*, 1977; *For Your Eyes Only*, 1981; *Money to Burn*, 1983; *Never Say Never Again*, 1983; *Silence of the Lambs*, 1991; *My Father the Hero*, 1994; *The Crew*, 1994; *L'Enfant d'Eau*, 1995; *Flipper*, 1996; *Zeus and Roxanne*, 1997.

Barbados: *Island in the Sun*, 1957; *Blacksnake*, 1973; *The Tamarind Seed*, 1974; *The Thunder Point*, 1996; *Guttaperc*, 1998.

Belize: *Dogs of War*, 1980; *South Pacific 1942*, 1981; *Mosquito Coast*, 1986; *Caribe*, 1987.

Bermuda: *That Touch of Mink*, 1962; *The Deep*, 1977; *White Squall*, 1996; *Mixing Nia*, 1998.

British Virgin Islands: *Muppet Treasure Island*, 1995.

Cayman Islands: *The Firm*, 1993.

Dominica: *The Mercenary Game*, 1983; *The Seventh Sign*, 1988.

Grenada: *Island in the Sun*, 1957.

Guyana: *Green Mansions*, 1959; *Operation Makonaima*, 1972; *If Wishes Were Horses*, 1976; *Mustard Bath*, 1993.

Jamaica: *All the Brothers Were Valiant*, 1953; *20,000 Leagues Under the Sea*, 1954; *Island in the Sun*, 1957; *Sea Wife*, 1957; *Passionate Summer*, 1958; *Dr. No*, 1962; *The Confession*, 1964; *A High Wind in Jamaica*, 1965; *In Like Flint*, 1967; *The Mercenaries*, 1968; *The Harder They Come*, 1972; *Live and Let Die*, 1973; *Papillon*, 1973; *Smile Orange*, 1975; *Rockers*, 1978; *Children of Babylon*, 1980; *Eureka*, 1981; *Countryman*, 1982; *Return to Treasure Island*, 1985; *Club Paradise*, 1986; *In Like Flynn*, 1985; *Clara's Heart*, 1988; *Cocktail*, 1988; *Milk and Honey*, 1987; *Passion and Paradise*, 1988; *Hammerhead*, 1988; *Lord of the Flies*, 1988; *The Mighty Quinn*, 1989; *Popcorn*, 1991; *The Lunatic*, 1990; *Marked for Death*, 1990; *Sankofa*, 1990;

Prelude to a Kiss, 1992; *Wide Sargasso Sea*, 1993; *Scam*, 1992; *Cool Runnings*, 1993; *Legends of the Fall*, 1994; *Klash*, 1996; *The House Next Door*, 1995; *Dancehall Queen*, 1997; *Shattered Image*, 1997; *The Man Who Knew Too Little*, 1997; *How Stella Got Her Groove Back*, 1998; *Belly*, 1998; *Third World Cop*, 1999.

St Kitts: *Missing in Action II*, 1985; *Hot Resort*, 1985.

St Lucia: *Dr. Dolittle*, 1967; *Superman II*, 1980; *Water*, 1985.

St Vincent: *White Squall*, 1995.

Trinidad and Tobago: *Heaven Knows, Mr. Allison*, 1957; *Affair in Trinidad*, 1952; *Fire Down Below*, 1957; *Swiss Family Robinson*, 1960; *The Right and the Wrong*, 1970; *The Caribbean Fox*, 1970; *Operation Makonaima*, 1972; *Bim*, 1974; *Bacchanal Time*, 1979; *Gold of the Amazon Women*, 1979; *Man from Africa*, 1982; *Obeah*, 1987; *Turn of the Tide*, 1988; *The Last Island*, 1991; *Innocent Adultery*, 1993; *Men of Gray II*, 1996; *The Panman*, 1997; *Enter the Black Dragon*, 1998; *Angel in a Cage*, 1998.

US Virgin Islands: *Lord of the Flies*, 1963; *Weekend at Bernie's II*, 1993; *The Shawshank Redemption*, 1994.

Bibliography

Alcazar, Annabelle. 'Wanted. Investors with Imagination'. *BWIA Caribbean Beat* 30 (March/April 1998).

Anthony, Michael. *Parade of Carnivals of Trinidad, 1838–1989*. Port of Spain: Circle Press, 1989.

Basdeo, Amrita. 'Indian Cinema in Trinidad: Role and Impact'. Caribbean Studies Thesis, UWI, St Augustine, 1997.

Beaton, Norman. *Beaton but Unbowed: An Autobiography*. London: Methuen, 1986.

Bloomfield, Valerie. 'Caribbean Films'. *Journal of Librarianship 9* (October 1977).

Bogle, Donald. *Toms, Coons, Mulattos, Mammies, and Bucks: An Interpretative History of Blacks in American Films*. New York: Bantam, 1974.

Bourne, Stephen. *Black in the British Frame: Black People in British Film and Television 1896–1996*. London: Cassell, 1998.

Braithwaite, E. R. *To Sir, With Love*. London: Bodley Head, 1959.

Brathwaite, Edward. *History of the Voice*. London: New Beacon Books, 1984.

Cameron, Kenneth. *Africa on Film*. New York: Continuum, 1994.

Cartey, Wilfred. *Whispers from the Caribbean*. Los Angeles: UCLA/CAAS, 1991.

Cham, Mbye, ed. *Ex-Iles: Essays on Caribbean Cinema*. Trenton: Africa World Press, 1992.

Cham, Mbye and Andrade-Watkins, Claire, eds, *Blackframes: Critical Perspectives on Black Independent Cinema*. Cambridge: the MIT Press, 1988.

Chanan, Michael. *The Cuban Image: Cinema and Cultural Politics in Cuba*. Bloomington: Indiana University Press, 1985.

Clarke, Sebastien. *Jah Music: The Evolution of the Popular Jamaican Song*. London: Heinemann Educational Books, 1980.

Combs, Richard. 'Review of *The Right and the Wrong*'. *Monthly Film Bulletin* 38 (1971).

Cooper, Carolyn. *Noises in the Blood: Orality, Gender and the 'Vulgar' Body of Jamaican Popular Culture*. London: Macmillan, 1993.

Daily Express. 'Righting the Wrong', 21 December 1970.

De Boissiere, Ralph. *Crown Jewel*. London: Picador, 1981.

Gilroy, Paul. *'There Ain't No Black in the Union Jack': The Cultural Politics of Race and Nation*. Chicago: University of Chicago Press, 1987.

Givanni, June. 'Les Reines du Dancing / The Queens of Dancehall'. *Ecrans d'Afrique* 21/22 (3rd–4th quarter 1997).

Griffith, Fitzgerald. 'Film Censorship in Trinidad and Tobago, with reference to *Bim*: A Case Against Censorship'. Caribbean Studies Thesis, UWI, St Augustine, 1978.

Hill, Errol. *The Trinidad Carnival: Mandate for a National Theatre*. Austin: University of Texas Press, 1972.

Hingoo, Asha. 'The Impact of Indian Films on Trinidadians'. Caribbean Studies Thesis, UWI, St Augustine, 1975.

Hodge, Merle. *Crick Crack Monkey.* London: André Deutsch, 1970.

Jacobs Carl. 'Trinidad's Pioneer Movie-Maker'. *Sunday Guardian.* 29 November 1970.

Jaikaransingh, Ken. 'Film Censorship in Trinidad and Tobago: Development, Analysis, Issues'. Caribbean Studies Thesis, UWI, St Augustine, 1992.

Julien, Isaac. 'Soul to Soul: Isaac Julien talks to Amy Taubin about *Young Soul Rebels.*' *Sight and Sound* 1,4 (NS).

King, Bruce. *Derek Walcott and West Indian Drama.* Oxford: Clarendon Press, 1995.

Leab, Daniel. *From Sambo to Superspade: The Black Experience in Motion Pictures.* Boston: Houghton Mifflin, 1976.

Lieber, Michael. *Street Life: Afro-American Culture in Urban Trinidad.* Cambridge: Schenkman, 1981.

Lovelace, Earl. *The Dragon Can't Dance.* London: Longman (Caribbean Writers Series), 1986.

———. *Salt.* New York: Persea Books, 1996.

Luengo, Anthony. 'Patrons of Empire'. *Vistas* (a publication of the NCB Group in Association with U.W.I. Faculty of Arts) 5, 1 (March–May 1998).

Manuel, Peter, with Kenneth Bilby and Michael Largey, *Caribbean Currents: Caribbean Music from Rumba to Reggae.* Philadelphia: Temple University Press, 1995.

Martin, Michael T. (ed.), *Cinemas of the Black Diaspora: Diversity, Dependence, and Oppositionality.* Detroit: Wayne State University Press, 1995.

Mast, Gerald, Cohen, Marshall, and Braudy, Leo (eds). *Film Theory and Criticism.* New York: Oxford University Press. 1992.

Mercer, Kobena. 'Black Film, British Cinema'. *Black Film, British Cinema.* London: Institute of Contemporary Arts, 1988.

Microsoft Cinemania 96. CD. Microsoft Corporation 1992–5.

Milner, Harry. 'Crime in Films'. *Sunday Gleaner,* 18 June 1972.

Monaco, James. *How To Read A Film: The Art, Technology, Language, History, and Theory of Film and Media.* Revised Edition. New York: Oxford University Press, 1981.

Morrison, Toni. *Playing in the Dark: Whiteness and the Literary Imagination.* New York: Vintage Books, 1992.

Naipaul, V. S. *The Middle Passage.* Harmondsworth: Penguin Books, 1969.

———. *Miguel Street.* Harmondsworth: Penguin Books, 1971.

———. *A House for Mr. Biswas.* Harmondsworth: Penguin Books, 1992.

———. *A Turn in the South.* New York: Vintage International, 1990.

Nair, Supriya. 'Expressive Countercultures and Postmodern Utopia: A Caribbean Context.' *Research in African Literatures* 27, 4 (Winter 1996).

Nizer, Louis. *My Day in Court.* New York: Doubleday, 1961.

Ové, Horace. 'Reflections on a Thirty-Year Experience'. *Black Film Bulletin* 4,2 (Summer 1996).

Paddington, Bruce. 'Where Have All the Movies Gone?' *BWIA Caribbean Beat 4* (Winter 1992).

———. 'Television and Video Production in the Caribbean'. In Cham, Mbye. *Ex-Iles* (1992).

Persad, Sophia. 'A Look at the Local Film Industry'. Caribbean Studies Thesis, UWI, St Augustine, 1966.

Pick, Zuzanna M. *The New Latin American Cinema: A Continental Project.* Austin: University of Texas Press, 1993.

Pines, Jim. 'The Cultural Context of Black British Cinema'. In Cham, Mbye and Andrade-Watkins, Claire. *Blackframes* (1988)

———, (ed.) *Black and White in Colour: Black People in British Television since 1936*. London: BFI Publishing, 1992.

Pines, Jim and Willemen, Paul (eds). *Questions of Third Cinema*. London: BFI, 1989.

Poitier, Sidney. *This Life*. New York: Knopf, 1980.

Ramdass, Harry. 'The Movies in Trinidad'. Caribbean Studies Thesis, UWI, St Augustine, 1983.

Ramnarine, Indra. 'The Cinema: Role and Content in Trinidad'. Caribbean Studies Thesis, UWI, 1977.

Rohlehr, Gordon. *My Strangled City and Other Essays*. Port of Spain: Longman Trinidad, 1992.

Rony, Fatimah Tobing. *The Third Eye: Race, Cinema, and Ethnographic Spectacle*. Durham N. Carolina: Duke University Press, 1996.

Rostant, Rory. 'Star Struck'. *Sunday Guardian Lagniappe Magazine*, 31 December 1995.

Russell, Kathlyn. 'Give me film, says Derek Walcott.' *Daily Express*, 4 September 1983.

Sherzer, Dina (ed.), *Cinema, Colonialism, Postcolonialism*. Austin: University of Texas Press, 1996.

Shohat, Ella and Stam, Robert. *Unthinking Eurocentrism: Multiculturalism and the Media*. London and New York: Routledge, 1994.

Stuempfle, Stephen. *The Steelband Movement: The Forging of a National Art in Trinidad and Tobago*. Philadelphia: University of Pennsylvania Press, 1995.

Thelwell, Michael. *The Harder They Come*. New York: Grove Weidenfeld, 1980.

———. '*The Harder They Come*: From Film to Novel'. In Cham, Mbye. *Ex-Iles* (1992).

Walcott, Derek. *Remembrance and Pantomime*. New York: Farrar, Straus and Giroux, 1980.

———. *Collected Poems*. New York: the Noonday Press, 1986.

Warner, Keith Q. 'Film, Literature, and Identity in the Caribbean'. In Cham, Mbye. *Ex-Iles* (1992).

Warshow, Robert. 'Movie Chronicle: The Westerner'. In Mast, Gerald, Cohen, Marshall, and Braudy, Leo. (eds). *Film Theory and Criticism*. New York: Oxford University Press, 1992.

Waters, Anita M. *Race, Class, and Political Symbols: Rastafari and Reggae in Jamaican Politics*. New Brunswick: Transaction Publishers, 1989.

Wilson, David. 'Review of *Pressure*'. *Monthly Film Bulletin* 45 (1978).

Wilson, Kennedy. 'On Location'. *Caribbean Travel and Life*, June 1996.

Winkler, Anthony C. *The Lunatic*. Kingston: Kingston Publishers, 1987.

Index